THE ENCYCLOPÆDIA
of
Ball Juggling

COMPILED, WRITTEN AND ILLUSTRATED BY
CHARLIE DANCEY

THE ENCYCLOPÆDIA OF BALL JUGGLING
Copyright © 2003 Charlie Dancey.
All rights reserved.

Published by Butterfingers, Devon.
+44 (0)1647 441188
mailbox@butterfingers.co.uk

First published in 1994.
Second edition published 1996.
Revised and reprinted 1997.
Reprinted 1998, 2000, 2001.
Third edition published 2003.

The author does not claim to be able to perform all the tricks
in this book.

Cover design, illustrations and typesetting
by Charlie Dancey.

http://www.dancey.net
charlie@dancey.net

Body text and headings set in Garamond,
other text in **Gill Sans**.

Printed by Goodman Baylis, Worcester.

A C.I.P. catalogue record for this title is available from the
British Library.

ISBN: 1 898591 13 X

Welcome to THE ENCYCLOPÆDIA OF BALL JUGGLING

JUGGLING TRICKS *look* difficult when you first see them and they *feel* difficult when you first try them; *but they're easy once you can do them!*

How else could they look so smooth?

Most juggling tricks involve doing more things at once than you can consciously think about – so a certain amount of self-programming, or practice, is required. To do this, you'll first need to understand *what* it is you are trying to do, and then work out *how* you're going to fool your hands into doing it – this is what THE ENCYCLOPÆDIA OF BALL JUGGLING is here to help you do.

This book contains detailed descriptions of literally hundreds of juggling tricks and patterns. It also contains special tips and hints that turn the seemingly impossible into the achievable.

Beginners will find a nice friendly section called **How to Juggle Three Balls** to get them started. Experts can dive straight into the more exotic stuff like the **Mills' Mess**.

The fact is that most complex juggling tricks are really just simple moves in disguise. The legendary **Mills' Mess**, for example, can be learnt by starting with a simple trick called the **Windmill** (which is a **Three Ball Cascade** with **Over the Top** and **Under the Hand** throws added) and then reversing its "windmilling" direction every three throws.

This technique of building up complicated moves from simple ones is the key to learning to juggle – by breaking tricks down into simple building blocks you can acquire new tricks far more effectively than you would by "diving in at the deep end" and trying to learn something like the **Mills' Mess** from scratch.

This is why the ENCYCLOPÆDIA is written in alphabetical order and this is why it's fanatically cross-referenced throughout. You don't so much *read* this book, you *surf* it!

You'll find that juggling tricks are described with words, diagrams, cartoons and several different forms of

Juggling Notation. This is deliberate overkill. The notations are extremely useful tools, especially for inventing new tricks and patterns, but you don't have to have a degree in advanced mathematics to be a juggler. **Beginners** will prefer simple cartoons and plain text, while jugglers at the five-ball stage will enjoy turning a string of numbers like **5151713151** into an aerial dance in the key of three balls (see **High-Low Shower**).

Finally, you don't need to master every trick in this book to be a great juggler.* The best juggling is what *you* do best, not what others do – so aim for invention and dare to be different!

If you manage to invent a new trick then do write and tell me all about it. Who knows? It could be included in a future edition of THE ENCYCLOPÆDIA OF BALL JUGGLING!

Charlie Dancey
August 2003
charlie@dancey.net

---

*I can't juggle all this stuff either – if I'd written a book solely about the stuff that I can do it would have ended up a lot smaller!

Acknowledgements

It would be quite impossible to name all the jugglers who have contributed to the material in this collection. All I can do by way of thanks is to applaud the wonderful free generosity of all jugglers, almost without exception, when it comes to sharing, comparing and exploring their skills with others. Long may it continue to be this way.

My thanks also go to all the people who helped me in special ways to put this book together. In particular:

Scott Harrison and Dominic of Captain Bob's Circus, who bought and paid for the first two copies, when I was only about a quarter of the way through the job – encouragement that I really needed;

Ray Bowler, artist and sculptor, of Trebarwith Strand in Cornwall. Ray lent me his studio flat in overlooking his Art Garden and the Atlantic beyond. It was there that I sat down and drew all the pictures and enjoyed Ray's amazing hospitality, for which he accepted only conversation and assistance with his quartz crystal solaire in return;

Peter Douglas of Tantra Computers in Bristol, the man with the Macs, for freely given help, advice and time on his computers;

Mad Pete, of Skate Naked, who particularly wanted to be mentioned because he's just basically like that and he showed me a trick once;

Haggis McLeod, with whom I have juggled for more years than I care to remember, for technical suggestions and improvements;

Dr. Colin Wright for timely advice both on mathematics and copyright issues;

Sean and Kati for explaining their work in such detail;

Laurie Collard of Butterfingers for having the faith to publish the first edition.

Contents

Contents

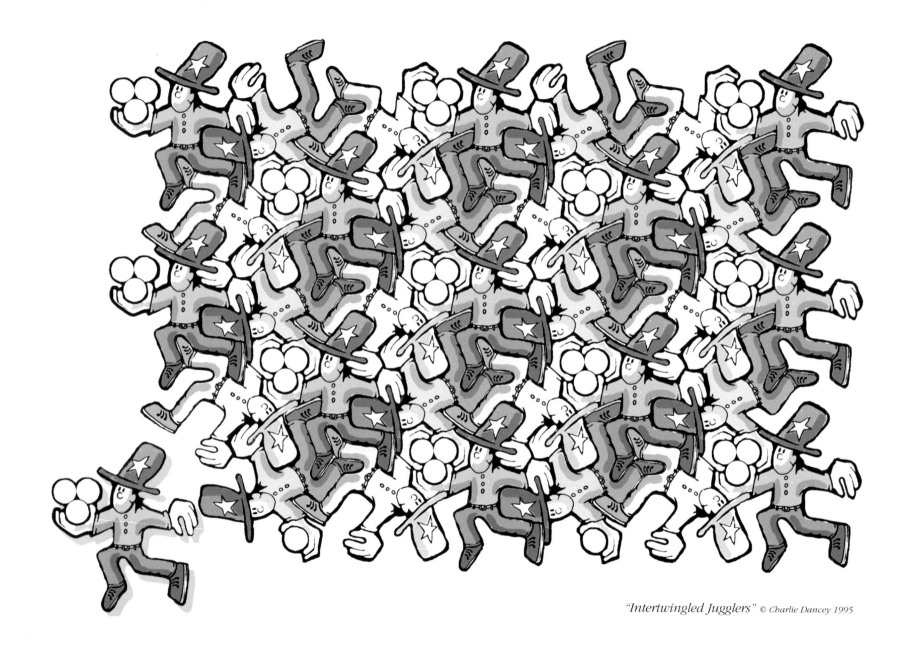

"Intertwingled Jugglers" © *Charlie Dancey 1995*

THE ENCYCLOPÆDIA
of
Ball Juggling

COMPILED, WRITTEN AND ILLUSTRATED BY
CHARLIE DANCEY

Aardvark

Nocturnal, timid, defenceless and about the size of a pig, the **Aardvark** has strong hole-digging claws, ears like a donkey and a long, sticky, termite-eating tongue.

The **Aardvark** is the sole member of the genus *Tubilidentata* and gets its curious name from the Afrikaans (Dutch South African) word for *Earth Pig*, or *Dirt Hog* if you prefer. **Aardvarks** still don't get to vote in South African elections.

Most encyclopædiae seem to have an **Aardvark** lurking in their first few pages, so why should THE ENCYCLOPÆDIA OF BALL JUGGLING be any different?

My point is this; the ENCYCLOPÆDIA is in alphabetical order so you can look stuff up easily – now go surf for some cool tricks!

Abracadabra

Abracadabra, also known as the **Disappearing Ball**, is a magic trick for the three-ball juggler – one moment you are juggling three balls, and in a flash one has vanished.

•Hold one ball in your right hand while juggling **Two in One Hand** using the normal *rolling out* style.

Now, keep the **Two in One Hand** going while carrying the right-hand ball in a circle so that it **Orbits** one of the **Two in One Hand** balls each time it is thrown. The orbit goes down through the middle of the pattern and up on the outside. Make the **Orbit** really exaggerated and show off the held ball, with fingers outstretched, just as you would do if juggling a **Yo-yo** or a

Fake. Since you are only **Orbiting** *one* of the **Two in One Hand** balls, you make one full orbit for every *two* throws of the left hand. **Orbiting** and juggling **Two in One Hand** at the same time feels a bit like trying to pat your head and rub your stomach at the same time, but you'll get there with practice.

Now for the sleight of hand! As you make an **Orbit** you *place* the held ball into the back of your left hand and *keep orbiting with an empty right hand*. Although this happens right under the noses of your audience – they won't see it! They are watching what *you* are watching – your empty right hand. The ball seems to have vanished!

*The **Orbit**...*   *Two balls approach the right hand...*   *It's gone!*

Do a couple of empty **Orbits** and then, as your empty right hand passes close to your left, throw a **Multiplex** (your left hand throws two balls at once) so that one ball follows the **Two in One Hand** path and the other does a sneaky little hop up into your right hand. The ball has reappeared!

The principal difference between jugglers and magicians is that while magicians *conceal* their skills, jugglers *flaunt* theirs. **Abracadabra** is a trick that crosses the line between these two disciplines. To get the best effect you must practise relentlessly until the trick is as smooth and as natural looking as possible. Your left hand should keep the **Two in One Hand** going evenly at all times, while your right hand should move in exactly the same way whether full or empty.

Finally, as every magician knows: you must never show your audience how it's done and never repeat it 'just one more time'.

Airtime

Airtime is the time that a ball spends in the air between a throw and a catch. If you want a ball to stay in the air for longer, then you have to throw it higher (unless you are juggling with **Bouncing Balls,** in which case you can simply let a ball bounce more than once before the catch).

For a ball to have double the **Airtime** you need to give it *four times* the height. This is because the height of a throw increases by the *square* of the **Airtime**.

Correspondingly, to get a ball to stay in the air for three times as long you need to throw it *nine times* as high. No wonder **Numbers Juggling** gets so difficult!

Throws are described in this book using the numbers 1, 2, 3, 4, 5 and so on from **Siteswap Notation**. It's important to realise that the **Airtime** of a throw is always *one less* than its number. So 1's have no **Airtime**, 2's spend one **Beat** in the air, 3's spend two **Beats** in the air and so on.

If you juggle the four-ball pattern **Five-Three** your right hand throws 5's (four **Beats** of **Airtime**) while your left hand throws 3's (two beats of **Airtime**). This

means that balls leaving your right hand need to spend twice as long in the air as the balls leaving your left hand, so the right hand needs to throw *four times as high* as the left.

Many jugglers find it useful to call out the weights of the throws they are using as they juggle – so if you see somebody mumbling to themselves as they juggle a complicated **Siteswap** that's probably what they are doing!

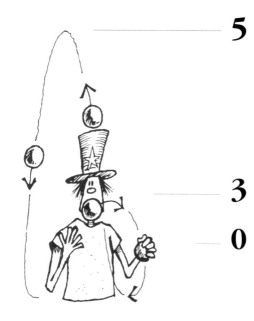

Airtime

Arches

This pattern is a charming distortion of the **Three Ball Cascade**, well within the capability of even the newest three-ball juggler. All you need are three balls and the ability to juggle **Over the Top**.

• Juggle a **Three Ball Cascade** and alter the shape of the pattern so that one ball crosses back and forth as normal, the next goes back and forth **Over the Top** of that one, while the third ball rides **Over the Top** of the whole pattern. Concentrate on keeping the low ball low, the middle ball in the middle and the high ball high.

You may find it helpful to practise **Arches** with three differently coloured balls. As you develop your skill with the pattern you will find that the balls start to *pour* from side to side, rather like a **Mills' Mess**.

By carefully adjusting the timing and shape of the **Arches** pattern a little you will find that you can transform it, by degrees, into an alternate-sided **Slow Shuffle**. The principal difference between the **Slow Shuffle** and **Arches** is that in the shuffle the *middle* ball is "slammed", that is, thrown *downwards* into the catching hand.

Asynchronous

This term is gobbledegook for *not at the same time*, it derives from the gobbledegook prefix "a-" (meaning *not*) and "synchronous" (meaning *not asynchronous*).

In juggling terms you'll sometimes hear **Siteswap**-heads speaking about **Asynchronous** patterns – they really mean patterns in which the hands *take it in turns to throw* (these being the only kind of patterns that **Siteswap** can handle without turning into degree-level algebra).

The **Three Ball Cascade** is an **Asynchronous** pattern. The **Box** is a **Synchronous** pattern.

*The **Arches** pattern.*

Backhand Catch

• Throw a ball as you normally would in a **Three Ball Cascade** but catch it on the back of your hand. With no fingers to grip the ball you'll need to follow it down so that it lands very gently. It's quite possible, though almost stupidly difficult, to juggle three balls using **Backhand Catches**. Squashy beanbags are obviously much better for this than hard balls.

• A more secure and reliable **Backhand Catch** is the **Fork,** in which the ball comes to rest between the open vee of your index and middle fingers. The advantage of this technique is that you still have two fingers and a thumb free to hold another ball under your hand.

Backwards

Almost all juggling patterns can be juggled **Backwards** so that they appear as they would if they were filmed and then played back in reverse. The best-known example of a **Backwards** pattern is the three-ball **Reverse Cascade** – a perfect reversal of the ordinary **Three Ball Cascade**. All you have to do is to juggle a **Three Ball Cascade** with every ball thrown **Over the Top**.

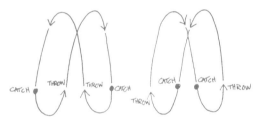

*Normal and **Reverse Cascade** shapes.*

If you look at a pattern written in **Ladder Notation** you can see it **Backwards** by simply turning the chart upside down and reading the throw symbols as catches and vice versa. **Siteswap Notation** is not so helpful when you are trying to reverse a pattern.

Taking **Five-Three-Four**, the complex four-ball pattern, as an example:

534534...

You might expect the reverse of this to be:

435435...

(which is just the same string of numbers in the opposite order). Surprisingly, it turns out that this sequence of numbers is not juggleable! The problem arises because **Siteswap Notation** takes no account of *hold time* (the time that balls spend in the hand). It turns out that when you juggle this pattern **Backwards** you get *the same sequence as before!*

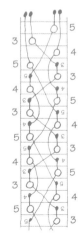

*This chart shows the pattern **Five-Three-Four**. If you turn the page upside down and read the throws as catches and the catches as throws you'll see that the throwing sequence of the **Backwards** pattern is still* **5 3 4**, *just as before!*

Reverse Chops are an interesting example of what happens when you reverse the sequence of a pattern. **Mills' Mess** stays the same when juggled **Backwards** – and I'm not sure *what* happens if you reverse **Rubenstein's Revenge**.

***Behind the Back** juggled **Backwards** is a great idea – throw from the front and catch balls blind behind your back. See **Behind the Back** for more about this.*

*Finally – what every juggler needs is for someone to work out how to reverse a **Drop**.*

HUP!

Backwards

Balls, Clubs and Rings

Balls, Clubs and Rings are the three classic props of **Toss Juggling**. Almost any object that you pick up and throw into the air will behave either like a ball, a club or a ring.

Stones, apples, small kittens, socks, car keys and crumpled paper heading for the litter bin all behave like balls. They are thrown any old way up, taking no account of **Spin**, and they are caught in a wrap-around grip.

Umbrellas, french bread, hammers, knives and cucumbers all have to be thrown and caught like clubs. They spin end over end and are caught in a handle grip.

Berets, records, plates, frisbees, playing cards, trays and other flat objects behave like rings. They are thrown with flat spin and caught by the edge.

THE ENCYCLOPÆDIA OF BALL JUGGLING deals with the techniques of juggling ball-type objects. **Spin** is normally irrelevant to ball juggling except when using **Bouncing Balls**, where carefully applied **Spin** can cause balls to change direction on the bounce, and when balancing balls on the end of your finger like a basketball player (see **Spinning Ball**).

Ball Surfing

Ball Surfing is a three-ball trick in which balls roll up (and down) your arms. It's a **Contact Juggling** move.

• Start by juggling a **Three Ball Cascade**. The move begins like a **Flick Off** – as a ball approaches your right hand you miss a throw and let the approaching ball land on the back of your right hand. From here it *rolls* all the way along your right arm, right up to your elbow where it drops off into your waiting left hand. The left hand throws its ball straight up in order to make the catch.

Here's the secret – it's not so much the ball that rolls up your arm, as your *arm* that rolls under the ball.

Be sure to learn **Ball Surfing** on both sides. You'll find that **Beanbags** are not the best prop for this sort of move, because they have an uneven roll; use stage balls!

• You can extend the trick by getting balls to surf back *down* your arm in the opposite direction – as one goes up, another comes down.

Start as before, catching the ball on the back of your arm and rolling it up to the elbow. As the surfing ball drops off you exchange it for the one in your left hand which rolls back down towards your hand.

Do this continuously on both sides and you have an awesome pattern!*

*The only way to make it any more incredible would be to perform it in a G-string and finish it off with a back somersault or two and a couple of rude jokes – but then if you were doing that why would you bother to juggle at all?

Banana

Yellow comedy fruit, now available all year round! Yes – you *can* juggle **Bananas**. For the basic edible juggling techniques, see **Eating the Apple.**

•If you decide to eat a **Banana** while juggling, remember that it is *cheating* if you peel it *before* you start to juggle. Once you have peeled it, make sure that the skin ends up somewhere obviously dangerous – for example, near the wheel of your parked unicycle. You can get a lot of comic mileage out of this fruit.

•Having peeled your **Banana** and recklessly disposed of its wrapper you have the option of breaking it in half, while juggling, and impressing your audience with your **Four Ball Fountain** skills. To go back to a three-object pattern – toss one piece high and catch it in your mouth.

Beach Ball Juggling

The **Beach Ball**, or any other huge ball, is hardly the ideal juggler's prop. Far too big, far too light, and a terrible bounce. But you can use them to juggle really *big* patterns.

•Get three huge balls and a partner and juggle a giant **Three Ball Cascade** between you. You throw each ball *under* the approaching ball, just as you normally do when juggling three. A **Reverse Cascade** is also possible.

•If you really want to steal the show on stage at a juggling **Convention** you may as well start practising your *Giant Juggling Routine*. Jugglers like to see tricks – so don't just stick to the plain old cascade. The **Box** and the three-ball **Half Shower** work well, so does a **Five-Three** if you

can manage four balls between you. If you want a standing ovation then your big finishing routine will simply *have* to be a **Mills' Mess** – this involves a lot of running around to mimic all of those **Under the Hand** throws!

Burke's Barrage is a much easier option; in the normal pattern it's your hands that take turns to make big sweeping carries over the top of the pattern. With beach balls you simulate the carries by running around *behind* your partner.

•More than two jugglers can play at **Beach Ball Juggling**. The simplest pattern for any number of jugglers is a **Domino Pattern**. Say there are three of you: A, B and C. Stand in a line with one ball each, A starts with an extra ball which gets thrown to B, who throws in turn to C who throws back to A. Thus there is always one ball in the air and a chain reaction of throws that goes round and round.

Beach Ball Juggling

Beanbags

Jugglers love beanbags. When they drop they stay dropped – unlike balls, which roll away (usually under the sofa) or **Bouncing Balls** which drive you completely nuts.

The advantage of **Beanbags** *is their dead drop. Their disadvantage is that, being squashy, they are rarely round. So every throw is made with a slightly differently shaped object which causes a small amount of wander in their flight paths.* **Beanbags** *are the right props to use when you are learning a trick, but balls are much smoother and more elegant in the air when your trick is more reliable.*

URK!

Good quality **Beanbags** are available in a wide range of usually garish colours. This is great for telling which ones are yours after the **Big Toss Up** at a juggling **Convention** when there are several thousand items of juggling equipment lying amongst the feet of the assembled throng. Buy yourself whatever mad combination of colours you like – or take my advice.

I would recommend a matching set of light coloured or white beanbags. Buy one or two more than you think you can juggle. That way, if the dog eats one you will still be able to juggle *and* you leave yourself room for improvement. So for a **Beginner** it's four, for a four-ball juggler it's five. You might also consider adding one ball of a different colour on top of your basic set – useful for those complicated tricks in which you need to work out just exactly where a particular ball is going.

Light colour is important. White, fluorescent and luminous balls are the easiest ones to see, so you may as well give yourself that advantage. For stage work white is best, because that's what lighting technicians like!

Beanbags are made to many different patterns. Most of the good ones are built to a four-segment pattern from stretchy simulated leather and are stuffed with birdseed. Really good quality ones have a lining of nylon stocking material which gives extra durability, roundness and squish.

There are many other designs, and the variation and ingenuity that has been applied to the simple problem of making something round out of flat material is quite incredible. Some are made to cube patterns, some are octahedrons, there are tetrahedrons (humbug shapes – very easy to make at home), and there is the two-segment pattern as used for tennis balls and Hacky Sacks. **Beanbags** also come in a ridiculous range of novelty shapes, penguins, pigs, vegetables and stars to name but a few.

Many jugglers start off by making their own, but later on nearly everyone buys them because they just don't have the *time* any more, they're too busy juggling!

The best material for a home-made beanbag is probably thin supple leather, something that the commercial manufacturers don't seem to offer – perhaps they believe that all jugglers are vegetarians?* For stuffing you can use birdseed (like the professionals), rice (heavy), barley (a little lumpy) or millet (very squishy). I know one itinerant juggler who was so poor one day that he split open his home-made beanbags and cooked up a meal.

*Many jugglers, I know, *are* vegetarians, no offence intended!

Beat

Despite having been juggled with for six months the mixture of rice, barley and aduki beans was still fine for the pot.

A useful low-budget alternative to the **Beanbag** is a surgically altered tennis ball. Standard tennis balls are *terrible* for juggling; poor grip, useless bounce and much too light. How they play tennis with them I will never understand! Take a tennis ball and cut a small X in it with a sharp knife. Push open the hole and half-fill the ball with rice, barley or whatever you can find in the kitchen cupboard. The hole is self-closing so you don't have to glue it shut. The result is a ball with a dead drop and a good weight for juggling.

Did you know that you can build bridges out of beanbags?

Juggling has rhythm, and you can measure off the rhythm in **Beats**. Each "rung" of the ladder in **Ladder Notation** represents one **Beat** of time.

In the **Three Ball Cascade** there is one throw (and one catch) every **Beat**. Listen to the slap of those beanbags and you can hear the rhythm! Each throw is a 3 which has two **Beats** of **Airtime**. Balls spend one **Beat** in the hand and the hands are alternately full for a **Beat** and empty for a **Beat**.

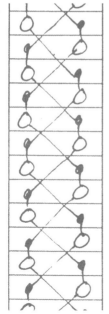

*A section of the simple plait of a **Three Ball Cascade** shown as a **Ladder Notation** chart divided into **Beats** by each "rung" of the ladder.*

*Everything works out very neatly into whole numbers of **Beats** – two beats of **Airtime** for each throw, one **Beat** of hold time and one **Beat** of empty time. Note that it would be quite possible to make throws and catches a little earlier or later without destroying the logic of the pattern.*

You don't *have* to juggle to such a tight and precise schedule but you'll find that human beings, being naturally rhythmical creatures, seem to automatically lock on to this style. You *can* juggle with long hold times and short empty times, you *can* juggle the other way round, but the even, whole-numbered scheme represents the middle way – the most perfect, the smoothest and the most natural pattern.

I should stress here that I'm not trying to suggest that the "whole number of **Beats**" idea is a *rule* about juggling – there are no rules in juggling! You are free to throw those balls into the air just about any way you like. You will notice though that the person who wins the five-ball endurance competition at the next **Convention** is juggling a very rhythmical (and most likely whole-numbered) pattern.

In alternate throw patterns there is usually one throw every **Beat**. When the hands throw simultaneously they normally throw every two **Beats**. In patterns with more complex throwing orders, like *right-right-left-left* it gets more complicated, but a simple rule of thumb (not a real rule of course) is that it is *very rare* for one hand to make more than one throw every two **Beats**.

Beat

Beginner

If you're a complete **Beginner** then this is your lucky day. You *can* learn to juggle, even from a book!

• Don't waste any more time. Your mission, should you choose to accept it (and you'd be a fool not to) is to look up **How to Juggle Three Balls** and follow the instructions that you will find there (which are in friendly cartoon format).

The trick you'll be learning first is called a **Three Ball Cascade**.

The **Three Ball Cascade** is the gateway to juggling. After that there are a million possibilities; many are simple variations on the **Three Ball Cascade**, others are completely different patterns. Who knows, you may *really* get the bug and embark on the single-minded crusade of **Numbers Juggling**, the aim of which is always to get one more ball in the air than the number you last thought of.

The art of juggling is as infinite as music in its possibilities. It is a wonderful mixture of play, performance, sport and dance – and it is *good* for people.

In recent years juggling has emerged from a dark age of secrecy and obscurity, rising

to massive popularity. The jugglers of the past were cagey creatures, fearful that others might learn the tricks of the trade and put them out of work. Today's jugglers are keen to share their skills with you – so don't be afraid to ask.

You may not have noticed, but a lot of juggling patterns are named after things that water does: like **Cascades, Fountains** and **Showers** (I hadn't noticed either, until it was pointed out to me by a legendary mathematical juggling genius Dr. Colin Wright).

He also also remarked on a fourth watery term, which you (as a **Beginner**) are about to find out all about. That would be the **Drop**.

Now look up **How to Juggle Three Balls** and remember that juggling is about as hard to learn as riding a bicycle – with the special advantage that it's not *you* that falls off!

Behind the Back

Yes – you *can* juggle **Behind the Back**. It may seem impossibly difficult at first, but remember: you aren't used to doing *anything* behind your back. The secret is to take it in stages.

• Start by working with one ball only.

The standard **Behind the Back** throw (the one you use in a **Three Ball Cascade**) leaves your right hand and rises alongside your left shoulder and is caught in the left hand (and vice versa of course).

*Pick up one **Beanbag** in your right hand and start experimenting with this throw. The correct action is very relaxed; let your throwing arm hang loose and swing in a lazy ape-like arc. Your throwing hand should not touch your back.*

Practise until the direction in which the ball travels ceases to be a mystery. It's helpful to *visualise* the flight of the ball. Some jugglers have claimed that working with a bunch of keys helps, because they tinkle as they fly, giving you more of a clue as to their whereabouts.

• With two balls it's possible to juggle a pattern that looks very much like *three balls* juggled **Behind the Back** – it's a bit of a cheat, but who cares?

Take one ball in each hand and start by throwing **Behind the Back** from the right so that the ball lands *back in your right hand*.

Now do exactly the same move with your left hand. Then *left-right-left-right* and you have it!

• Here's the trick that you *really* want to learn – how to throw **Behind the Back** in a **Three Ball Cascade**.

Start by getting a very smooth, very slow and very relaxed **Three Ball Cascade** running.

Now you must *really watch* each ball as it peaks. Normally you would do this without thinking about it, but for **Behind the Back** you need to be *consciously aware* of where you are looking. It's vital that you spot every ball at the peak of its flight – the most common mistake jugglers make with this trick is that they fail to spot one ball, which promptly hits the floor.

Move your head from side to side in time with the pattern and drill your eyes right into those balls.

Now start to mentally *get in time* with the action of your right hand, *catch-throw, catch-throw* – when you throw **Behind the Back** the throwing action seamlessly flows from the catch. You do *not* pause for a moment, think about it, and *then* throw the ball!

Continued overleaf...

Behind the Back...

With an utterly smooth movement, your right hand catches a ball and keeps it moving at a constant speed around **Behind the Back**. It then releases it so that it rises alongside your left shoulder. It's important that you keep looking to your *right*. If you don't then you are almost certain to drop the next right-hand catch.

You only look to your left as the **Behind the Back** ball peaks.

Then you have to flick your head back again to your right to spot the next ball!

Keep your shoulder low, keep relaxed and keep trying! When you can do the throw one way, try it the other way. Then try all the usual combinations: every right, every left, same ball every time and finally *every* throw. In the full **Behind the Back** pattern your head will need to *flick* from side to side to catch a glimpse of each ball as it peaks.

• Here's another **Behind the Back** move in which you make a throw *and a catch* behind your back.

Juggle a **Three Ball Cascade** and throw what *looks* like a left self 4 (as if you were going into **Two in One Hand**) – actually you are going to catch this in your right hand.

*While the 4 is in the air you make a right-hand throw **Behind the Back**, catching the 4 with your right hand while it's still behind you.*

You could, alternatively, make that **Behind the Back** throw a *behind-the-back-and-under-the-arm* throw – rather like juggling the **Contortionist**.

• Next – **Behind the Back** juggled **Backwards!** Instead of throwing balls behind your back and catching them in front, you throw from the front and *catch them* **Behind the Back** – it's a blind catch.

Throw a ball high on the exact centre line of your body while your other hand waits, palm upwards, at the base of your spine. The throw should be aimed to hit your forehead. At the last moment you tip your head forwards, out of the ball's way. If all goes well the ball will drop right into your waiting hand.

Practise this with one ball until it's solid, and then try working it into a cascade. As ever, work on every possible combination: every right, every left, same ball every time and every single ball.

• The ultimate **Behind the Back** trick is to juggle a **Three Ball Cascade** *entirely* behind your back, so that you never see the balls at all. This takes serious dedication to master. The cascade should be very low and tight, exactly as you would juggle if you were doing **Blind Juggling**.

When juggling entirely behind your back you should try to avoid getting into the habit of bouncing the balls off your back – although this enables you to "see" the balls by feel it just doesn't look as good, and once you get used to it, it's a very hard habit to break.

Continued overleaf...

Behind the Back...

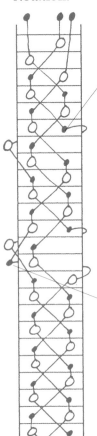

It's possible, with a little imagination, to show a **Behind the Back** throw in **Ladder Notation.**

Here the right hand catches a ball as normal and then sweeps it behind the back (represented by the ball line going behind the chart) before throwing…

*…and next is the **Behind the Back** swap move from the first column on the previous page.*

*After a normal **Behind the Back** throw, the right hand carries a second ball back again.*

*The base pattern is, of course, the familiar plait of the **Three Ball Cascade**.*

Big Toss Up

The **Big Toss Up** is a magic moment at every juggling **Convention**. Hundreds, or even thousands of jugglers assemble in a huge crowd, all furiously juggling as many objects as they can manage. On a countdown from ten they all throw everything they have as high as they possibly can. It's *the* major photo-opportunity of every convention.

Very little of what goes up gets caught!

Binocular Bounce

The **Binocular Bounce** is a classic comic move for **Bouncing Balls**.

•*Juggle three **Bouncing Balls** in the air. Throw one straight up, really high, and hold the other two over your eyes so that they look like a pair of giant eyeballs or binoculars. Follow the ball down with your "binoculars", then follow it up again as it bounces. Catch it and continue the cascade.*

•Since you can't actually *see* the ball, you may as well invert the logic of the gag and look *up* as the ball goes down, then *down* as the ball goes up, before "discovering" the ball and resuming the cascade.

Blind Juggling

Blind Juggling is the art of juggling *without looking*.

• Kneel on the floor so the balls don't have so far to drop. This also quells the fear of height that your hands immediately develop when you shut your eyes and juggle.

Start with your eyes open, juggling a **Three Ball Cascade** as low and as smoothly as you can, stretching your fingers right out for the catches. Now shut your eyes and keep juggling at exactly the same speed. It really helps if you *visualise* the flight paths of the balls. Whatever you do, don't move your head, because as soon as you do, those balls will sail past your hands as if they weren't even there!

If you perform this trick in front of an audience, bear in mind that they will all think you are cheating unless it is totally obvious that you can't see a thing. Ordinary blindfolds are no good because *everybody* knows that you can peep past the edge – after all *they* would! Use a bucket, preferably a steel one. People *believe* in buckets!

• A completely different sort of **Blind Juggling** involves two jugglers. Start by getting a partner to juggle a **Three Ball Cascade** while you stand face to face.

Catch every ball from their pattern at the peak of its flight and *place* it into their catching hand. As soon as this pattern is running your partner can shut their eyes!

Try it – it feels so *weird!*

Boston Mess

The **Boston Mess** is the first cousin of the **Mills' Mess**. It *looks* complicated but it really isn't that hard to learn.

The idea behind the pattern is simple; in a normal **Three Ball Cascade** the balls move from side to side and your hands stay put, but in the **Boston Mess** the balls stay put, bobbing up and down in three columns while the *hands* criss-cross underneath them. Every right-hand throw is still caught by the left and vice versa, just as in the **Three Ball Cascade**. So in a sense the **Boston Mess** *is* a **Three Ball Cascade** juggled in a strange shape.

• As a warm-up to the full pattern juggle a **Reachover** (look it up) on the right-hand side of a **Three Ball Cascade**. Notice that the balls get juggled in three vertical columns briefly, before the pattern goes back to its normal shape. If you do continuous **Reachovers** on one side, you have the **Boston Mess**.

Continued overleaf...

Boston Mess...

• In case the **Reachover** method of learning the **Boston Mess** doesn't work for you here is a complete breakdown of the pattern, throw by throw. The pattern repeats every six **Beats**. Start with two in the right hand, one in the left and imagine three columns in front of you.

Beat one: The right hand throws the first ball in the right-hand column.

Beat two: The left hand throws in the left column and crosses *over* the right hand to catch the ball on the right.

Beat three: The right hand throws *under* the left wrist into the middle column and moves to catch the left-hand ball.

Beat four: The left hand throws the ball on the right and moves to the middle column to catch the middle ball.

Beat five: The right hand throws the ball on the left up and crosses *under* the left wrist to catch the ball in the right column.

Beat six: The left hand throws the ball in the middle column and moves to catch the ball in the left-hand column.

That's the whole sequence!

Note that the pattern is asymmetrical – the left hand always travels *over* the right. You can, if you wish, juggle the same sequence with the left hand travelling *under* the right, or even alternate between six beats with left over right, followed by six beats with right over left.

Then you can reverse the *entire symmetry* of the pattern and work on the mirror image version. Variations like this are good for you, as a juggler, because they are exercises in ambidexterity but are completely lost on audiences, who find the **Boston Mess** totally bamboozling in any guise. If you want to impress *them*, concentrate on smooth throws, tight, well-defined columns and the *lowest* pattern you can possibly manage.

• If you can juggle **The Fastest Trick in the World** then try combining it with the **Boston Mess** – make every catch a **Snatch**. This is an awesome trick!

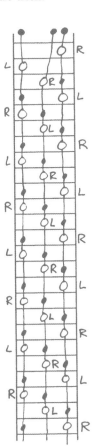

*A chart of the **Boston Mess**. Note that each ball stays in its own column while the hands move back and forth across the pattern. Apart from the strange shape, the **Boston Mess** is otherwise identical to the **Three Ball Cascade**.*

*The four-ball version of this pattern is much simpler – it's just a **Four Ball Fountain** juggled in columns. See the entry for **Pistons**.*

Bouncing Balls

Bouncing Balls add a new dimension to your juggling. To begin with you can juggle downwards as well as upwards! Miss a catch and make out that you *meant* it to happen that way. You can juggle five, six or even more balls off the floor far more easily than you can in the air and you can make throws with massive **Airtime**, simply by allowing balls to bounce several times before the catch.

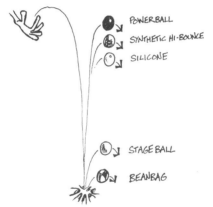

POWERBALL

SYNTHETIC HI-BOUNCE

SILICONE

STAGE BALL

BEANBAG

To be useful to a juggler, **Bouncing Balls** need to have a bounce of 75% or better when dropped from three or four feet (one metre). In other words, they should bounce back up to at least three-quarters of the height that they were dropped from. The best bounce you are likely to find in a ball is around 85%. There is no such thing as a ball with 100% bounce.

The hideously expensive *silicone balls* are the very best you can get. They don't have the best bounce (usually under 80%) but the feel, the finish and their perfectly engineered roundness makes the silicone juggling ball the Rolls Royce of juggling balls. Many professional jugglers use them even for non-bouncing routines.

Juggling shops sell cheap high-bounce balls with a relatively poor finish but terrific bounce. These are probably the best choice for the beginner (keep the silicone for professional work!) – you can buy a whole set of these for the cost of just *one* silicone ball.

Next, you need a good floor. There is no greater expert on floors than the **Bouncing Ball** juggler; some solve the problem by carrying around their own slab of marble. I find that the very best surface of all is a smooth, polished wooden parquet floor laid over concrete, such as you often find in school halls. It's also worth checking out airports and shopping malls because they often have huge polished stone floors. Unfortunately, they also have security guards who tend to take a dim view of juggling, which they instinctively see as a threat to the clean and safe consumer experience.

Learning ball-bouncing tricks can be infuriating. When your pattern gets out of control those balls just explode in all directions. If God had meant us to juggle **Bouncing Balls** then He would have put our feet on pointing backwards.

Enough of the pitfalls! Get yourself some **Bouncing Balls**, find a good piece of floor well away from hills, ponds, dogs and downward-leading staircases, and make a start! The first tricks to try are the **Three Ball Bounce** (which is the **Bouncing Ball** version of the **Three Ball Cascade**) and the **Column Bounce** (equivalent to juggling **Two in One Hand**) – the rest follows from there!

*If God had meant us to juggle **Bouncing Balls** He would have put our feet on backwards!*

Bouncing Balls

Bouncing Beast

The **Bouncing Beast** is a curious creature that you can fashion from six **Bouncing Balls**. This is not a juggling trick, just something weird and wonderful that you can do!

• You need six balls (ideally silicone) and a smooth floor. Make a **Pyramid** with four balls, which will hold together due to the high surface friction of the balls. This is the beast's head. Now locate a fifth ball in the centre of one face of the pyramid – this is the body. The sixth ball is placed between the fifth ball and the floor, forming the tail. Let go of everything and the **Bouncing Beast** will stay intact with the body forming a bridge between the head and the tail.

Now gently stroke the *body* in the direction of the **Bouncing Beast's** tail and the whole structure will roll across the floor as a unit.

Incredible!

Box

The **Box** is a **Square Juggling** trick for three balls*. It never fails to impress!

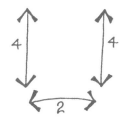

In the **Box** one ball rises and falls in a column on the left, another rises and falls on the right and the third ball swaps from hand to hand across the bottom of the pattern. This gives the pattern its characteristic U-shape. Both hands throw simultaneously which makes it a difficult pattern to learn because the hands have to make different throws at the same time – one hand throws a 4 into one of the columns while the other throws a 2 across the bottom. Even trickier, on the next throw the same thing happens the other way around!

It's quite a knack! One way to learn the pattern is to build it up, practising first with one ball, then two, and finally putting the whole thing together. Another method

*The term **Box** is also used to describe a collision-prone **Passing Pattern** arrangement for four jugglers standing in a square. Each juggler passes to the person diagonally opposite them.

is to start with a simpler pattern and transform it into a **Box** by degrees. This can be done from **Right Middle Left** or the three-ball **Half Shower**.

Once learnt, the pattern seems to have as many possibilities for variation as the **Three Ball Cascade** itself, though this is largely unexplored juggling territory. If you are hoping to invent a great new trick by teatime then the **Box** is as good a place as any to start!

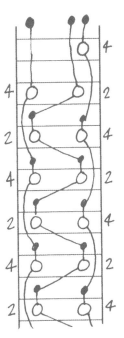

Ladder Notation chart of the **Box**.

The pattern is started by throwing a single 4 (in this case from the right hand). Both hands throw together and each ball stays in its own part of the pattern.

Here's how to learn the **Box** by adding one ball at a time.

• Start with just one ball in your right hand. Throw a 2 to your left, and then throw a 2 straight back. 2's are so low that they are almost horizontal. Do this a few times until it feels easy and natural.

• Next, put one ball in each hand and practise throwing *L shapes*. Your right hand throws a snappy little 2 straight across to your left hand and *at exactly the same time*

your left hand throws a 4 straight up to itself. Thus the 2 arrives in an empty left hand just as the 4 peaks and starts to descend. At this moment the left hand throws the crossing ball straight back as a 2 to the empty right hand. Time this throw so that the right hand catches the 2 at exactly the same moment that the left catches the 4.

Learn to throw perfect *L-shapes* on both sides before moving on to three balls.

• For the complete **Box** pattern you start with two balls in the right hand and one in the left.

The first throw is a solitary 4, thrown straight up from the right hand to itself. This is just to get the pattern going; from now on every throw will be an *L-shape*, just like the two-ball exercise.

After the single 4 both hands throw an *L-shape* to the left, just as you did with two balls, followed by an *L-shape* to the right. Then you just keep going, throwing *L-shapes* to alternate sides.

Notice that each of the three balls remains in its part of the pattern, one ball on each side and the third ball echoing back and forth across the bottom of the pattern.

When a **Box** is juggled well, the height of the 4's matches the width of the 2's and the juggler's head flicks from side to side in time with the pattern, watching the 4's as they peak.

Continued overleaf...

Box...

• Here's how to turn a three-ball **Half Shower** into a **Box** in case the first method didn't work for you.

The three-ball **Half Shower** uses simultaneously thrown 4's and 2's just like the **Box** – but it is always one hand that throws the 4's, while the other hand throws 2's. That's the key!

Juggle the **Half Shower** in one direction for a few beats and then *reverse* it, without stopping, so that the balls are travelling the other way around. Work on these direction changes until you can change direction on *every* throw, and now, as if by magic, you are juggling a **Box**.

• Many jugglers find a left-handed **Half Shower** a pretty tough proposition in its own right, so here's a route to that tricky old **Box** that starts from the stunningly simple pattern **Right Middle Left**.

Juggle **Right Middle Left** as you normally would, all three balls rising to exactly the same heights. Then gradually reduce the height of the *middle* throws until they are as low as you can possibly manage. You'll find the timing of the pattern gets a bit lumpy but, if you are lucky, it suddenly "snaps" into a **Box**. It worked for me!

These two pattern conversion techniques are evidence of the complex intertwingled family tree of juggling patterns. Many patterns seem to be close relatives of each other – perhaps *every* pattern is another in disguise?

Once you can juggle the basic **Box** pattern it's time to start working on variations. Here are some ideas to get you started.

• Try juggling the **Box** and switching into right- and left-handed three-ball **Half Showers** juggled at exactly the same tempo: say, two throws of **Half Shower** to the right, two throws of a **Box**, then two throws of a left-handed **Half Shower**. Rinse and repeat. Sequences like this have a pleasing rhythm – invent your own!

• Juggle the **Box** with one odd coloured ball. It will be in one of the three "positions" of the **Box** – either bobbing on the right, bobbing on the left, or crossing from side to side at the bottom.

Practise changing the position of the odd ball by putting in occasional **Half Shower** throws.

Alternatively, you'll find that you can move the ball around by putting in one round of **Two in One Hand** at the right moment. Apart from moving the ball around (which might be very amusing if it was part of an **Eating the Apple** routine) these variations can lead you to create interesting new patterns.

• If you have **Bouncing Balls** you can juggle the **Box** as a bouncing ball pattern. The 4's are **Force Bounces** straight down, while the 2's remain as air throws*.

For a real fingertwister try mixing 4's in the air with 4's thrown as bounces – a real exercise in mind over muscle!

*The legendary Luke Burrage claims that this pattern can be juggled in a single vertical line, one hand above the other, so the **2**'s go *up* and *down* instead of left and right to create a *One Dimensional **Box***.

• Mix **One-up Two-up** throws into your **Box** pattern. As you throw a 4 in the normal **Box**, think of it as a *one-up*, follow it with a *two-up* thrown with the other two balls, and then go back into the **Box**.

• Juggle a **Box** and then *miss out a 2,* but keep the rest of the pattern going. The hand that *should* have thrown the 2 then catches a 4 in a **Fork** briefly before tossing it back up again to resume the **Box** pattern.

Keep doing this trick on alternate sides and you have a very deft piece of ball manipulation indeed!

2 BALL

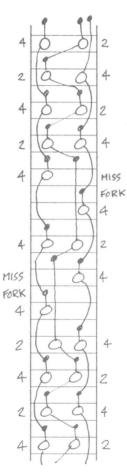

This chart shows a **Forked** *stop on the right, followed by a* **Forked** *stop on the left, juggled in a* **Box**.

• You can juggle **Chops** in a **Box** too! Here are three simple steps that will get you there.

Step One: Juggle a normal **Box**, concentrating on the 2 ball, the ball at the bottom of the pattern. Break the rhythm briefly by throwing the 2 ball as a right self 4, just as you did in the "moving balls around" exercise earlier. Effectively your right hand goes into **Two in One Hand** for one throw, causing the 2 ball to swap places with the right-hand 4 ball. It's easy.

Step Two: Make that **Two in One Hand** throw go *under* the left wrist and back to the right hand. This is **Under the Hand** in a **Box** – a pretty respectable trick in its own right!

Step Three: Concentrate on the evasive move that your left hand instinctively makes as your right throws **Under the Hand**. Develop this small dodge into a full-blown **Chop**. When you can do it on one side, learn it on the other, then juggle **Chops** on alternate sides and jugglers will crowd round you asking technical questions!

See **Four Ball Box** and **Luke's Shuffle** for even more ideas.

Box

Burke's Barrage

Burke's Barrage, **Mills' Mess** and **Rubenstein's Revenge** – these are all flashy three-ball patterns with crossed hand throws, twiddly bits and attention-seeking alliterative names. Faced with patterns like these you have three choices: learn them, ignore them and work on the simple stuff, or invent something incredible and *name it after yourself** – that's what Ken Burke did.

If you decide to learn them then you'll be pleased, I'm sure, to hear that **Burke's Barrage** is the easiest of the trio. When you untangle the wheeling paths of the hands in this pattern you'll discover that it is really just **Right Middle Left** tied in a knot.

Burke's Barrage is a **Four Two Three (423)** pattern, so the throwing order is *right-right... left-left...*

•Start your practice by warming up with a few minutes of **Right Middle Left**. This gets the throwing order and tempo of the pattern firmly imprinted on your brain.

*The Author did this with a trick named **Dancey's Devilment**. Unfortunately he missed out the bit where he actually *invented* anything – hence he ended up with a cool name, *but no trick to go with it!* There has been confusion ever since.

Here's the secret – **Burke's Barrage** is simply a **Right Middle Left** distorted in such a way that the *4-balls* are thrown with your arms crossed as **Under the Hand** throws.

To put it another way: the *right* and *left* throws from **Right Middle Left** are made on the *wrong side* of the pattern by means of crossing your arms – that's all there is to it!

•Here's a cool way of getting into it. Place two balls in your right hand, and one in the left. Cross your right hand *under* the left. That's the starting position.

Now try the first two throws, and the first catch.

Throw an **Under the Hand 4** straight up, then uncross your hands and throw an **Over the Top 3** from your right hand, then immediately catch the **4** by crossing your right hand over your left.

Let the 3 hit the floor!

•OK, now do *exactly* the same exercise **mirrorwise**. Finally, put those two moves together and you have it.

Once you have the basic scheme of the pattern taped you should work on the way in which you catch the **4**'s – try to make them into nice exaggerated **Snatches** that feel like outside **Chops**. This is just a point of style, but plenty of people will say you aren't "doing it right" until you do it this way.

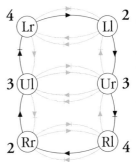

Burke's Barrage is a *shape distortion of* *Four Two Three (423).* *This Mills' Mess State Transition Diagram shows how it works.*

•It has been observed that **Burke's Barrage** is a **423** juggled with **Mills' Mess** hand movements (though there are several ways of making this combination. Only the one shown here is **Burke's Barrage**).

•**Burke's Barrage** can also be juggled as a spectacular **Gandini Pattern**: look up **Four Two Three (423)** for instructions.

NOTE: This pattern was incorrectly described in earlier editions of THE ENCYCLOPÆDIA OF BALL JUGGLING. The "wrong" version can now be found under **Charlie's Cheat**.

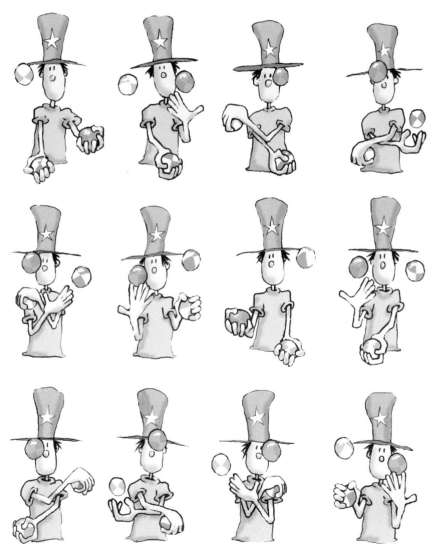

Burke's Barrage
*with three balls.
It's a **423** tied in
a knot!*

*The four-ball
version uses very
similar hand
movements,
there's just more
stuff in the air
above.*

• It's possible to juggle a four-ball **Burke's Barrage**. To do this we need a four-ball base pattern with the same throwing order as **423**, and it turns out that **Five Five Two (552)** fits the bill perfectly.

• Start with two balls in each hand and lead with a **Reverse Cascade 5** from the left hand.

1. Throw an **Under the Hand 5** from the right hand, then uncross your hands and throw a **Reverse Cascade 5** from the right again.

2. Throw an **Under the Hand 5** from the left hand, then uncross your hands and throw a **Reverse Cascade 5** from the left again.

Go back to step 1 and repeat. It's tricky, but not *that* tricky. Your main problems will be collisions, and failing to throw proper **5**'s (hence running out of time underneath them).

Once you get it **Solid** you could easily convince your friends that it's a **Four Ball Mills' Mess** (if you felt like being dishonest). It certainly looks like one!

See also **Four Two Three (423)**, **Fake Mess**, **Charlie's Cheat**.

Burke's Barrage

Capacity

The **Capacity** of a juggling pattern is the number of balls it can hold. It's interesting to note that if both your hands are throwing 3's you are juggling a pattern with a **Capacity** of three balls (the **Three Ball Cascade**). If both hands throw 4's you are juggling four balls, if it's 5's then it's five balls. Neat, isn't it?

It gets better. If one hand throws **5**'s while the other throws **3**'s you are juggling four balls – it's a **Five Three (53).** The **Capacity** of a two-handed pattern turns out to be the *average* of the throw weights being used (barring **Gaps** and **Multiplexing** of course). This rule also works for complicated patterns like **Five Three One (531)** (three balls) and **Five Three Four (534)** (four balls).

In **Passing Patterns** the **Capacity** is the average throw weight multiplied by the number of jugglers. For example, when passing a seven-ball **Two Count** each juggler is throwing 4's with the right hand and 3's with the left, giving an average of three and a half. Multiply this by two, because there are two jugglers, and you get seven – the right answer!

It's quite interesting to look at exactly how a particular number of balls fit into a juggling pattern. Let's consider the **Three Ball Cascade**.

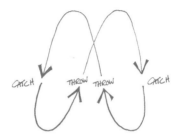

In this pattern three balls chase each other around in a figure-eight shaped path. Each ball takes six **Beats** of time to complete the circuit. This can be drawn as a simplified chart (a *Circuit Diagram* perhaps) looking rather like a railway track.

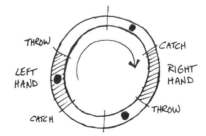

The actual shape of the cascade is ignored and the diagram simply shows a circular track divided into six **Beats**.

The arrow shows the direction that the balls take around the track, and the two shaded regions represent the time that the balls spend in the hands. The balls themselves are denoted by the three black blobs that are spread *equally* around the track. We imagine them to be moving clockwise as the pattern is juggled, always equally spaced like well-scheduled trains.

It's another form of juggling **Notation**!

The diagram, as drawn, represents one moment of time in the **Three Ball Cascade.** At the particular instant shown here there is one ball in the left hand, one about to be caught in the right, and the third ball just leaving the right. If you compare this with a real **Three Ball Cascade**, or with a cascade written in **Ladder Notation**, you'll find that the circuit diagram is giving an accurate picture of where the balls are at one instant.

What the circuit diagram demonstrates is that, in a **Three Ball Cascade**, the balls are separated from each other by two **Beats** of time. It turns out that nearly all juggling patterns behave like this.

It follows from this discovery that the **Capacity** of a pattern is *half the number of* *beats* in the circuit, because that's the only way you can keep all the balls separated by two **Beats** of time.

It's a good exercise, when armed with a new theory, to try it out the other way round to see if it *really* works. So we'll see if we can work out how to do **Four Ball Juggling** on paper.

The first step is to map out a circuit of eight beats. This gives us enough space to draw in four balls, each separated by our legal minimum of two beats.

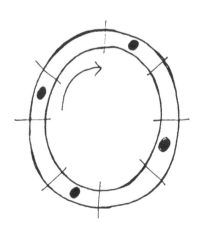

Next, the *hold times* need to be shaded in – but there are a number of possible ways of doing this.

44

If the hands are placed evenly, the diagram shows a pattern with **4**'s going each way. However, by moving the hands *closer together* on the diagram you can create patterns with uneven throws. The possibilities here are **5**'s and **3**'s, **6**'s and **2**'s and finally **7**'s against **1**'s.

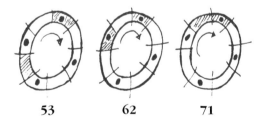

53　　　**62**　　　**71**

71 is a **Shower**, **62** is a **Half Shower**, **53** is of course the well-known pattern **Five Three**, and **44** is four balls juggled with simultaneous, equal height crossing throws (see **Four Ball Juggling**).

In each case you can determine whether the patterns use simultaneous or alternate throws. If the diagram shows both hands holding at the same time it's a simultaneous throw pattern; if one is holding and the other empty it's an alternate throw pattern.

The diagram did not produce a **Four Ball Fountain** because **Fountain** patterns contain *two* circuits – in this case two independent **Two in One Hand** patterns. Each of those circuits is four **Beats** long, giving them a **Capacity** of two balls each.

If you go back to the circuit diagram for three balls you'll see that there are three possibilities for the arrangement of the hands, corresponding to the **Cascade** itself, the **Half Shower** and the full **Shower** (**33**, **42** and **51**).

Class dismissed!

Capacity

Cascade

A **Cascade** is a symmetrical juggling pattern for two hands and an odd number of balls. You can't **Cascade** an even number of balls no matter how hard you try!

*Three and Five Ball **Cascades***.

The hands throw alternately in a **Cascade**; every throw crosses and every throw rises to the same height. The balls cross each other's paths in the middle of the pattern like a motorcycle display team. **Cascades** are the simplest and most symmetrical patterns for odd numbers of balls and since most would agree that *real* juggling starts at three, the **Three Ball Cascade** is generally considered to be the simplest, most elegant and obvious juggling pattern of all.

In a normal **Cascade** each ball is thrown *under* the approaching ball, as opposed to a **Reverse Cascade** in which balls are thrown *over*.

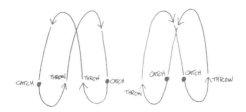

Cascade** and **Reverse Cascade.

For *even* numbers of balls the simplest patterns are the **Fountains**. In these patterns each hand *independently* juggles half the balls in the pattern.

For *any* number of balls you can juggle a **Shower** pattern; one hand throws balls across while the other hand **Feeds** them back. As you add more balls to the **Shower** patterns they get very high very quickly.

Causal Diagrams

Causal Diagrams were invented by the well-known club-passing "guru", Martin Frost. This system has two great advantages over other systems of notation; firstly it shows how a juggling pattern *feels* to the juggler, and secondly it can describe large and complicated patterns without resembling the wiring diagram of a telephone exchange.

Martin developed the idea as part of his excellent work on **Passing Patterns**. I happen to think that this is an excellent way of looking at solo patterns too.

The key to understanding **Causal Diagrams** is to realise that while **Ladder Notation** and **Siteswap Notation** attempt to record the movement of every object in a juggling pattern, **Causal Diagrams** simply track the movement of the juggler's *problem*. Let me explain what I mean by that.

At any given moment in the **Three Ball Cascade** the juggler has a *problem* – there is one more ball than there are hands. The *problem* approaches the hand and it *causes* the juggler to make a throw – which, in turn, creates a *new* problem heading for the other hand.

A **Causal Diagram** tracks, not the motion of the balls, but the motion of the *problem* that *causes* the balls to be thrown.

Here's a **Ladder** chart and a **Causal Diagram** for a **Three Ball Cascade**,

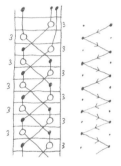

*The **Ladder Notation** resembles a braid of three strands of hair; the **Causal Diagram** of the same pattern gives a single line that zigzags from right to left.*

Each line in the **Causal Diagram** leads from one throw to the throw that is *caused* by it. The little dots are simply place markers so you can read off the succession of **Beats** in the pattern.

To my way of thinking, the **Causal Diagram** accurately models the *feel* of juggling three balls. I'm convinced that this zigzag line is far closer to the image of the pattern in the juggler's mind than the braid of three in the **Ladder** chart. How about you? Perhaps the **Causal Diagram** for the **Box** might further convince you.

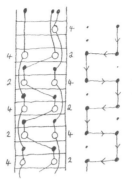

*The **Box** in **Ladder Notation** and as a **Causal Diagram**.*

Notice how the **Box's** crossing 2's cause *simultaneous* self 4's to be thrown, hence the causal arrows representing these throws travel *horizontally* across the chart.

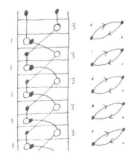

*A **Two Ball Shower** in **Ladder Notation** and as a **Causal Diagram**.*

According to this **Causal Diagram** the action of throwing a **3** with the right hand *causes* the left hand to throw a **1** (a **Feed**) one **Beat** later. This seems fair enough (you need to empty the hand in order to catch the **3**), but how about the idea that the throwing of a 1 by the left hand *causes* the right hand to throw the selfsame **3** a **Beat** *earlier?!*

This isn't as crazy as it seems – here's the logical answer: *in order to place a ball directly into your right hand you have to have emptied it first!*

So these curious time-travelling arrows do make sense after all, and the **Causal Diagram** has captured the spirit of the two-ball **Shower** perfectly.

Each arrow in a **Causal Diagram** starts from the point at which a throw is made and ends at the point at which a *caused* throw is made. Notice that the arrow for a throw of weight **3** always moves *one* beat down the chart, while a **4** moves *two* beats down the chart, and so on. This leads to a simple mathematical rule:

Each arrow moves down the chart two beats less than the weight of the corresponding throw.

That's why the **2**'s in the **Box** converted to horizontal arrows, moving *zero beats* down the chart. It's also why the **1**'s move one **Beat** *up* the chart (one minus two equals *minus one*).

Numerically adept readers will already have guessed that 0's (**Gaps**) produce arrows that move *two beats up* the chart.

27

...Causal Diagrams

Here are three more examples of fairly well-known patterns: from left to right they are 534, 531, and 504.

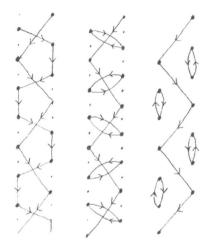

Here's the next mathematical rule for **Causal Diagrams**:

The number of paths down the chart is equal to the number of objects in the pattern, minus the number of hands.

Think of it this way – the surplus of balls over hands is the number of *problems* that a juggler has to deal with in a pattern.

This seems to fit perfectly well for the **Three Ball Cascade** diagram (one line zig-zagging), the three-ball **Box** (one line

square-waving) and the four-ball **534** pattern (two lines criss-crossing) but what about the two-ball **Shower**, **531** and **504** diagrams? All these charts are complicated by the fact that arrows are moving *up* as well as *down* the chart.

In the two-ball **Shower** there should, by rights, be *no arrows at all* because the number of balls minus the number of hands is zero, hence (in theory) no *problem* to deal with! – therefore *nothing to juggle!*

The answer to this is that there is indeed *nothing to juggle*, but the juggler decides to juggle anyway by throwing a **3**, creating a *problem* where there was none. The payoff is that the juggler then un-creates the problem by throwing a **1**; thus producing two causal arrows that cancel each other out. To put it more simply, arrows that move up the chart cancel out arrows moving down the chart.

This cancelling-out idea can also be applied to the charts for **531** and **504** which contain closed loops. Once the loops are taken out of the picture the two patterns are revealed for what they are – three-object patterns.

Causal Diagrams really come into their own when applied to **Passing Patterns.** This is what Martin Frost invented them for. Martin drew his diagrams with time running from *left to right* which is the conventional mathematician's way of doing things. (I draw **Causal Diagrams** of solo patterns vertically because they sit more easily next to **Ladder Notation**.)

Here's a two-person, six-object **Four Count**. Each juggler's throws are represented by a single row of circles, labelled L and R, and the passes are denoted by arrows that cross from one juggler to another.

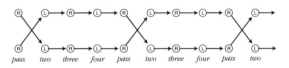

One very convenient feature of a **Causal Diagram** for a passing pattern is that the distance an arrow moves along the chart happens to tell you exactly what type of throw it is. An arrow that travels down by one beat is a **Single**, two beats for a **Double**, three beats for a **Triple,** and so on.

Here's the **Right-Left-Triple!**[CCJ]* combination thrown in a **Four Count**. Notice that while the **Singles** all move just one beat along the chart, the **Doubles** move along by two and the **Triples** by three, making it very easy to work out what's going on. The dotted lines simply mark the "normal" sequence for reference.

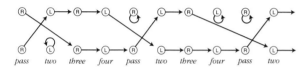

pass   two   three   four   pass   two   three   four   pass   two

This trick creates some spaces in the chart during which a juggler simply holds a ball for a beat or two. A hold like this is denoted by a "2" in **Siteswap** which *should* convert mathematically into an arrow that moves *zero beats* down the chart. Hence they are drawn with arrows that lead back onto their own tails!

The **2**'s are shown as causal arrows that *cause themselves* – what does this mean? It means that you are holding an object *because* you are holding an object.

Mathematics may seem crazy but it *does* make sense!

*The little CCJ superscript indicates that **Right-Left-Triple!**[CCJ] is a trick you can look up in this book's companion volume, THE COMPENDIUM OF CLUB JUGGLING.

Charlie's Cheat

In previous editions of THE ENCYCLOPÆDIA OF BALL JUGGLING the three-ball pattern **Burke's Barrage** was incorrectly described. Instead of writing about Ken Burke's original trick the author presented an elegant description of a *time-reversed* **Follow**. Since nobody else seems to have staked a claim to this trick the author has cheekily called it **Charlie's Cheat**. The single difference between the two is this: in **Charlie's Cheat** the **2**'s are carried over the top of the pattern, whereas in **Burke's Barrage** they are carried *through*.

•Here's an easy way to learn it. Juggle a **Yo-yo** on one side. Now change sides. Then change sides on every throw of the *yo-ball*.

•Keep going and concentrate on the *string-ball* (still changing sides) and start to stretch the imaginary string until you are making huge, elaborate, exaggerated arcs. That's **Charlie's Cheat**!

•The legendary Luke Burrage* has invented an amazing trick which allows you to juggle **Charlie's Cheat** at the *same time* as **Burke's Barrage.**

You use *five* balls and juggle **[44][22]3**. The **[44]**'s are column **Multiplexes**,

*http://lukeburrages.thingonthe.net

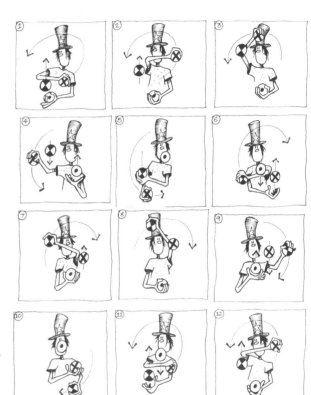

thrown **Under the Hand**. The **[22]**'s are *double* holds. You swing the **[22]**'s *between* the two **Multiplexed** balls. You see, when you go *under* it's **Burke's Barrage**, and when you go *over* it's **Charlie's Cheat** – so now you're doing both!

See also **Four Two Three (423)**, **Fake Mess**, **Follow**.

Charlie's Cheat

Chin Trap

•Throw a ball up out of a **Three Ball Cascade** and trap it between your chin and your collarbone. You'll need to turn your head to one side. It helps to make the throw from as close to your stomach as possible.

In this position you can pause and give the ball a little kiss before dropping it back into the cascade.

•As with any simple trick you simply *must* try all the combinations; every right, every left, same ball every time, and every ball. The trick combines well with the **Orangutan**, **Off the Head** and other body moves.

Chop

A **Chop** is a violent catch that slices through the middle of a juggling pattern like an axe.

This is a very important technique, and although you may be able to learn to **Chop** *reasonably* well without too many problems, developing really *elegant* **Chops** is something you can work on for a long long time.

Chops are fundamental to many complex juggling patterns, so you'd better get started!

•Juggle a **Three Ball Cascade** as normal. Now catch a ball with your right hand at the *peak* of its flight and sweep it downwards and to the left, passing *over* the following throw from your left hand. As the chopped ball reaches the bottom left of the pattern the chopping hand stops dead and throws the ball more or less straight up. Then continue the cascade as normal.

This is not an easy move to get right and it won't look or feel right until it feels smooth and natural. This means lots of practice. The best way of developing a good **Chop** is to begin by making **Under the Hand** throws a lot in your **Three Ball Cascade**.

Notice that as you throw **Under the Hand** with your right hand, your *left* hand moves out of the way a little (you'll find that you do this quite subconsciously). The key to the **Chop** is to exaggerate that small evasive movement until it becomes a huge slicing sweep.

It feels awkward at first, but be assured that as soon as it starts to *feel* smooth, it will also be *looking* smooth.

• When you can **Chop** on both sides you should work on **Chopping** every single ball – it is so different to the **Cascade** that the resemblance is hard to spot. In the fully **Chopped** pattern the balls rise vertically in two columns and all the sideways movement of the balls is taken up by the **Chops**.

• A variation of the **Chop** is the *outside* **Chop**. Instead of chopping through the middle of the pattern the chopped ball is taken all the way to the opposite side of the pattern. The outside **Chop** is a key move to mastery of the infamous **Rubenstein's Revenge**.

• A difficult and amazing variation is the *reverse* **Chop** – awesome when juggled as a continuous pattern.

Juggle a **Reverse Cascade** with three balls, and as a ball from your left hand peaks you catch it with your right hand and carry it up, over and to the right of the pattern and continue. Learn this on both sides and then go for *every* throw. The final pattern is a fully **Backwards** version of continuous normal **Chops** in a **Three Ball Cascade**.

Familiarity with **Chops**, especially *outside* **Chops**, will stand you in good stead when working on crossed-hand patterns.

See also **Under the Hand, Turnover, Reachover, Reachunder.**

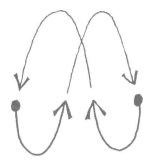

Cascade shape.

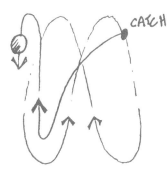

*A **Chop.***

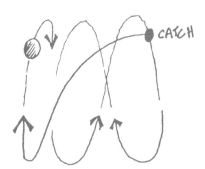

*An outside **Chop.***

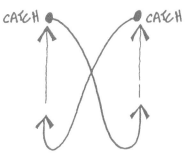

*Continuous **Chops.***

Chop

Cigar Box Moves

Cigar Box Juggling is a highly energetic and comical form of juggling. The cigar box juggler works with three boxes, starting with one in each hand and the third gripped precariously between them. Once upon a time they would have been real cigar boxes, but nowadays jugglers use custom-made wooden boxes with special high-grip ends.

Cigar box juggling has a stop-start style, unlike **Toss Juggling** which tends to be continuous. The juggler might toss the middle box into the air with a couple of side spins, swap the two other boxes from hand to hand and then catch the middle box between them again, thus returning to the start position – ready for the next move which might involve trapping the middle box behind the back, and so on.

Sounds simple? Try it – it's very hard and highly skilled work. You don't have to have cigar boxes though, because many of the cigar box juggler's tricks can be juggled with balls instead, especially if you have three large stage balls.

•The simplest cigar box move is the *Trap*. Start by juggling three balls as normal, then throw one up and catch it by trapping it between the other two. This puts you in the equivalent to the cigar box juggler's starting position and it stops your juggling dead in its tracks.

•Now for the tricky stuff! Release the right-hand ball, **Snatch** the middle ball downwards and *trap* the right hand ball. (To get away with this you'll need to "float" the balls in mid-air for an instant – it's all in the knees!) Phew! You have just done a trick that cigar boxers call a *takeout*.

The *takeout* looks impossible, but it's actually not that difficult to do (don't you just *love* tricks like that?). When you have mastered takeouts on both sides try taking out the middle ball *upwards*.

•No problem, huh? Right, now float the balls in empty space again and release all three. While they hover for that oh-so-brief moment your right hand *takes out* the far left-hand ball, whizzes it right to the other end of the row and back to the starting position. It's just like the *takeout*, but you are taking out the far end ball instead of the middle one.

• A characteristic of cigar box juggling is that you can keep extending moves to ever more improbable realms of difficulty. For example, hop all three up, cross your hands and take out *both* end balls, then uncross your hands and trap.

• Still not tricky enough for you? Float all three balls, release with your left hand and hang on with your right. As your left hand lets go, **Feed** the right-hand ball into it, then take out the left-hand ball with your right hand and back to the trap. Got you that time!

• When you can do all that try adding some **Under the Leg**, **Behind the Back** and **Fork** moves for good measure.

The stop-start style of **Cigar Box Moves** works very well in performance because you can pause between tricks and make eye contact with your audience and hype up whatever move you plan to attempt next.

Claw

The action of swiping a ball out of the air, palm downwards. What some call a **Claw** this book lists as a **Snatch**.

Cold Start

Doing a trick from a **Cold Start** means starting from rest, with all the balls in your hands.

Three-ball jugglers usually find it easier to perform tricks from a **Hot Start**, juggling a **Three Ball Cascade** and then adding tricks to the running pattern. Always using the **Three Ball Cascade** can result in a lot of very samey juggling, so consider using other base patterns like the **Box** and **Five Three One (531)**.

Cold Start

Column Bounce

The **Column Bounce** is a **Bouncing Ball** technique that can be applied to patterns for two, three, four, five or even more. The simplest **Column Bounce** is a two-ball bounce – the **Bouncing Ball** equivalent of juggling **Two in One Hand**.

•In the two-ball **Column Bounce** both balls bounce on the *same spot* and they rise and fall in a perfect vertical line, hence the name.

Start with two **Bouncing Balls** in your favourite hand. Lift the first ball a few inches into the air and let it drop to the floor. As it rebounds, *lift* the second ball into the air directly above it. Now quickly turn your hand to **Snatch** the first ball out of the way before they collide. Keep repeating this exchange and you are juggling a two ball **Column Bounce**.

The throws, or *lifts*, should be very slow and gentle. The catches, or **Snatches**, are quick, almost violent – it's a bit of a knack. The two balls should rise together in perfect unison and you'll find that it helps a lot if you *listen* to the rhythm of the pattern.

When your **Column Bounce** is solid you have opened the door to some truly amazing patterns. A **Column Bounce** pattern is almost always the easiest way of juggling a given number of **Bouncing Balls** – once you have that knack!

•Juggle a two-ball **Column Bounce** while holding a third ball in your spare hand. Then let your hands take turns to juggle the pattern (still bouncing each ball on the same spot) and you have a three-ball pattern using two hands and one column (see **Three Ball Bounce**). It's a kind of **Slow Cascade**.

•To juggle four balls you just do a two-ball **Column Bounce** in both hands at the same time. Take your pick of simultaneous or alternate throws.

Lift. **Snatch!** *Dodge.*

To extend to higher numbers you just apply the following simple rule. Add the number of hands to the number of columns you are juggling, and that's how many balls you can fit into the pattern (the **Capacity**).

Thus one column plus one hand makes a two ball pattern. Two hands plus one column makes a three-ball pattern, three columns plus two hands makes a five-ball pattern (see **Five Ball Column Bounce**), three columns plus one hand gives a **Four in One Hand Bounce** and so on – the floor's the limit.

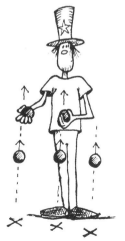

*A **Five Ball Column Bounce**.*
The five balls are juggled in three columns with two hands – three plus two equals five!

Comet

A **Comet** is a fun juggling object. Find three silk scarves and tie them around a set of balls or beanbags so that a long tail is left trailing. Now juggle them!

Comets are especially amazing if you make them from **Bouncing Balls** and fling them at the floor from time to time – somehow it seems surprising when a **Comet** bounces.

Contact Juggling

In contrast to **Toss Juggling**, which is the business of manipulating objects by *throwing* them, **Contact Juggling** is concerned with manipulating objects *without* throwing them; rolling balls up and down your arms, around your head, through your hands and so on. It's a very highly skilled branch of juggling and is quite mesmeric to watch.

Contact Juggling falls largely outside the scope of THE ENCYCLOPÆDIA OF BALL JUGGLING although you will find a few **Contact Juggling** moves amongst all the throws and catches in these pages. See **Fork** and **Ball Surfing** for a couple of examples.

Contortionist

There are many ways of making juggling more difficult than it actually is – but the **Contortionist** takes the biscuit.

•Take three balls, put your right arm behind your back and all the way around to the left side of your body and under your left arm, so you can *see* it. Now juggle a **Three Ball Cascade** in this position.

•It gets worse. Throw a ball out of that contorted position so that you can catch it and continue with your *left* arm behind your back – the mirror image of the previous move.

•Finally, dare to attempt what few ever master. Juggle a **Three Ball Cascade** with *both* arms wrapped around your back.

See also **Eric's Extension**.

Convention

There are few sights more impressive than the one that greets you when you walk into the main hall at a Juggling **Convention**. A multicoloured haze of balls, clubs and general juggling paraphernalia seethes over the heads of the assembled jugglers.

If you haven't been to a **Convention** already then you simply *have* to go to the very next one. In one long weekend your mind will be saturated with more juggling than you've ever dreamt of.

Juggling **Conventions** take place all over the world. In the USA they tend to be large, well-organised and sensible affairs. In the UK (where I live) they tend to be large, well-organised and fairly silly.

You can find out when and where **Conventions** are taking place by visiting the web sites listed under **Internet Resources.**

Cranes

This is *the* all-time classic **Gandini Pattern**. A masterpiece of **Square Juggling** for two jugglers and five balls.

•Stand side by side with your partner and practise with just one ball to begin with, so you can both get familiar with the route taken by the balls.

You catch a falling ball with your inside hand, carry it across your body to the outside and toss it vertically up to your outside hand (which pretends to be a tower crane). The crane then carries the ball over to your partner's juggling space and drops it – whereupon your partner mirrors what you just did.

•OK, now do it with five balls.

HINT: It's a **Domino Pattern** and it will help if you can both juggle the **Factory**.

Cross Arm Cascade

• Take three balls, two in one hand and one in the other. Now cross your arms and juggle.

• You'll probably find yourself juggling a **Reverse Cascade** (it's easier) so make sure you try a normal **Cascade** as well (it's harder).

• And don't forget to try each version in both right-over-left and left-over-right crossage.

Cross Arm Tennis

This is the name of a **Four Two Three (423)** pattern in which the 3-ball is thrown back and forth from a crossed-hand position. It's now generally accepted that this pattern is so similar to the **Fake Mess** that it is, in fact, the same thing.

Really pedantic jugglers might argue that in the **Fake Mess** the *2-ball* is swung under the pattern (as if *faking* a throw) while in **Cross Arm Tennis** this move is omitted.

This is a minor point of style – the real point being that if you have learnt to juggle one, then you have also learnt the other.

Does that make them the same pattern?

I'm not sure, and since I'm terrified of pedantic jugglers I have included entries for both.

See also **Fake Mess**, **Tennis**, **Four Two Three (423)**.

The original sketch of **Dancey's Devilment.** *Note that at least one ball is doing something that is clearly impossible.*

Dancey's Devilment

In the original edition of THE ENCYCLOPÆDIA OF BALL JUGGLING I wrote:

Dancey's Devilment: A mythical juggling pattern of brain-bending complexity and subterfuge. It came to me in a dream but the memory of just precisely what it was faded infuriatingly as I woke in the morning.

I seem to remember that it was a four- or five-ball pattern with the looping features of **Rubenstein's Revenge** combined with **Multiplex** throws of varying kinds. Complex, interwoven and visually hypnotic, this may be the lost chord of ball juggling. Should you accidentally discover this trick, please write and tell me what it was.

To my amazement people took this seriously and **Dancey's Devilment** has taken on a life of it's own. Supposedly sane jugglers all over the world argue about the exact details of the trick. If you search the Internet you'll find videos of people *actually doing it.* Strangers have walked up to me at **Conventions,** done weird stuff with balls and then asked me if they have got it right!

I have no idea! The fact is that I have a trick named after me that I *can't actually do!* So here's something I've been itching to say ever since I started this job.

"If you want to learn this trick you'll have to work it out for yourself! So there!"

Dancey's Devilment

Difficulty

Sometimes people get the wrong idea about juggling, thinking that the basic idea is to do something horrendously difficult just to prove that you can. From this point of view the greater the **Difficulty** of a trick, the better it is.

"How many balls can *you* juggle?" – is therefore the question that jugglers get asked most often. There are scores of **Numbers Jugglers** out there who would never have begun their war against **Gravity** if they had just known how to answer that question. The right answer is, of course, "One more than you."

Since we all like to know just exactly how brilliantly clever we are I have devised a simple formula for working out *Dancey's Juggling Index* – a fair way of grading the difficulty of juggling a given number of balls in a given number of hands. The formula only works well for simple patterns, like the **Cascades** and **Fountains** since it takes no account of frilly bits like **Behind the Back**. The simplest, most obvious (and incorrect) formula would be:

$$d = b/h$$

In plain English, the **Difficulty** is *the number of balls divided by the number of*

hands. This doesn't paint a very fair picture since **Two in One Hand** gets the same score (2) as a **Four Ball Fountain**. Everyone knows that juggling four is harder than juggling two, so the formula needs a little modification. The correct calculation is:

$$d=b/(h + h/b)$$

– which has an authoritative sort of symmetry to it.

A nice feature of the *Index* is that anything that gets a score of less than 1 is not really juggling. One ball in one hand gets 0.5, two balls in two hands gets 0.6666 (well it *is* harder, just not *much* harder). One hundred balls in one hundred hands gets 0.99. Real juggling starts at 1.0 on the scale of *Dancey's Juggling Index*. Three balls in

two hands (a **Three Ball Cascade**) gets 1.125 which is slightly less than the score for **Two in One Hand**, 1.3333.

Most of the comparisons you can read off from the table below seem to correspond well with the real world. Five-ball jugglers (2.08) can usually manage **Three in One Hand** (2.25) in their best hand. Similarly seven-ball jugglers (3.06) are normally happy with four in one hand (3.2). Four ball jugglers (1.6) find passing seven balls between two jugglers quite easy (1.53) and so on. If everything I have heard is true then I believe that the limit of human capability measures off at about 6.0 on this scale. And my score? You should know me better than to think that I would take such a thing seriously.

I showed the formula to a **Numbers Juggler** to see what they thought about it. "No good," was the comment: "*This* is what you want: d=(b/(h+h/b)) x **100!**"

		1	2	3	4	*Number of Balls* 5	6	7	8	9	10	11	12
	1	0.5	1.3333	2.25	3.2	4.1667	5.1429	6.125	7.1111	8.1	9.0909	10.083	11.077
	2	0.25	0.6667	1.125	1.6	**2.0833**	2.5714	3.0625	3.5556	4.05	4.5455	5.0417	5.5385
Hands	3	0.1667	0.4444	0.75	1.0667	1.3889	1.7143	2.0417	2.3704	2.7	3.0303	3.3611	3.6923
	4	0.125	0.3333	0.5625	0.8	1.0417	1.2857	1.5313	1.7778	2.025	2.2727	2.5208	2.7692
	5	0.1	0.2667	0.45	0.64	0.8333	1.0286	1.225	1.4222	1.62	1.8182	2.0167	2.2154
	6	0.0833	0.2222	0.375	0.5333	0.6944	0.8571	1.0208	1.1852	1.35	1.5152	1.6806	1.8462

*Dancey's Juggling Index to four decimal places for one to twelve balls and one to six hands. The **Five Ball Cascade** with its score of 2.0833 is marked in bold type. What's your score?*

Disappearing Ball

Well they do, don't they? Especially those very expensive silicone **Bouncing Balls** once they bounce out of the door and down the street. Any experienced juggler's front-room sofa has a couple of lost juggling balls lurking underneath in its dusty depths. There is also a juggling trick, listed in the *Encyclopædia* under **Abracadabra**, in which a ball vanishes before the amazed eyes of the audience.

Domino Pattern

• Get a box of dominoes and stand each of them on end forming a long line across the floor.

Knock over the first one (tee hee!) and a chain reaction starts. Each domino topples its neighbour and a wave of falling dominoes travels down the line.

This is great fun and seriously addictive! Major domino topplers spend *weeks* setting up huge complex patterns containing hundreds of thousands of dominoes. After many sleepless nights in terror of *sabotage* they enjoy the oh so brief satisfaction of watching the whole lot fall over in a few seconds.

It's completely mad! But I wouldn't have mentioned it in THE ENCYCLOPÆDIA unless it had something to do with ball juggling*.

Imagine an alien juggler with, say, eight arms arranged around its body. Feeling a little bored our interstellar friend decides to

*OK, yes, I admit the **Aardvark** thing.

have a quick juggle. It picks up nine balls, two in the right hand and one in each of its seven left hands – it's a right handed alien, OK?

The pattern starts with the right throwing to the first left hand, then that hand has to throw to the *next* left hand in order to clear itself for the catch, and so the chain reaction of throws runs around and around just like falling dominoes. This is a nine-ball **Domino Pattern**, a chain reaction of throws.

Continued overleaf...

39

Domino Pattern...

Domino Patterns are the simplest patterns for any given number of hands. They always use one more ball than there are hands; each throw triggers the next and the last hand throws back to the first.

The **Three Ball Cascade** is a **Domino Pattern** for two hands, and if you look up **One Count** you'll find a **Domino Pattern** for five balls and four hands.

• **Domino Patterns** are useful for **Beach Ball Juggling**. With beach balls you need to use *both hands* for throwing and catching, so a **Domino Pattern** for beach balls uses one more beach ball than you have jugglers.

Stand three jugglers, **A**, **B** and **C**, in a line, **A** gets two beach balls, **B** and **C** get one each. **A** throws to **B**, **B** throws to **C** and **C** throws back to **A**. That's all there is to it!

Double

Club jugglers tend to describe throws as **Singles**, **Doubles** and **Triples**, depending on how many turns a club makes in the air.

A **Single** is usually a 3, a **Double** a 4 and a **Triple** a **5** – so if you are translating from clubspeak to ballspeak you can be pretty sure that "throwing a **Double**" means throwing a **4**.

A notable exception to this is the cascade of five. Whether you are juggling balls, rings or clubs, every throw is a **5**, but the club jugglers tend to use **Double** spins because the pattern is a lot easier that way!

*The **Four Ball Fountain**.*

*Club jugglers normally use **Double** spins when juggling a four club fountain. As far as the ball juggler is concerned, every throw is a 4.*

Drop

An otherwise great book on juggling (which shall remain nameless) claims that *"a drop is a sign of progress"*.

This is not true. Unless you are throwing balls at the floor on purpose, a **Drop** is a sign of a mistake. The only progress involved was the ball's progress towards the centre of the earth – and even that has been stopped short by its meeting with the floor. Jugglers form only a small percentage of the world's population, but they are responsible for *most* of the world's **Drops**.

If you are performing in front of an audience it's a really good idea not to let them see you **Drop**. A practical way of achieving this is only to perform tricks that you can do *five times in a row* in practice without a mistake.

If you do **Drop** in a show there are only two things you can do – ignore it and carry on regardless or make a big thing out of it. Feeling guilty and awkward about a **Drop** is *out of the question*.

The "ignore and continue" method is only ever justifiable if you are working to taped music or for some other reason are unable to take a few seconds out of your scheduled routine to deal with the problem properly.

Making a big thing of it is the best method. *You* saw it hit the floor, *they* saw it hit the floor (secretly they were hoping it would). *Everybody* saw it hit the floor! There's no getting out of it.

Jugglers have, over the years, come up with literally hundreds of gags and one-liners, called *drop-lines* in the trade, which get wheeled out whenever there is a **Drop.** Here are some examples:

"I washed my hands today and I can't do a thing with them."

"OK, who threw that?"

"I also have a slightly longer version of this routine."

"I'm trying out a new finish."

"I'm also very good with two balls."

(POINTING AT BALL) *"Stay!"*

"Lucky that ball hit the floor, otherwise it would have kept right on going!"

"It's OK! That one was a spare."

(DROPPING EVERYTHING ELSE AND PLACING HANDS OVER ONE EYE) *"Aargh! I have something huge stuck in my eye!"*

"Don't worry about that, it was just a sudden gust of gravity."

And so on. Drop-lines are an art form in their own right, so much so that in the end you'll be putting *deliberate* **Drops** into your show, just so you can do all those gags you've been saving up.

Don't make a habit of using the same drop-lines every time (that's just a way of trying to avoid the situation) and *do make up your own*, rather than just copying somebody else's. Other people's lines may seem to *you* to be the funniest, but the best ones are *always* the ones you make up yourself.

If you ever find yourself completely flummoxed by a **Drop** and you really can't think of a single thing to say, just take a bow! You'll be amazed at just how well that works!

Drop

Dropswap

This **Floor Juggling** pattern, invented by Michael Karas, combines **One-up Two-up**, the **Box**, and a whole lot of carefully timed **Drops** and **Pickups** to produce a bewildering four-ball pattern.

You'll need to use **Beanbags**, unless you are lucky enough to be juggling on a sandy beach. If you can find four **Beanbags** of different colours, so much the better.

Now before trying to juggle we need to *think* our way through this pattern.

• Kneel down and place three beanbags in front of you, one in front of each knee, and one in the middle. Hold the fourth beanbag in your right hand.

This pattern is juggled in five columns; the three beanbags on the floor mark the middle three. Those three beanbags will always stay in their own columns, and all three of them will hit the floor from time to time (landing exactly where they are now). So note where they are, because that's where you'll be picking them up from. We'll call them the *left-ball, middle-ball* and *right-ball*.

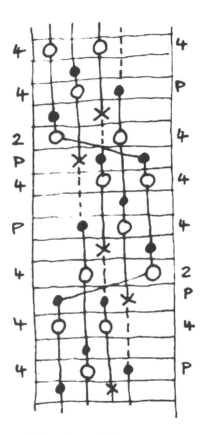

*A **Ladder** chart of the **Dropswap**. The **X**'s indicate the moment at which balls hit the floor. The dotted lines indicate time on the floor.*

The ball in your right hand is the only one that never hits the floor. We'll call it the *crossing-ball*.

It may help if you can find four differently coloured balls.

The *crossing-ball* will be tossed up on the far right of the pattern, caught, slammed across to the opposite hand, tossed up there and then slammed back. You can practice that if you want; the crossing throw is a **2** just like the crossing throw in a **Box**.

That's enough *thinking*, it's time to juggle.

• Arrange the balls into their starting positions: the *crossing-ball* goes in your right hand together with the *right-ball*. The *middle-ball* goes in your left hand. The *left-ball* stays on the floor.

That's the set-up – now let's do it!

(This is just the start.) Do a *One-up*, throwing the right-ball straight up in the right column with your right hand.

1. Do a **Two-up**, throwing the *crossing-ball* and *middle-ball* up on either side of the *right-ball*.

2. Do a *One-up* again with the *right-ball*, and catch the *crossing-ball* while picking up the *left-ball* with your left hand.

3. The *middle-ball* hits the deck – plop! Do a **Box** throw to the right (your right hand slams the *crossing-ball* across while your left hand throws the *left-ball* straight up).

4. Pick up the *middle-ball* with your right hand. The *right-ball* will hit the deck – splat!

We're now halfway through – we're going to repeat steps 1 to 4 mirrorwise.

5. Do a **Two-up**, throwing the *crossing-ball* and *middle-ball* up on either side of the *left-ball*.

6. Do a *One-up* again with the *left-ball*, and catch the *crossing-ball* while simultaneously picking up the *right-ball* with your right hand.

7. The *middle-ball* hits the deck – plop! Do a **Box** throw to the right (your left hand slams the *crossing-ball* across while your right hand throws the *right-ball* straight up).

8. Pick up the *middle-ball* with your left hand. The *left-ball* will hit the deck – splat!

You've now thrown the whole sequence, go back to step 1 and repeat.

It's going to take you a few tries to get this one right; there's something most disconcerting about deliberate **Drops**.

See also **Floor Juggling**, **Box**, **Robotic Drop**.

| 1 | 2 | 3 | 4 | 5 | 6 | 7 | 8 |

Dropswap

Dyer's Straights

A fiendishly knacksome pattern for three **Bouncing Balls** that taps out a pleasant rhythm on the floor.

Dyer's Straights uses single and double bounces and is juggled in four columns. Every throw is a **Force Bounce**, and the hands throw alternately. Once the pattern is running you will be making vertical downward throws into the four columns, *left-right-left* in the two right-hand columns followed by *right-left-right* in the two left columns. Your body will need to swing from side to side, as you juggle. It's a good idea to mime that sequence before trying anything foolish – like adding **Bouncing Balls**. Try it now and what follows will be infinitely clearer.

• Done that? Good. Now in the *left-right-left* and *right-left-right* throwing sequences the *first* two throws are snappy little **Self** throws. You throw the balls straight down and catch them as they wham back up into the throwing hand. It's good style to make them really punchy and quick. Practise these snappy throws with just two balls: *left-right* and *right-left*.

• You are definitely getting there now. The *third* throw in each sequence is allowed to bounce twice, so in the full pattern you'll

be juggling *leftsnappy-rightsnappy-left* in the two right-hand columns. Then you leave that last *left* to bounce twice while you swing your body to the left and juggle *rightsnappy-leftsnappy-right* in the left two columns. Your hands do not cross at any time!

• Here's the full pattern. Start with two in the right and one in the left, imagine four columns before you and mentally number them one to four from the left. You start the pattern by dumping the first ball, from your right hand, into column two, where it will bounce twice.

Now swing to the right and juggle *leftsnappy-rightsnappy-left* using columns three and four. That last *left* stays to bounce twice. Swing to the left, picking up the double-bounced ball in column two in your left hand as you go, and juggle *rightsnappy-leftsnappy-right*. That last *right* stays to bounce twice.

Just keep going and that's it!

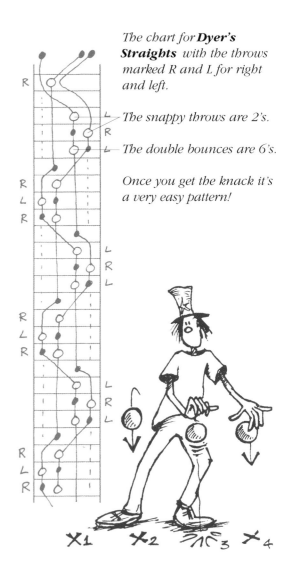

The chart for **Dyer's Straights** *with the throws marked R and L for right and left.*

The snappy throws are 2's.

The double bounces are 6's.

Once you get the knack it's a very easy pattern!

Eating the Apple

You've been practising your **Mills' Mess** all day and you've *nearly* got it after hours of nerve-knotting effort. Feeling dead chuffed you show a friend your new trick.

"Hmm, that's *quite* good!" they say, "But I saw this juggler the other day juggling and eating an apple at the *same time!* It was *incredible!*"

It's the simple tricks that get them every time. Forget the artistic technical moves – get right down to your audience's level and impress them with the *easy* stuff!

•Juggle a **Three Ball Cascade** with two balls and one apple.

(New Zealand Cox ones are best because they don't spray them with chlorofluoro-carbons and E numbers. They are also a good size.)

Now take a bite. The *hard* way is to wait until the apple is in your best hand, quickly whizz it over to your mouth and then throw it back into the pattern. This has to be lightning fast, you have about a fifth of a second, and you could lose teeth!

•Here's an easier method. Catch the apple in your right hand and *place* it in your mouth, gripping it with your teeth. Keep juggling the other two balls as a **Gap** pattern until the **Gap** comes to your left hand. Then take the apple out of your mouth with your left hand, biting off a chunk as it goes.

•Here is the easiest way of all. Juggle a **Three Ball Cascade**. As the apple arrives in your right hand, throw a **Self** 4 from the left. In other words, go into **Two in One Hand** in the left hand for *just one throw*. This gives you plenty of time to take a nice leisurely bite.

•Repeat whichever technique you are happy with until the apple is nearly all gone (this can take *ages*). Then throw the core high and catch it in your mouth for a neat finish. In performance you have to work fast to prevent the audience from becoming bored. Be messy! Ravenously savage that piece of fruit!

Continued overleaf...

Eating the Apple...

- If you juggle a ball, a fork and an apple you can use an alternative finish – eat about half the apple, then throw it up and catch it by impaling it on the fork.

- Other fruits, especially **Bananas** (which need to be peeled in the air using a combination of teeth and the **Two in One Hand** technique) can be eaten to good effect while juggling.

- It's perfectly possible, and very amusing, to eat an apple while juggling a **Passing Pattern**. You'll need to create **Gaps** in the pattern by throwing **4**'s and **5**'s (see **Three Count**, **Four Count** etc.).

- Alternatively, when working with another juggler, get them to juggle a **Three Ball Cascade** while *you* eat the apple.

It sounds boring, and it is, until you throw the half-eaten fruit *very high*, and **Steal** their pattern while the apple is still in the air. You end up with the cascade and your partner catches the apple and finishes it off for you.

Eggs

Yes – you *can* juggle with **Eggs!**

Eggs are great juggling props because they provide your routine with instant dramatic tension. The audience knows what will happen if you drop one and, of course, they are secretly hoping that you will.

Leaving aside your natural nervousness about working with such breakable balls, there is really no problem about juggling with **Eggs** – it's *stopping* that is the problem, especially if you attempt the *Five Egg Omelette* (sorry, *Cascade*).

To finish an **Egg** juggle you need to make an ultra-delicate catch that follows the last **Egg** almost all the way to the floor, thus minimising its impact on its brothers and sisters.*

Believe it or not, there is a **Bouncing Ball** pattern that can include **Eggs**. See **Six-Three-Three** to find out how this miracle is performed.

*Think about it!

Eric's Extension

Just when you thought the **Mills' Mess** was the ultimate in crossed-hand work, along comes Eric Urhane who adds an extra twist to the pattern. You'll need to be a master of the **Mills' Mess** to have even the remotest chance of pulling this trick off.

- Start with no balls at all, cross your left hand over your right, look at your left hand and say "Throw!" as you uncross your hands.

- Now look at your right hand and say "Throw!" while simultaneously crossing the right hand over the left.

- Now look at your left hand and say "Throw!"

So far so good: you've just *mimed* the first three throws of a **Mills' Mess**. Anyone with any sense would now repeat those movements mirrorwise to complete the pattern – but not Eric Urhane. He continues like this:

- Now tuck your right hand under your left (yes it does hurt), look at it and say "Throw!"

You have just added an extra twist to the **Mills' Mess**.

To continue the pattern you just unwind from here:

• While your hands are still double crossed you make a throw from the left hand and move your left hand to the right.

• Now throw from the right hand and uncross your hands.

• Throw from the left hand and cross it over the right.

• Throw from the right hand and then double-cross the left under the right (ouch again!).

You are now double-crossed on the opposite side.

You'll find that **Eric's Extension** produces *five* throws on each side of the pattern compared to the three throws of the **Mills' Mess**.

OK, so once you have the throwing sequence in your head you are ready to try adding some balls. The pattern, like the three-ball **Mills' Mess**, is just a **Three Ball**

Cascade juggled in a complex shape.

A good tip is to juggle the pattern higher than you normally would; this will make it easier to achieve the double-cross. It also helps if you have spindly arms – so if you are a body-builder you probably have no chance at all with this trick.

An easier way to juggle **Eric's Extension** is to juggle it as a **Gandini Pattern** and use two arms that are not connected to the same body.

• Find a partner and get them to stand on your left. Now hook your left arm under your partner's right. You will be using your left hand only, and your partner will be using their right hand only. It's a good idea to mime your way through the hand

movements a couple of times before adding the balls. You are A, and your partner is B.

To start, A makes a throw that loops to the left, leaving their left hand in front of B's body.

B makes a throw that also loops to the left, leaving your arms uncrossed.

A makes another left looping throw and crosses their left arm over B's right.

B makes another throw and adds another half twist.

A makes a final left looping throw.

Your arms are now fully twisted together in the exact mirror image of your starting position.

• Reverse the exercise with imaginary balls until you are both familiar with the sequence, then add some balls and do the real thing!

Eric's Extension

Excited State Pattern

An **Excited State Pattern** is a **Siteswap** pattern that can't be juggled from a **Cold Start**, as opposed to a **Ground State Pattern** which can.

The **Three Ball Shower (51)** is an **Excited State Pattern** because you can't just grab three balls and start throwing **515151.**

• Try it! You'll get an immediate collision as the first **1** will cause you to **Feed** a ball into a hand that is already holding a ball.

Instead you can go **5 2 51515151…**

Mind you, the rules of **Siteswap** aren't exactly laws of nature, they are just a set of mathematical rules which produce some interesting results if you play around with them.

You can, if you wish, **Feed** a ball into a hand that's already holding a ball. It's called a **Squeeze** or **Reverse Multiplex**.

Go look them up!

See also **Ground State Pattern**.

Extended Box

This pattern is an extension of the **Square Juggling** pattern, the **Box.**

• Before juggling an **Extended Box** you need to learn how to move a **Box** pattern *one frame to the right*. This might sound weird but it makes sense when you do it.

In the **Box** your hands throw simultaneously, the right throws a 4 while the left throws a 2, then on the next throw the left throws a 4 while the right throws a 2.

To move one frame to the right throw right 4 and left 2 *twice in a row* and then continue with a normal **Box**. You need to move the *whole pattern* to the right as you do this. It's a pretty good trick on its own and looks very perplexing to an audience.

• The full **Extended Box** pattern is simply a matter of moving one frame to the right and then one to the left and repeating. Try to keep a good square shape to the pattern and concentrate on making *three* well-defined columns in the air, instead of the normal two columns of the standard **Box**.

*A **Ladder Notation** chart for the **Extended Box**.*

Some charts are tricky to draw, requiring lines to be curved slightly so that they don't get all tangled up and unreadable – just imagine what the London Underground map would look like if it showed the real routes that the trains took!

Factory

The **Factory** (sometimes called the **Machine**) is a **Square Juggling** move – perhaps the *best* **Square Juggling** move there is.

The audience sees you juggling three balls, then one ball is raised straight up, as if by a crane, carried horizontally across the top of the pattern and dropped back in. The contrast of this very *square* move against the usual curves of juggling is what makes the trick so special. You can be guaranteed a good response from any audience when you juggle a **Factory**.

•Begin by juggling **Two in One Hand**, in columns, in your right hand. Your left hand, holding the third ball, mimics the rise and fall of the ball in the rightmost column. This is, in fact, the **Fake** (this is described on the next page).

As your left hand reaches the top it turns sharp right, travels across the top of the pattern and drops its ball at the far right of the pattern.

The left hand then zooms back to the left of the pattern and **Snatches** the left-most (formerly the middle) ball. Phew! That puts you back where you started, except that the balls have all swapped places in the pattern.

At first you should concentrate on just *doing* the trick – but as you get more solid you start to *perform* it. Start to exaggerate! Make a really crisp right angle and really *show off* the held ball.

•The **Factory** can be juggled on alternate sides, or continuously from one side. It looks very neat if you step to the side as you carry the ball. This can be used as a very flashy way of exiting, stage left!

Other **Square Juggling** moves that share the **Factory**'s right angled roboticism are the **Robotic Drop**, the **Robot Bounce** and, of course, the **Box**.

Fake...

...lift...

...across...

...Snatch!

Factory

Fake

This is a simple comedy trick, closely related to the **Yo-yo**. You need to be able to juggle a really solid **Fake** before you learn the **Factory** (previous page).

• Start by juggling **Two in One Hand** in columns in your right hand, while holding a third ball in your left hand.

Ready? Now move your left hand up and down so that its movement precisely mirrors the movement of the rightmost ball. The effect is that of juggling the pattern **One-up Two-up**, but you are *faking* it by *cheating* with one ball. It is

very important that you get the two outside balls moving precisely in sync. Exaggerate the "cheat" by holding the rogue ball between thumb and forefinger with your other fingers outstretched.

If you find this hard to do then warm up by just making any old movement with your free hand while juggling **Two in One Hand** in the other. Touch your head, touch your foot, swing your arm around. After this just going up and down will seem much easier.

The trick should be done with a suitably stupid expression on your face. If you are working in front of kids they will all shout, "You're not juggling that one!" This is the moment to swap the **Fake** onto the *other* side of the pattern.

"No, no! Now you're not juggling the *other* one!"

Avoid getting into any sort of discussion with the kids* but keep swapping from side to side so quickly that it's obvious that you must be juggling with *something* – then move on to the next trick. The best trick to follow a **Fake** with is the **Factory**.

*Discussing subtle points of performance with kids is a short route to a riot.

Fake Mess

This is a **Four Two Three (423)** pattern. Some call it **Cross Arm Tennis** but the name **Fake Mess** is a better description. It looks a if you are *faking* a **Mills' Mess**. Curiously, even though it is a lot simpler than the real thing, many jugglers with **Mills' Mess** skills don't know this one.

Here's how to learn it:

• Juggle **Right Middle Left** to warm up. Pay close attention to the *3-ball* (that's the middle ball).

• OK, now every time you catch the 3-ball with the left hand, position your left arm so that it's *crossed over the right*. Similarly, every time you catch it in your right hand, your right arm should be *crossed over the left*. The *3-ball* now travels back and forth with **Reverse Cascade** throws.

It's just a shape change.

• Got that? Now every time your left arm is crossed over, swing your right arm so it's *crossed under as if you are going to throw* **Under the Hand** (but don't throw the ball it's holding!)

• Likewise, when your right arm is crossed over, swing your left arm underneath.

That's all there is to it! It's a devilishly simple pattern, but can be a little tricky to get, especially if you can already juggle a **Mills' Mess** – you'll find your hands are keen to make all sorts of unnecessary throws out of pure habit.

• The **Fake Mess** has the rather unusual property of being a *time-reversed* version of itself. It is exactly the same forwards or **Backwards**.

See also **Mills' Mess**, **Follow**, **Right Middle Left**, **Four Two Three (423)**.

Fast Start

The **Fast Start** is a way of starting a **Passing Pattern**.

In a **Fast Start** the *very first throw* is a pass, as opposed to a **Slow Start** in which the jugglers make four self throws before the first pass.

Fast Starts are almost always used in situations where there are more than three balls per juggler.

Fast Start

Feed

In solo juggling a **Feed** is the action of one hand placing a ball directly into another, rather than throwing it. In terms of numbers, a **Feed** is a **1**, a throw with no **Airtime** at all.

The **Feed** is the throw on the *easy* side of a **Shower** pattern. A three-ball **Shower** uses **5**'s and **1**'s – that is **Five Ball Cascade** throws on one side, and **Feeds** on the other. A four-ball **Shower** uses **7**'s and **1**'s. A five-ball **Shower** uses **9**'s and **1**'s.

In **Passing Patterns** the word **Feed** has a different meaning. It is used to describe an arrangement of jugglers in which one juggler passes radially out to all the others – that juggler is **Feeding** the rest.

• The simplest **Feed** is an arrangement of three jugglers in vee formation; call them **A**, **B** and **C**.

A (who is going to **Feed**) stands facing **B** on the right and **C** on the left. All three jugglers start with three balls, two in the right and one in the left. They all start juggling together.

A juggles a **Two Count**, passing on every right-hand throw. The passes are aimed at **B** and **C** alternately. **B** and **C** juggle **Four Counts**, both passing to **A**.

Obviously, since **A** can only pass to one person at a time, only **A** and **B** pass on the first throw, **C** has to juggle two **Selfs** before passing the first ball.

A can throw any **Tricks** that would work in a **Two Count**. **B** and **C** can throw any **Tricks** that would work in a **Four Count**. The resulting chaos of balls can create an incredible display and is enormous fun to juggle.

While the **Feed** is good fun, it is perhaps *more* fun for the feeder than the fed. This is OK if **A** is a stronger juggler but really you should all swap around so that you all get the valuable practice at the *hard end*.

As an alternative you could juggle a more even arrangement, like the **Triangle**.

See also **Ten Ball Feed**.

Five Ball Bounce

The **Five Ball Cascade** can be juggled as a **Bouncing Ball** pattern. There are two basic styles, the **Reverse Cascade** style and the **Force Bounce**. Jugglers call both these patterns a **Five Ball Bounce**.

Reverse Cascade.

If you just want to juggle five **Bouncing Balls** and you don't care how you do it then you should look up the **Five Ball Column Bounce** which is *much* easier.

• The **Reverse Cascade** style is much more relaxed than the **Force Bounce**. Each ball is *lifted* over the approaching ball so that the paths of the balls cross on the way down.

Learning to bounce five balls is much like learning to juggle five in the air except that the balls travel downwards. You should follow the same path of practice described for the **Five Ball Cascade**. Start with the three- and four-ball exercises and then work your way up (or down) to the full pattern.

Fumbles and collisions are catastrophic. Balls bounce off all over the place, disappearing down drains, under the sofa and always in at least three different directions. Be kind to yourself by finding a really good practice area. Fence yourself in with cushions, furniture or whatever you can find so you won't have to run miles every time you drop!

You will find that the **Five Ball Bounce** is a gentler pattern than the **Five Ball Cascade** because so little force is required to keep it going. Every throw in the **Five Ball Cascade** has to be propelled three or four feet into the air while the **Bouncing Balls** only need to be *lifted* a few inches.

• The **Force Bounce** style is considerably harder. The downwards throwing action feels unnatural, and your hands tend to obscure your view of the balls. The balls cross each other's paths on the way *up* in the **Force Bounce**.

Force Bounce.

Continued overleaf...

Five Ball Bounce...

Any slight aiming errors in the **Force Bounce** tend to get magnified as the balls bounce from the floor (which is never quite perfectly level) and then you get collisions.

Juggling a three-ball **Force Bounce** *very fast* is good practice for five. With **Force Bounce** patterns *you* control the speed, whereas the speed of a **Reverse Cascade** bounce pattern is set by the height of your hands from the floor. Taller jugglers juggle slower **Reverse Cascade** bounce patterns!

One major advantage of the control you get in a **Force Bounce** is that you can juggle the pattern over floors that would be too dead for the **Reverse Cascade** bounce by throwing the balls harder to compensate for the poor bounce.

• When you can juggle both styles you can try changing from one to the other while juggling.

You'll find that a straight change from a **Reverse Cascade** to a **Force Bounce** causes collisions. The secret is to start a new pattern, a few inches closer to your body. The balls are *taken out* of the reverse pattern and *thrown into* the force pattern, moving into a new plane as they go.

• Changing from **Force Bounce** to the **Reverse Cascade** bounce is easier – just do it! Everything miraculously misses everything else.

• You can combine **Reverse Cascade** throws and **Force Bounce** throws to create some interesting rhythms – start by learning to throw one **Force Bounce** at a time in the **Reverse Cascade** and see where you get to!

• Changing from a **Force Bounce** into a **Five Ball Cascade** in the air is a great trick.

Throw three extra hard bounces, so that three balls **Flash** out of the pattern and rise above your head – from there it's straight into the **Five Ball Cascade**. The knack is to aim those three hard throws so that they don't spread too wide as they rise up through the pattern. Begin by practising three ball **Flashes**, bounced off the floor. When that's solid try the trick from a **Cold Start** – three balls in the right hand, two in the left. Throw your three-ball bounced **Flash**, watch the balls rise and go straight into the **Five Ball Cascade**.

• You can **Steal** five-ball bounce patterns. The most important ingredient is another five-ball bounce juggler. Stand face to face and get your partner to juggle the smoothest **Five Ball Bounce** that they can manage.

Take the balls *on the rise* to their hands. Your hands must stay below your partner's until the balls are entirely in your control.

You are in control as soon as you have caught the first three balls – the other two follow naturally. As with any other **Steal**, you must be positive and decisive when you move in or your partner will drop in anticipation!

• With **Bouncing Balls** you can make throws with massive **Airtime** by simply letting balls bounce *more than once*. Here's a trick that uses a 10, a throw you are very unlikely to see in the air!

From a **Reverse Cascade** bounce you can lift (rather than *throw)* a ball *straight up* on the right-hand side of the pattern. Let it bounce *twice* on the same spot while you keep the other four balls running in a **Five Ball Gap** pattern. *Don't* hold through the **Gap**, just keep going.

You'll find that the ball arrives back at your right hand (after its two bounces) at exactly the same time as the **Gap**. Grab it and continue the **Five Ball Bounce**. That throw was a right self 10! The corresponding trick in the air would involve throwing a ball five times higher than the cascade itself!

*This chart shows how a 10 fits into the scheme of a **Five Ball Bounce**. Really keen jugglers might like to attempt this in the air. The 10 will need to be <u>five times</u> as high as your **Five Ball Cascade**. See **Airtime** to find out why!*

Continued overleaf...

Five Ball Bounce...

Five Ball Cascade

The **Five Ball Cascade** is the purest five-ball pattern there is. It is a landmark in the juggling career of anyone who achieves it, the beginning (and for many the *end*) of **Numbers Juggling**. Whenever you see a **Five Ball Cascade** you can be sure of one thing – that juggler has been *practising* a lot.

Anyone can learn to juggle a **Five Ball Cascade** but, since humans were not designed with five-ball juggling in mind, it will *always* take a good deal of work to get there. There is no shortcut.

If you are looking for an easy way of juggling five balls you could "cheat" and learn **Five Ball Splits**, or pick up some **Bouncing Balls** and go for the **Five Ball Column Bounce**, or even a straight **Five Ball Bounce**. All these patterns are easier than the **Five Ball Cascade** juggled in the air. But, human nature being what it is, you want to be a *real* juggler, you want to feel good about yourself as you walk down the street, become the envy of your friends – you want to learn the **Five Ball Cascade**. It's a great thing to do, you *will* get there, and it really *does* feel good when you do. Just don't expect to do it in a couple of weeks! Read on.

• Here's another great trick that uses 10's, based on the **Reverse Cascade** bounce.

Juggle the **Five Ball Bounce** and then throw a right self **10*** immediately followed by a left self **10**. Now you juggle five throws of a **Three Ball Cascade**, in the air, while the two **10**'s bounce twice. If you stay on time you'll find that you can catch the **10**'s and go back into the **Five Ball Bounce** as if nothing had happened.

It looks amazing, as if you "forgot" you were juggling five balls for a moment! The secret is to keep the rhythm of the pattern absolutely steady throughout – the brief **Three Ball Cascade** is juggled at exactly the same tempo as the **Five Ball Bounce**. You'll also find, with *all* **Bouncing Ball** patterns, that *listening* to the bounces helps. Turn that music *down*!

• While working on your **Five Ball Bounce** you'll probably develop a taste for hanging out in shopping malls and airports where the floors are usually very good indeed. If you should locate a marble staircase then you can practise juggling your pattern up and down the steps.

*In **Siteswap Notation** throws over **9** are usually written as letters rather than numbers. So a **10** becomes an **A**, an eleven becomes a **B** and so forth. I've used numbers here because they make more sense in this context.

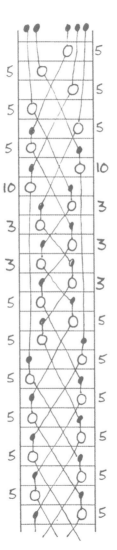

*How to throw two **10**'s in a **Five Ball Bounce**. You get to make five throws of a **Three Ball Cascade** as those two balls bounce twice.*

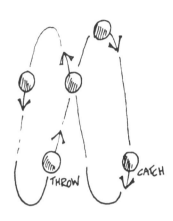

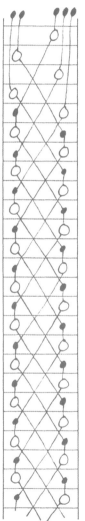

*The **Five Ball Cascade** – just like a **Three Ball Cascade** only higher!*

At any given moment there are four balls in the air, and it's absolutely guaranteed that when you first attempt the pattern your brain will be quite unable to make any sense out of the chaos that is happening in front of you – persevere and everything will slowly fall into place.

• Start your training with just three balls by juggling a three-ball **Shower** *both* ways around. This pattern uses 5's thrown from one hand and 1's (**Feeds**) from the other. The full **Five Ball Cascade** is, of course, 5's from both hands. By practising the **Shower** you are building up the skill in your hands to this level.

While working on the **Shower**, make a point of starting and stopping with three balls in one hand – you'll need this skill later so you may as well learn it now!

• The three-ball **Flash** is often reckoned to be good practice for five balls.

Juggle a **Three Ball Cascade** and then pump all three balls out to around four times their usual height (in other words, throw three consecutive **5**'s) – clap your hands once while they are all in the air and then continue the **Cascade**. Make sure you balance this practice by throwing both right-handed *and* left-handed **Flashes**.

*A chart of a right-handed three-ball **Shower**. This is good practice for the **Five Ball Cascade** because the right hand is doing exactly the same thing (throwing **5**'s) as it would if you were juggling five balls.*

Be sure to practise the left-handed version as well.

In this sequence all three balls start in the right hand and finish in the left.

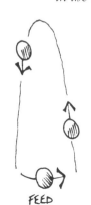

Continued overleaf...

Five Ball Cascade...

•You can also practise juggling three balls as if they were part of a full **Five Ball Cascade** – in other words, juggle the five ball pattern with two **Gaps**.

You start with three in the right hand and throw them exactly as if you were starting a three-ball **Shower** – the first ball should land in your left hand at exactly the same the moment as the third ball leaves your right hand.

As they are caught in the left hand you throw them back to the right in exactly the same way. If you juggle this correctly the three balls chase each other around like a snake. Every throw is a 5.

By the time you can actually juggle five balls all of these three-ball exercises will seem easy! So if you are having trouble with any of them you can't expect your **Five Ball Cascade** to work!

•Moving on up to four balls you can practise throwing *crossovers*.

Taking two balls in each hand, you lead off with four **5**'s as if you were starting the full **Five Ball Cascade**, *right left right left,* then catch all four.

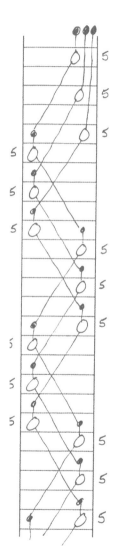

Snaking three balls around is good practice for the ***Five Ball Cascade****.*

All three balls start in the right hand which leads off exactly as it would in a three-ball ***Shower****.*

The first ball is caught just as the third ball is thrown and the balls then continue to play "follow the leader".

In **Siteswap Notation** *this is* **50505...**

Now do it the other way, *left right left right*. Don't disappoint yourself by trying to work with five until you have this trick solid!

•While you are training yourself to juggle five balls you should also spend some time working with some of the easier five-ball patterns, to "acclimatise" your brain to the magnitude of the problem.

Five Ball Splits, and the **Five Ball Column Bounce**, and the **Four Ball Drop** variant that uses five balls are all good patterns to work on.

•Throughout your training, right from the beginning, you should keep practising five ball **Flashes**. Pick up five balls and try to **Flash** them – five throws to a clean finish. You catch the first ball just as you throw the last one.

When you first try this you will have difficulty in even *seeing* the pattern – your brain is just not used to coping with five objects and it gets confused easily.

Keep plugging away at this, and all the three- and four-ball exercises, and one day you'll begin to see some semblance of order in the air in front of you.

Gradually the chaos of balls will start to take shape and you'll manage to **Flash** five.

From here on you are going to have all the problems that you had learning the **Three Ball Cascade** (remember that?) only a hundred times worse.

It's *very common* for the pattern to twist to one side or the other, just as it's very common for a beginner's **Three Ball Cascade** to run away from them. One hand throws too far forward and the other throws too far back.

You cannot fix this problem consciously. The only answer is relaxed and enjoyable practice. Your brain will eventually work out, all on its own, what is required *as long as you are nice to yourself!*

Concentrate on your stance, feet apart at shoulder width, shoulders dropped and stay relaxed. If the pattern moves to one side move with it – don't try to lean over sideways.

It really helps if you try to focus on what the *balls* are doing, rather than what your hands are doing. Relax, relax, relax. Enjoy the work and *always* take a break if you

feel frustrated or annoyed – you won't learn anything while you feel that way. Make sure you finish your practice on a high note! The better you *feel* about your progress, the faster it will be.

Pretty soon you'll be **Flashing** five, then you'll get up to about ten throws and be stuck there for ages. Pure luck can keep a **Five Ball Cascade** going that long, but only the subconsciously acquired skill of *correcting* the pattern will keep it going for longer. Slowly this skill will come and you'll be doing twenty to twenty five throws. One day you'll creep up past fifty and you'll know that you've made it!

When you *can* juggle a **Five Ball Cascade** it still feels hard, but in a different way. While learning you are trying to *make* yourself do it; when you can do it you *watch* yourself doing it instead. A moment's lapse of concentration and the pattern will collapse, but it's a *passive* concentration rather than an *active* one that keeps the **Five Ball Cascade** in the air.

Most solid five-ball jugglers can demonstrate the trick without any fear of dropping, but there are *very few* who can juggle a **Five Ball Cascade** for ten minutes

without a drop – as you will see when you watch or participate in the *Five Ball Endurance Contest* which is a regular feature of the games held at every juggling **Convention**.

It's a hard road, but *anyone* can do it, including and especially *you*. Enjoy!

Continued overleaf...

Five Ball Cascade...

...tricks!

When you can juggle a **Five Ball Cascade** there is still more to learn! Here are just a few ideas. For more, check the other five ball patterns in THE ENCYCLOPÆDIA. For example: **Five Ball Splits**, **One-up Four-up** and **Vesuvius**.

•Just as you can reverse a **Three Ball Cascade** so you can reverse the five-ball pattern so that you throw on the *outside* and catch on the *inside*, throwing every ball **Over the Top**. You need to have a solid **Reverse Cascade** before attempting the **Five Ball Mills' Mess**, and anyway, it *looks good!*

•Try a **Flash Pirouette** in the **Five Ball Cascade**. You only **Flash** three balls, holding the other two in your hands as you make the turn.

•For a flashy start to a **Five Ball Cascade**, throw a very high **Self** from your right hand. Then, as it descends, start the cascade with the other four balls so that the high ball drops into the pattern just perfectly – a lot easier than it sounds!

This trick can also be thrown from a running **Five Ball Cascade**.

Throw one ball high, and as it drops go into a **Five Ball Cascade.**

Five Ball Column Bounce

If you can do a **Four Ball Column Bounce** you'll be able to learn this – even if you never thought of yourself as a five-ball juggler!

Five balls are juggled in three columns using the easy peasy (once you've got the knack) **Column Bounce** technique. The hands throw simultaneously and the pattern is juggled similarly to **Spreads**, first two throws to the right and then two throws to the left.

•Start by placing three balls in your *left* hand and two in the right. This is a slightly unusual start, since the first move is to the *right*.

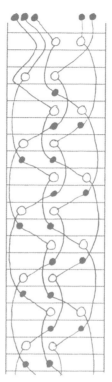

*A chart of the truly elegant **Five Ball Column** bounce showing the unusual start – three in the left and two in the right.*

The lines representing the flight paths of the balls are curved in order to keep the chart readable.

*In **Siteswap Notation** it's a **(6,4x)(4x,6).***

Imagine three columns before you, right, middle and left.

The first two (simultaneous) throws are made in the right and middle columns, then you sweep to the left and throw into the left and middle columns (at this stage your right hand is making the first *exchange*).

Then you sweep right again and make exchanges in the right and middle columns. Thus the pattern continues, sweeping to the left and right alternately. On *every* throw a ball is delivered into the middle column.

All three columns rise and fall in sync and on every bounce three balls hit the floor. The balls in the outside columns bounce twice and the ball in the middle column bounces once. The trick is to keep those balls moving absolutely vertically, which means *no sideways movement of the hands at all* at the instant of the throw.

When you can juggle a solid **Five Ball Column Bounce** you are ready for the even more incredible **Six Ball Column Bounce** which is juggled using the same technique, but in four columns instead of three.

Five Ball Gap (55550)

A **Five Ball Cascade** can be (and often is) juggled with one missing ball, in other words, with a **Gap** or a hole in the pattern.

If you are learning to juggle five you may find the **Five Ball Gap** slightly easier than the full-blown cascade. You'll certainly find yourself doing it naturally on those many occasions when you lose a ball out of the pattern.

•Juggle a **Five Ball Cascade** with only four balls. Because of the missing ball the throwing order of the hands goes *right-left-right-left-**Gap**-left-right-left-right-**Gap*** and so on. That's **55550** in **Siteswap**.

In the **Five Ball Cascade**, as in any pattern, every throw is made just in time to empty a hand for the next catch. Now, since one of the balls you are catching is *imaginary* you don't *have* to throw every ball at every opportunity. *Not* throwing a ball is called "*holding through the gap*". If you hold through the **Gap** in the **Five Ball Gap** you end up with the unusual throwing order *right-left, left-right, right-left*. This useful pattern is described under **Five Five Two (552)**.

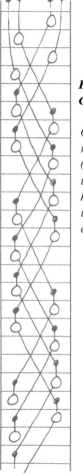

Five Ball Gap patterns.

On the left is the normal pattern (55550) in which your hands throw whenever they can.

On the right the hands hold through the Gap, throwing only when they have to – (552).

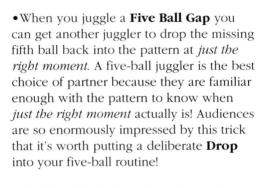

• When you juggle a **Five Ball Gap** you can get another juggler to drop the missing fifth ball back into the pattern at *just the right moment*. A five-ball juggler is the best choice of partner because they are familiar enough with the pattern to know when *just the right moment* actually is! Audiences are so enormously impressed by this trick that it's worth putting a deliberate **Drop** into your five-ball routine!

• The **Hat Finish** from five balls and **Mopping your Brow** are two tricks that use a brief **Five Ball Gap** pattern and you can also use **Gap** technology to perform the incredible feat of **Eating the Apple** while juggling five.

You'll remember (or you are about to look it up) that in order to eat an apple in a **Three Ball Cascade** the secret was to either do it the *hard* way (i.e. just *do* it!) or to do it the easy way – by throwing a furtive 4 with your left hand to create a **Gap** in the pattern giving your right hand time to carry the apple to your mouth while you take a bite.

"Just doing it" in a **Five Ball Cascade** is completely out of the question, whatever footwear you prefer – there simply is not enough time.

Here's the method that works. Juggle four balls and an apple as a **Five Ball Cascade**. Watch the apple as it reaches your left hand and palm the *next* ball through your left, thus forcing the pattern into a **Five Ball Gap.**

When the apple arrives in your right hand there is no ball following it so you get two whole **Beats** (about half a second) to take a chunk out of it and resume the **Cascade**.

← HELD BALL

Five Ball Mills' Mess

The **Five Ball Mills' Mess** is one of those patterns that is legendary by name alone. You don't even need to *see* it to be impressed. When juggled well, and there are very few who can manage it, the impression is of five balls being run through a blender.

The **Five Ball Mills' Mess** is a distortion of a **Five Ball Cascade**. Every throw is a crossing **5** but the hands wind and unwind in characteristic **Mills' Mess** style. Three throws pulse from one side of the pattern, then three throws pulse from the other. All the catches are more or less in the middle of the pattern.

Those pulses of three throws on each side create the effect of three balls chasing each other in a lazy arc at the top of the pattern. First snaking one way, and then the other.

Continued overleaf...

*Three throws of a **Five Ball Mills' Mess** being made on the right-hand side of the pattern (from our point of view). For the full sequence these are followed by three identical throws on the left-hand side. Notice the "snake" of three balls that appears at the top of the pattern. Learn the pattern by building it up from a five-ball **Reverse Cascade** with **Under the Hand** throws added. All catches are more or less in the middle of the pattern.*

63

Five Ball Mills' Mess...

Five Ball Splits

Five Ball Splits is a **Multiplex** pattern for five balls. It's one of the easiest ways of juggling five balls there is.

•Start your training for the **Five Ball Mills' Mess** by warming up with a few hundred throws of **Five Ball Cascade** and then unwind with a hundred throws of five-ball **Reverse Cascade**.

•Now start working on **Under The Hand** throws in the **Reverse Cascade** pattern.

You catch a ball in the right hand, throw it *under* the left wrist straight up the side of the pattern, and then continue cascading. You need to be able to juggle this move smoothly and reliably on both sides.

•The complete **Five Ball Mills' Mess** is simply a **Reverse Cascade** of five balls, juggled with an **Under the Hand** throw on every *third* beat.

Did I say "simply"?

•**Bouncing Ball** jugglers can juggle the pattern off the floor using the **Reverse Cascade** style of **Five Ball Bounce** as the base pattern. The procedure is exactly the same. You need to develop a very solid **Under the Hand** throw to have any chance of success at all.

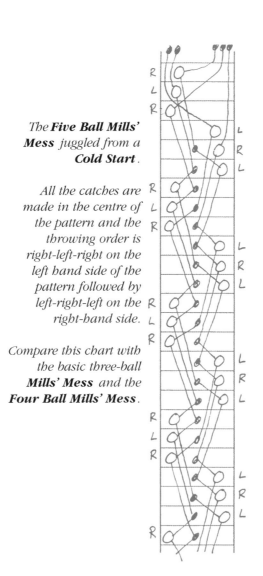

*The **Five Ball Mills' Mess** juggled from a **Cold Start**.*

All the catches are made in the centre of the pattern and the throwing order is right-left-right on the left hand side of the pattern followed by left-right-left on the right-hand side.

*Compare this chart with the basic three-ball **Mills' Mess** and the **Four Ball Mills' Mess**.*

•Start with three balls in the right hand and two in the left.

Throw a highish two-ball split **Multiplex** from the right hand. As the two balls peak throw a second two-ball split **Multiplex** from the left hand that passes right through the middle of the first one. Now continue to throw splits from alternate hands, always just as the previous pair start to fall, and always through the middle.

*Each **Multiplex** is thrown through the middle of the last one.*

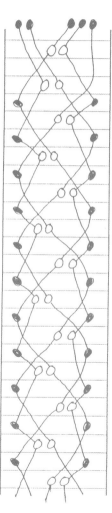

Five Ball Splits is one of those patterns that seems to work itself out for you - you'll find that you don't need to think too much about the catches – and you may be surprised to find that there are always two balls in your throwing hand when you need them.

The tempo of the pattern is the same as the **Slow Cascade**: *all the throws are* **4**'s *and there is one throw every two beats.*

• An interesting extension of this pattern uses *three-ball* **Multiplex** throws and results in a *seven-ball* pattern. In this version every throw delivers three balls, two are split, just as before, and the third does a lowish "hop" straight back into the throwing hand. That's two **4**'s and a **3.**

Start with four balls in the right and three in the left. The four balls need to be held in a **Pyramid**. The starting throw is a right to left **4** thrown with the single ball that forms the top of the **Pyramid**. This is just to get the pattern started.

Next you follow with a three-ball **Multiplex** from the left, then from the right, and so on. It sounds like a nightmare but really you are juggling *exactly* the same pattern as **Five Ball Splits** with two extra balls tacked onto the side of the pattern. You need to get the throw heights of those two extra balls just right, otherwise you will be trying to catch two balls in one hand at the same time – which is nearly impossible. The "extra" balls must be thrown as **3**'s (half the height of the splits) to arrive in the right time window.

See also **Seven Ball Splits** which is something else again!

The seven-ball version of **Five Ball Splits** *is not nearly as difficult as you might think. For readablity the* **Multiplexes** *have been drawn at the sides of the chart though they are usually thrown centrally. Note the single throw at the start.*

Five Ball Splits

Five Five Five One (5551)

The **Five Five Five One (5551)** is a
four-ball pattern that is a logical extension
of the **Four-Four-One (441)**. It is based
on a **Five Ball Cascade** juggled with a
Gap, in other words with only four balls.
Every time the **Gap** reaches a hand, the
other hand **Feeds** a ball into the space.

• Start with two balls in each hand and
lead off into a normal **Five Ball Cascade**.
After throwing three **5**'s (*right-left-right*)
your right hand will be empty, the **Gap**
having arrived there. At this moment your
left hand **Feeds** its ball into the empty
right. Or to put it another way, your left
hand throws a **1**. Now just keep going,
55515551 and so on.

Unlike the **441** you'll find that every **Feed**
is from *left to right*, making the pattern
asymmetrical. It's good to practise the
pattern both ways. You can combine it
with the **Five Ball Gap** to produce
symmetrical sequences.

• If you are really keen you might try
making those **Feeds** go **Behind the Back**
or **Under the Leg**.

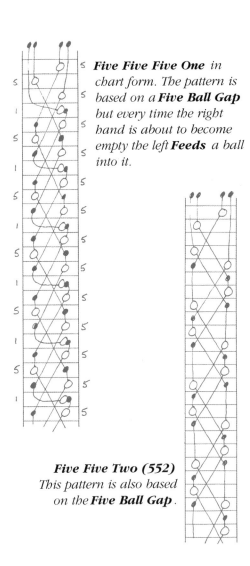

Five Five Five One in
*chart form. The pattern is
based on a* **Five Ball Gap**
*but every time the right
hand is about to become
empty the left* **Feeds** *a ball
into it.*

Five Five Two (552)
*This pattern is also based
on the* **Five Ball Gap**.

Five Five Two (552)

Gosh! Aren't there a lot of patterns that
start with a **5?** This is *very* useful piece of
four-ball manipulation that uses **Gap**
technology. You can drop into this pattern
easily if you lose a ball out of a **Five Ball
Cascade**.

It's a good one to work on if you are still
working up to five balls because it will get
you used to throwing **5**'s.

The throwing order is *right-right...left-left*,
just like that clever three-ball pattern called
Four Two Three (423). This means you
have time to scratch your nose while juggling it, and you can use either hand to do
so!

• Start with two balls in each hand and
lead with a **5** from the left. Now proceed
with two **5**'s from the right, followed by
two **5**'s from the left, and continue ad
infinitum.

Being closely related to **423**, you can lay
this sequence on top of a **Mills' Mess
State Transition Diagram** to generate all
sorts of amazing crossed-hand patterns
with *four balls!* Even a four-ball **Burke's
Barrage** is possible! Go look it up!

See also **Five Ball Gap**.

Five Three (53)

The **Five-Three (53)** is a four-ball pattern in which the balls cross. Club jugglers often call it **Triple Singles** because they juggle their equivalent pattern by throwing high **Triple** spin throws from one hand while throwing low **Single** spin throws from the other. The **Five Three** is a very useful and versatile pattern and you really should learn it.

As the name suggests, one hand throws **5**'s, as if it was juggling a **Five Ball Cascade** and the other throws **3**'s, as if it was juggling a **Three Ball Cascade**. Since four comes midway between five and three it's not much of a surprise to find that four balls fit perfectly into such an arrangement. The pattern is asymmetrical because one hand always throws **5**'s while the other always throws **3**'s. The hands throw alternately.

•If you can already juggle a solid **Four Ball Fountain** you might like to learn this pattern from a **Hot Start**. Get the fountain going (juggling **44444...**), and then flip into this pattern. You lead into it with a **5**, so the sequence goes:

4444535353...

•To do a **Cold Start**, put two balls in each hand and lead with a **5**.

The most common problem is that of not throwing the **3**'s low enough; they should reach only about half the height of a **4** and a *quarter* the height of the **5**.

It's tempting to learn the pattern only one way round. Right-handed jugglers tend to prefer **5**'s from the right and **3**'s from the left. Don't fall into the trap of neglecting your weak side! If you learn this pattern on both sides you will open the door to all sorts of variations on four-ball juggling: patterns like **Five Three Four (534)** and **Four Ball Tennis**.

•As your **Five Three** pattern becomes more solid concentrate on getting a really smooth tempo and flipping between **Four Ball Fountain** and **Five Three**. *Listen* to the slap of the balls, which should sound like a metronome with no perceptible change of rhythm as you move from one pattern to the other. If the rhythm becomes at all irregular it means that you are getting

the throw heights wrong; it's *almost certainly* the **3**'s that are being thrown too high.

•You can also juggle the pattern as a **Bouncing Ball** pattern, in which case the **5**'s are thrown as bounces and the **3**'s are air throws.

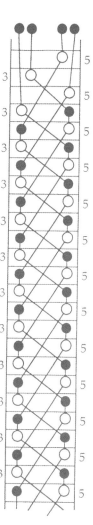

Five Three Four (534)

Five Three Four (534) is a four-ball pattern that uses three different weights of throws, **5**'s, **3**'s and **4**'s. If you are the sort of person who is familiar with thinking of patterns in terms of **Siteswaps** then all you need to know is that the throwing sequence is:

534...

The **5**'s and **3**'s cross while the **4**'s are self throws.

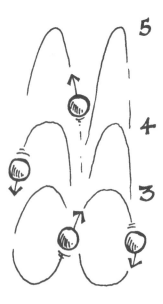

Mere mortals may need a little more guidance to learn the pattern so here's how to build up to it in stages.

• *Step One:* Start by juggling a **Four Ball Fountain** for a couple of minutes to warm up. Then juggle a **Five Three (53)** for a while. **Five Three** is an asymmetrical pattern and it is really going to help if you can juggle both the right- and left-handed versions.

Juggle the **Four Ball Fountain** again; you will find that it's easy to "change gear" into a **Five Three** and then drop back into the fountain. Practise this both ways – that is, going into both right-handed and left-handed **Five Threes**.

• *Step Two:* Practise going from the **Four Ball Fountain** into **Five Three** for *just two throws*. So that you juggle:

4444 53 4444...

Do this on both sides until it's smooth and solid. The **5**'s and **3**'s should drop back into the pattern in *perfect time* – the rhythm of balls slapping into the hands staying quite constant. If it doesn't then you are getting the throw heights wrong.

• *Step Three:* Juggle a **Four Ball Fountain** and throw **53** from the right, dropping straight back into the **Fountain** – but as the **5** lands in your left hand throw a **53** from the *left*. Keep this going so that the same ball is thrown as a **5** each time. The sequence you are juggling becomes:

534445344453444...

This is in fact, **Four Ball Tennis**, juggled without the **Over the Top** throw.

• *Step Four:* This time, throw the **53** from the right and return it *one throw earlier than before* from the left. So the **5** from the left is thrown *under* the **5** from the right. This is the full-blown **Five Three Four**.

If you think you are getting the sequence of throws right but the pattern *still* doesn't work it's the actual throw heights that are wrong. Keep those **3**'s low!

Five Three Four is a pattern that has been independently invented by many different people using **Juggling Notation** and computer simulated juggling. Unlike many of the patterns that the techno-jugglers come up with, this pattern has one great advantage – it is actually juggleable!

There is a closely related seven-ball **Passing Pattern** for two jugglers that uses a similar mix of throws – see **Seven Ball Passing** for more about this.

The **Ladder Notation** for the pattern makes a very pretty chart which looks almost as convoluted as the real thing!

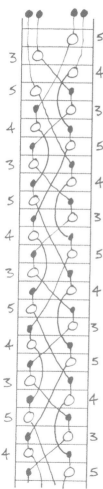

Five Three Four.

You may have noticed that **Ladder Notation** *highlights the similarity between many juggling patterns and plaits or knots.*

The **Three Ball Cascade** *resembles a plait of three, so much so that if you were to tie three ribbons to three juggling balls and juggle them you would find yourself plaiting the ribbons! To unplait them again you use a* **Reverse Cascade** *of course!*

On the right is a Celtic knot design based on **Five Three Four**.

Five Three Four (534)

Five Three One (531)

The **Five Three One (531)** is a three-ball pattern that uses three different weights of throws; **5**'s, **3**'s and **1**'s. The **1**'s are **Feeds** – one hand puts a ball directly into the other. It's a very busy pattern, and looks much more complicated to the spectator than it feels to the juggler.

•Warm up by juggling a two-ball **Shower** (**313131...**) a few dozen times, both ways.

Now pick up the third ball and try the first three throws of the **Five Three One** start-ing from the *right*. All you have to do is throw a **5** from the right and then juggle one "round" of a left handed two-ball **Shower** underneath.

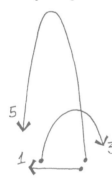

Next try the same sequence starting from the left – a **5** from the left and one round of a two-ball **Shower** underneath. Finally put the two halves together: **531** starting from the right, and then **531** starting from the left. It will help if you note that the *fed* ball is always thrown as the next **5**.

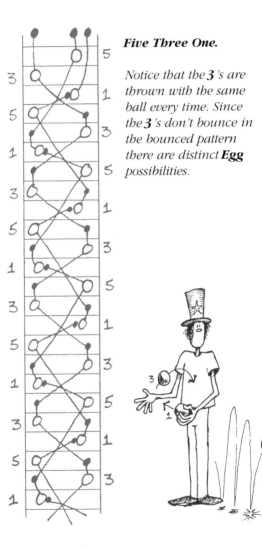

Five Three One.

*Notice that the 3's are thrown with the same ball every time. Since the 3's don't bounce in the bounced pattern there are distinct **Egg** possibilities.*

•**Five Three One** is an excellent **Bouncing Ball** pattern. Unlike most other three-ball bounces, which are rather slow, this pattern keeps your hands moving quickly – despite having only three balls to work with.

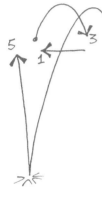

With **Bouncing Balls** you juggle the pattern almost exactly as before except that every **5** is now a bounce instead of an air throw. It may take you a little while to get the sequence into your head, and then a little while longer to get it from your head down those nerves to your hands, but once it "clicks" you'll find that you can keep it going all day!

•In the bounced **Five Three One** you can let one ball bounce several times, instead of just once, keeping the other two balls running in a tiny two-ball **Shower** pattern. When the bouncing ball starts to run out of momentum after two or three bounces, just gather it up and go back into **Five Three One.**

Flash

Throwing up all the balls you have in your hands (and catching them again) is called a **Flash**. If a juggler says that they are *flashing five balls* they generally mean that they can throw the first five throws of a **Five Ball Cascade**.

If they say that they can throw a *five-ball Flash* they mean that they can throw all five balls so that *both hands are empty for a moment*.

A three-ball **Flash** is needed for the **Flash Pirouette** (next entry). Apprentice five-ball jugglers spend a lot of time **Flashing** five balls.

•While eavesdropping on two **Numbers Jugglers** you might hear something like this:

"How's your seven?"

"Solid. Eight's coming on and I'm flashing nine now."

"Hear about Ivan Tumakalov?"

"Yeah – flashing fourteen!"

Doesn't it feel good to know that even if you can't match the skill of these godlike super-beings, you can at least understand what they are talking about?

Flash Pirouette

•Juggle a **Three Ball Cascade** and then throw a high **Flash**, making a full 360 degree pirouette before catching the balls and continuing. Tricky stuff! Try to get all three balls aloft *before* you start to make the turn, otherwise they tend not to fly straight. In performance a good way of presenting the trick is to build up to it in stages. First turn a pirouette under one ball, then pirouette under two, and finally all three.

•Five-ball jugglers can try throwing a three-ball **Flash Pirouette** out of their pattern, turning with a ball in each hand before catching and resuming their **Five Ball Cascade**.

Flick Off

The **Flick Off** is a simple trick for three-ball jugglers.

•Juggle a **Three Ball Cascade**. As a ball approaches your right hand you flick it back to the left with the first two fingers of your right hand, instead of making the usual exchange.

Your right hand is holding a ball, palm downwards, as it does the **Flick Off**. It's easy!

•A variation is to **Flick Off** the ball with the underside of your wrist. Try all the combinations you can think of on both sides, mixing in similar moves like **Off the Elbow** – these may be easy moves but they look very cool.

Flick Off

Floor Cascade

Now you can make use of all those **Drops**! The **Floor Cascade** is the **Floor Juggling** version of the **Three Ball Cascade**. It involves *no throws at all!*

• Kneel down on the floor and place two beanbags on the floor, a few inches apart, one in front of each knee. Hold a third over the right-hand floored beanbag and grasp (but don't pick up) the left-hand beanbag.

That's the starting position.

For the first "throw" you pick up the left hand beanbag *at the same time* as placing the held beanbag exactly in its place. *Clomp!* Now let go of the clomped beanbag and grasp the right-hand floored beanbag.

For the second "throw" pick up the right-hand beanbag at exactly the same time as the left hand clomps its beanbag down in

its place – the left hand then moves to grasp the left-hand beanbag. The pattern then repeats. It might seem ridiculously simple but it leads on to some truly amazing fun.

• Find a partner and kneel face to face, both in the starting position for two **Floor Cascades**. You should arrange yourselves so that the beanbags on the floor form a neat square.

Now juggle a **Four Count** passing pattern. You both juggle **Floor Cascades** in time, but **Every Other** right hand "throw" (or "clomp" if you prefer) is a pass, so you clomp it to your partner instead of yourself.

• Once you can do that you are ready to attempt any **Passing Pattern** for any number of jugglers that uses three balls per juggler. Try the **Triangle** for a giggle.

Floor Juggling

In normal **Toss Juggling** you try to keep the balls off the floor as much as possible. In **Floor Juggling** you make use of the floor. It's a style of juggling that positively *enjoys* drops – get it out of your system! If the beanbags *want* to be on the floor (mine usually do) then let them!

The simplest **Floor Juggling** pattern is the **Floor Cascade** (previous entry) which can be used as the basis for converting **Passing Patterns** into an easy format.

Other interesting **Floor Juggling** patterns are the **Four Ball Drop** and the **Robotic Drop**.

Foot Catch

Beanbags are best for the **Foot Catch,** and you will find that some shoes work better than others – how about working barefoot so that your feet get a chance to enjoy juggling too?

•Throw a ball and catch it on the top of your foot, just behind your toes. It helps to put in a **Knee Bounce** on the way down to your foot. It's a very satisfying catch. Once you have the ball on one foot, try hopping it over to the other before kicking it back up into your pattern.

Force Bounce

A style of ball-bouncing in which balls are thrown at the floor, rather than being lifted into the air and allowed to fall. It's also called "active bounce" or "power bounce".

In **Force Bounce** patterns for odd numbers (**Cascades**) the balls cross each other's paths on the way *up*, after the bounce, as opposed to the gentler **Reverse Cascade** style in which balls cross on the way *down*. These two ways of juggling a bounce pattern are *time-reversed* equivalents of each other, just as the **Three Ball Cascade** and three-ball **Reverse Cascade** are.

See **Three Ball Bounce**, **Five Ball Bounce**.

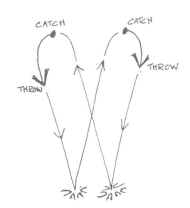

Follow

The **Follow** is a shape distortion of **Four Two Three (423)**. In the **Follow** the *3-ball* is thrown **Under the Hand**.

When this pattern is juggled elegantly it feels, to the juggler, as if the *2-ball* (the held ball) is "following" the *4-ball* – hence the name.

The **Follow** is a close relative of the **Fake Mess**. It's an easy one to juggle once your hands have worked out what they are supposed to be doing. As with all patterns based on the **423** sequence, the throwing order is *right-right left-left*.

•If you can juggle a **Turnover** then you will need only very simple instructions: just juggle continuous **Turnovers** on alternate sides.

If that doesn't work for you we can try another way. (We just need to *fool* your hands into doing the right thing.)

•Juggle **Tennis** for 128 throws (or thereabouts). In **Tennis** you toss the **4**'s right up the middle, while the **3**'s go back and forth **Over the Top**.

Continued overleaf...

Follow...

...Follow

- OK now, we're going to make one teensy change to **Tennis** – juggle the **3**'s as **Under the Hand** throws instead of **Over the Top** throws. (Imagine that the **Tennis** ball has become a rabbit that is sneaking under the net.)

- Finally we make one more change: as you throw each **Under the Hand** throw you are to make an *Outside* **Chop** with the hand that's on top.

You'll know when you've got it right!

- If you arrange your pattern so that the **2** is held as if by a crane, you can end up with a very interesting pattern that resembles an upside-down **Yo-yo** pattern.

The **Follow** is very similar to the **Fake Mess**, the principle difference being that in the **Fake Mess** the held ball (the *2-ball*) is carried *under* the pattern instead of *over*.

- If you *time-reverse* a **Follow** you end up with **Charlie's Cheat**.

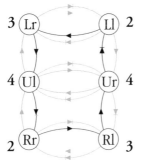

*A **Mills' Mess State Transition Diagram** shows how the **423** sequence is combined with hand crossings to create the **Follow**.*

See also **Four Two Three (423)**, **Fake Mess**, **Yo-yo**, **Mills' Mess**, **Charlie's Cheat**, **Turnover**.

Forehead Catch

- Juggle a **Three Ball Cascade** of squishy beanbags. Throw one up and catch it on your forehead then tip it off with a nod of your head and carry on juggling. Experts can catch hard balls, even bouncing balls, in a **Forehead Catch**.

- Juggle a **Four Ball Fountain** and throw one of the four balls into a **Forehead Catch** and carry on juggling the other three as a **Three Ball Cascade**. As the applause fades, tip the ball off your head and go back into the four-ball pattern.

*The **Follow** .*

Fork

The **Fork** is a way of holding a ball on the back of your hand, so that it rests in the open vee between your index and middle fingers. The **Fork** leaves two fingers and a thumb free, so you can hold another ball in the same hand at the same time.

• Try juggling a **Three Ball Cascade**, stopping with one ball in each hand and the third in a **Fork**, then restarting the pattern. The forked stops add an interesting punctuation to the rhythm of the cascade.

At first you will want to work with the squidgiest beanbags you can find, but once you have the knack you shouldn't have any trouble with hard balls.

*• Practise the **Fork** while juggling **Two in One Hand**, starting and stopping from the **Fork** position. If that feels solid you can move right on to the **Four Ball Fountain**, putting in forked stops and starts on alternate sides.*

A pause in a juggling routine – now what?

*• Here's a two-ball move that starts and ends with a **Fork**. Both balls are thrown together in a column – **Snatch** the top ball and catch the bottom ball in a **Fork**.*

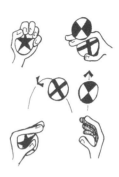

*• Here is a three-ball move which, if repeated on alternate sides, produces a **Forked** cascade. The lower and tighter you juggle this trick – the better it looks! Only two balls get thrown at a time.*

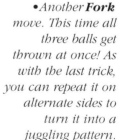

*• Another **Fork** move. This time all three balls get thrown at once! As with the last trick, you can repeat it on alternate sides to turn it into a juggling pattern.*

Fork

Fountain

The **Fountain** patterns are to even numbers what the **Cascade** patterns are to odd numbers. **Fountains** are the simplest patterns for an even number of balls. It just isn't possible to juggle an odd number in a **Fountain**.

The hands throw alternately, each juggling half the balls in the pattern *independently*. Non-jugglers generally do not realise that the balls don't cross from one side to the other. The balls are thrown on the inside and caught on the outside (*rolling out*) to give the **Fountain** effect.

A **Four Ball Fountain** is juggled simply by juggling **Two in One Hand** in *both* hands at the same time.

The next possible fountain, of six balls, is a rare sight, because so few jugglers get past five. It is juggled by working two independent **Three in one Hand** patterns. An eight-ball fountain (very rare indeed!) requires you to be able to juggle four balls in either hand.

You can juggle a **Fountain** in reverse, just as a **Cascade** can be reversed, simply by throwing the balls on the outside and catching them on the inside (*rolling in*).

*The shape of a **Fountain**, which can be juggled in reverse, just as a **Cascade** can.*

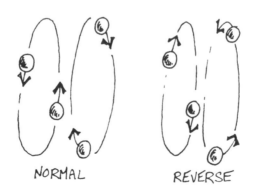

NORMAL   REVERSE

Four Ball Box

A couple of variations of the **Box** can be juggled with four balls. Both hands throw together, just as they do in the standard three-ball **Box,** but instead of throwing **4**'s and **2**'s they throw **6**'s and **2**'s.

In the first variation both hands make the same throw at the same time, juggling **(6x,6x)(2x,2x).**

***Four Ball Box**, throwing **2**'s blind.*

Four Ball Column Bounce

•Start with two in each hand. Both hands throw **6**'s straight up and then *swap* the balls that are left by throwing two simultaneous crossing **2**'s. Collisions, collisions! One of those **2**'s has to go in front of the other! As soon as the **2**'s have swapped sides they get thrown up as the next pair of **6**'s and so the pattern continues.

You need to be able to throw those swapsies (the crossing **2**'s) *blind*, so you can watch the **6**'s as they peak.

The second variation has both hands making different throws at the same time. First the right throws a **6** while the left throws a **2**, and then the same thing repeats from the other side. See **Six Two** for more possibilities.

Using the **Column Bounce** technique for **Bouncing Balls** you can easily juggle four balls. The idea is exactly the same as for juggling four balls in the air – juggle **Two in One Hand** in both hands at the same time.

•Start with two **Bouncing Balls** in each hand and juggle two **Column Bounces** simultaneously side by side. Concentrate on getting both hands working perfectly in time.

•You can play with the pattern by putting in crossed-hand catches, crossed-hand throws, or both!

•By letting two balls bounce twice you gain enough time to swap the balls in your hands with a couple of nifty simultaneous **2**'s (like a **Four Ball Box**). If you are fast you might be able to do this on single bounces.

•You can juggle four **Bouncing Balls** as **Spreads** too. Two balls bounce in two columns to the right and the other two bounce in two columns to the left – try making the pattern wider and wider. When it gets too wide to cope with, you can always let the balls bounce twice or more! With a bit of running around you can get the pairs of columns a *long* way apart!

Continued overleaf...

Four Ball Column Bounce...

The **Four Ball Column Bounce** can also be juggled as an alternate throw pattern, just like a **Four Ball Fountain** in the air.

Juggle two **Two in One Hand** bounces *out of phase* with each other.

When you juggle this pattern you will find that you can easily change gear into a **Six Three Three (633)** bounce. The **6**'s are bounces and the **3**'s are air throws.

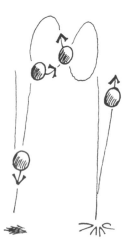

From the **Six Three Three** bounce it's easy to shift up another gear into a **Four Ball Fountain** juggled in the air.

•When juggling the **Four Ball Column Bounce** with alternate throws you'll find that it is possible to put in **Under the Hand** throws.

Juggle the bounce pattern in two columns out of phase with each other. Put in a right-hand throw *under* the left wrist – this starts a new column at the left of the pattern. Step to the left and continue the pattern in its new position, one "space" to the left of where it started.

You'll find that your left hand has to make two consecutive throws immediately after the **Under the Hand** throw to sort everything out.

Juggle this trick continuously on alternate sides and you will find yourself juggling a very slow and complicated pattern that looks and feels quite like a **Mills' Mess**.

•Keen **Bouncing Ball** jugglers can substitute **Behind the Back** bounces for those **Under the Hand** throws.

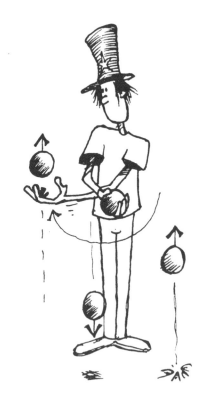

*The **Four Ball Column Bounce** with an **Under the Hand** throw. Here a ball has been swiped out of the right-hand column (from your point of view) creating a new column on the left.*

Four Ball Drop

This is a comic four-ball **Floor Juggling** trick for the three-ball juggler. You need to use **Beanbags** because it involves deliberate drops and you don't want things rolling away.

The trick appeals to those with a childish sense of humour – in other words *everybody*. It's also virtually impossible to mess it up in performance because you are *supposed* to be dropping everything.

•Take four beanbags and kneel on the floor. Place one beanbag in front of your right knee and juggle a **Three Ball Cascade** with the others.

Here comes the tricky bit. Watch your right hand catching – watching? OK, now as a ball approaches your right hand *ignore it and pick up the ball on the floor instead.* You have to do this by "mind over habit" because every nerve in your body screams at you to *catch that ball!*

After the pick up, the ball you ignored should sail down to the floor, replacing the ball that was there before. If you simply cannot persuade your hands to do this trick then look up **Picking Up** and learn the tricks there first.

•When you can manage a **Four Ball Drop** you should try picking up *every time*, so that you are continuously dropping balls on the right-hand side of the pattern. Instant comedy!

•Next learn the trick on the left-hand side. When you can do that, you should attempt the hilarious *Five Ball Drop:* put one ball in front of each knee and juggle three in the air above them. You can put in as many drops and pick ups as you like; one side, the other side, alternate sides and the ultimate – both sides on every catch! This is practically a **Five Ball Cascade**.

•Try combining the **Four Ball Drop** with pick ups and put-downs as described in **Picking Up** for an instant comedy routine. Start with three balls in the air and one by your right knee, now *put down* a ball by your left knee – keep juggling until the **Gap** reaches your right hand and *pick up* on the right. I leave the rest to your imagination.

See also **Dropswap, Floor Juggling.**

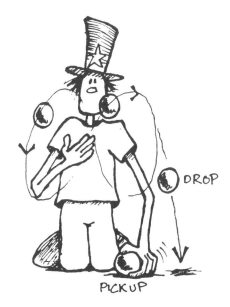

DROP

PICKUP

Four Ball Drop

Four Ball Fountain

The **Four Ball Fountain** is the basic **Four Ball Juggling** pattern. **Fountain** patterns only work for even numbers, just as **Cascades** only work for odd numbers. There is no such thing as a *Four Ball Cascade*.

In the **Four Ball Fountain** every throw is a **4**. While there is no *correct* height for any juggling pattern (height depends on the speed at which you are juggling), beginners will find it best to work on throws a little over head height.

•Take two balls in each hand and juggle two independent **Two in One Hand** patterns at the same time, with the hands throwing alternately. The balls should be *rolling out* – that is with the throws on the inside and the catches on the outside.

It's very hard for an observer to tell that the balls *don't cross from hand to hand*.

A good tip for beginners is to *lead with your weakest hand*. Everybody is better at **Two in One Hand** on one side, usually the right, so lead with your left – it really does help you to get the pattern started!

•Just as you can juggle three balls in a **Reverse Cascade** so you can juggle four

balls in a *Reverse Fountain*. All you have to do is juggle those two **Two in One Hand** patterns *rolling in* – throws on the outside and catches on the inside. This feels quite unnatural, but it is the basis for the **Four Ball Mills' Mess**.

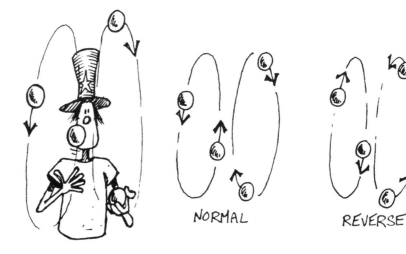

*The general shape and size of the **Four Ball Fountain** and its reverse.*

NORMAL   REVERSE

*A chart of a **Four Ball Fountain** showing clearly that it consists of two entirely independent **Two in One Hand** patterns.*

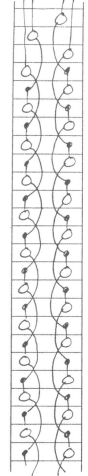

Four Ball Juggling

The basic beginner's **Four Ball Juggling** pattern is the **Four Ball Fountain** – see the previous entry.

In the **Four Ball Fountain** there are two independent **Two in One Hand** patterns running, and since the balls never cross from side to side it doesn't really matter (from the point of view of keeping balls in the air) whether the hands throw alternately or simultaneously, or even completely out of time with each other.

• Juggle four balls by working two **Two in One Hand** patterns with the hands throwing *simultaneously*. Since both hands are throwing and catching at the same time it doesn't matter whether your hands throw to themselves or across the pattern (as long as they make up their minds and do the same thing).

If you do use crossing throws there is a bit of a collision problem at the top of the pattern. If your aim is anything like mine then all you have to do is aim for a hit – and they'll miss!

• Alternating between crossing throws and self throws looks wonderful – some jugglers call this an *Umbrella* because that's what it looks like!

Juggling four balls with a mixture of crossing and self throws. Aim for a hit and they'll probably miss!

• Now here's a point of style and general juggling technique. In your forthcoming four-ball routine you may wish to change from a **Four Ball Fountain** proper (alternate throws) to the simultaneous throw pattern, and perhaps back again.

Many jugglers do this change very badly, by kludging the rhythm of the pattern for a few beats while they *force* a change from one style to the other. This is messy and it doesn't look or feel very good.

All you have to do, to make the change either way, is throw one self **5**, and the pattern will gracefully and immediately switch from one mode to the other. A **5** is about double the height of a **4**.

Just as there are many ways of juggling three balls, so there are just as many, if not more, patterns for four.

See also **Five Three (53), Six Three Three (633), Six Two (6x,2x), Five Three Four (534), Pistons, Spreads** and **Four Ball Mills' Mess.**

Four Ball Juggling

Four Ball Mills' Mess

The **Mills' Mess** is more a pattern for the *hands* than the balls. Although the 100% genuine original **Mills' Mess** is a three-ball pattern, the underlying technique can be applied to four balls, five balls, and beyond. It's the crossing and uncrossing of the arms that makes the **Mills' Mess** what it is. A three-ball **Mills' Mess** is a distortion of a **Three Ball Cascade**. A **Four Ball Mills' Mess** is a distortion of a **Four Ball Fountain**. In both cases the *logic* of the juggling pattern stays the same – only the *shape* is changed.

• Warm up by throwing a few hundred throws of a reverse **Four Ball Fountain**, that is, a **Fountain** juggled so that the **Two in One Hand** throws are *rolling in* (throws on the outside and catches on the inside). This is your base pattern and you need to have it completely solid.

Aim to get every ball caught more or less exactly in the middle of the pattern.

• Now practise throwing **Under the Hand** from the reverse **Fountain**.

When you throw a ball **Under the Hand** you are simply altering the *route* that the ball takes – it still gets caught by the hand that was expecting it. It might help to use two balls of one colour and two of another to save you wondering whether everything is going where it is supposed to.

• Here then, is the devastatingly simple secret of the **Four Ball Mills' Mess** – if you can juggle one **Under the Hand** throw on every *third* beat you are juggling a **Four Ball Mills' Mess** (or something *very* similar that is currently unknown to juggling science).

If that explanation doesn't work for you then go back to the "miming" exercises for the three-ball **Mills' Mess**; the throwing sequence is *exactly* the same for four balls – it just looks a lot more confusing in the air. The logical structure of the four-ball pattern is unchanged – every right hand throw is caught by the right hand and every left hand by the left. The hands still throw alternately and every ball rises to the same height.

Don't try to *think* about it too much, just *do it!*

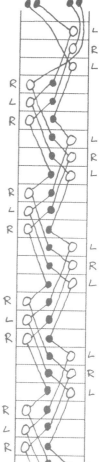

*The **Four Ball Mills' Mess** in chart form with the throws labelled R and L for right and left. Compare this with the three- and five-ball versions of the **Mills' Mess.***

The sequence on the left shows six throws of the pattern. It's very unlikely that anyone could actually learn the trick from a sequence of drawings like this, but they might just help to show you where you are going wrong!

Four Ball Mills' Mess

Four Ball Tennis

In **Four Ball Tennis** it looks like you are juggling three balls and playing catch with yourself at the same time. A *tennis-ball* sails back and forth over the top of the pattern while you juggle three below it.

Four Ball Tennis is most effective when you use one ball that is differently coloured (or much larger than the other three) as the *tennis-ball* – perhaps a football.

• Juggle a **Four Ball Fountain,** starting with the "tennis" ball in your right hand.

As the "tennis" ball leaves your right hand throw it as a **5, Over the Top** of the pattern. This throw is immediately followed by a low crossing **3** from the left – then resume the fountain. Thus you are inserting one round of a **Five Three (53)** into the **Fountain**. For the **Siteswap** literate the throwing sequence is:

4444 53 4444...

The **5** is thrown with the *tennis-ball*. Practise this move on the right and the left. If you are having trouble with the timing of the pattern then it's probable your **3**'s are being thrown too high – nearly everybody does this at first!

• To juggle the full pattern you just throw a **53** from the right, and as the *tennis-ball* lands in your left hand you throw it back as a **53** from the left. The complete **Four Ball Tennis** pattern in **Siteswap Notation** is written as:

444 53 444 53 444 53 ...

For the maximum effect, work on really emphasising the *tennis-ball* by throwing it as high and as wide as possible while keeping the other three balls low and tight.

See also **Five Three (53), Five Three Four (534).**

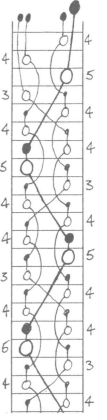

Four Ball Tennis (with the "tennis" ball suitably emphasised) showing how the whole thing fits together.

The pattern **Five Three Four (534)** *is very similar to this.*

Four Count

A **Four Count** is a **Passing Pattern** in which every fourth throw is a pass. Since most jugglers are right handed this usually means that *every other* right hand throw is a pass – hence it is often called *Every Others*.

The **Four Count** is perhaps *the* most popular passing style. Not as slow and boring as a six count, not as frantic as a **Two Count** and it favours the right hand. On top of all that it's *four-time,* like 99% of all popular music – so that funky juggling rhythm just gets right into your head!

• Stand face to face with your partner, three balls each and about five feet apart. You both juggle **Three Ball Cascades** – making *every other* right-hand throw to your partner's left hand instead of yourself. Most jugglers prefer to begin with a **Fast Start**, so that the *very first throw* is a pass. Alternatively you can use a **Slow Start**, in which you both juggle a few throws of **Three Ball Cascade** to get synchronised, before starting to pass to each other. As you juggle together, get the rhythm going in your heads by counting off your throws – chant out loud if you wish:

PASS-two-three-four-
PASS-two-three-four-

...and so on. Try to keep the passes at the same height as your self throws – there is a natural tendency to emphasise the passes by throwing them too high which makes the rhythm of the pattern irregular and lumpy.

• If you **Drop** a ball you don't have to stop. Dropping creates a **Gap** in the pattern, so that at any moment one juggler has three balls while the other has only two. Threeball *keeps going* while Twoball waits. Threeball then passes to Twoball and the situation is reversed. Thus, on every pass, the **Gap** moves from one end of the pattern to the other.

As soon as the **Gap** gets near the dropped ball, Twoball can pick it up and resume passing on the next *PASS* beat. That's why it's so important to keep the count going in your head! Throwing in the dropped ball at any old time doesn't work!

When you have learnt to recover from drops in the **Four Count** the fun really starts because you can keep going whatever happens.

• In the plain vanilla **Four Count** every pass is a **3** from your right hand to your partner's left hand, but it doesn't have to be that way!

On the *PASS* beat you can throw a **4** to your partner's *right* hand instead. They'll probably drop it in surprise the first time – where did *that* one come from?

When you receive one of these right to right **4**'s, you just pass it straight back to your partner as a normal **3** pass, on the next *PASS* beat. That doesn't make sense on paper I know, but if you are actually *doing* this you'll know exactly what I mean. The **4** needs to be a little over twice the height of the normal throws (**3**'s), otherwise the rhythm of the pattern will be broken.

Continued overleaf...

Four Count...

You can make the right to right **4** pass on *any* pass beat, regardless of what your partner is doing; they could be throwing one to you at the same time!

•The right to right 4 pass adds *syncopation* to the pattern, in other words you are playing around with the rhythm without actually breaking it. Many other non-standard, syncopated throws are possible too!

On the *three* beat (that is the right hand throw *between* passes – you are still counting, aren't you?) you can throw a right to left **5** to your partner's left hand. The **5** needs to be about four times as high as the **3**'s if it is to arrive at the right time. Throwing this trick gives you a brief **Gap** on your side of the pattern – long enough to turn a pirouette!

•You can throw a right to right self 4 on the *three* beat.

•You can throw a left to left **4** as a pass on the *four* beat. You get the **Gap**.

•A left to left self **4** on the *two* beat works.

•A left to right **5** pass on the *four* beat works too!

All of these syncopations can be combined in any order, without warning your partner, and the pattern will hold together. But if you throw any of these **Tricks** on the *wrong* beat you'll find that two balls arrive at the same hand at the same time, causing a **Drop**.

There are many other possibilities for variations in the **Four Count**, far too numerous to catalogue. Have fun discovering them all!

Four Four Eight

The **Four Four Eight** is the ambidextrous equivalent of the **Three Three Ten**. It is a **Passing Pattern** routine for two jugglers and six balls.

Unlike the **Three Three Ten** which is usually juggled with right-hand passes only, you will be making passes from both hands in the **Four Four Eight**. This is useful practice and generally good for your juggling. Far too many jugglers neglect their left hands when passing.

Also, because the **Four Four Eight** is a routine, rather than just "juggling till you drop" there is at least the possibility that you will get the satisfaction of a clean finish!

•Stand facing your partner, three balls each, two in the right hand and one in the left. Start juggling together, counting off the rhythm as you go: *RIGHT* means a pass from the right hand, LEFT means a pass from the left hand.

One-two-three-four-RIGHT
One-two-three-four-LEFT
One-two-three-four-RIGHT
One-two-three-four-LEFT
One-two-RIGHT
One-two-LEFT
One-two-RIGHT
One-two-LEFT
RIGHT-LEFT-RIGHT-LEFT
RIGHT-LEFT-RIGHT-LEFT

Phew!

From a **Slow Start** you have juggled four passes of a *five count*, four passes of a **Three Count** and eight **One Counts**. Then (optionally) you both throw a ball high, turn a pirouette and bow to tumultuous applause.

The **Four Four Eight** is a fairly complex sequence to remember, so before committing it to gravity it might be a good idea to rehearse the sequence as a **Floor Juggling** pattern which eliminates any possibility of **Drops** (though you are still free to make *mistakes*) – see **Floor Cascade**.

Four Four Eight

Four in One Hand Bounce

Juggling four balls in one hand is a very difficult trick. **Solid** seven-ball jugglers can usually juggle four in their best hand – four balls in one hand having about the same level of **Difficulty** as seven balls in two hands.

Juggling four in one hand as a **Column Bounce** pattern, however, is much easier than juggling four in the air.

Warm up by juggling a **Three in One Hand** column bounce using the faster style, so that one column is falling as the other is rising and each ball bounces only once.

•The four-ball pattern is juggled in three columns. Start with four balls in your least useless hand. The throwing sequence is *right-middle-left-middle-right..* and so on.

Deliver the first ball into the right-hand column, the second into the middle and the third into the left column. The third ball should rise in time with the right-hand column. So far that's *right-middle-left* and you have got the pattern started. Now continue the throwing sequence *..middle-right-middle-left-middle-right..* making exchanges as you would in any other **Column Bounce** pattern.

The key is to keep the outside columns rising in unison while the middle column moves in opposite time. The motion of the balls resembles **One-up Two-up**.

You will have trouble keeping all those columns from crashing into each other – I never said it was *easy*, just a lot easier than juggling four balls in one hand in the air. You'll also notice (if you have time) that the outside columns bounce twice, while the middle column bounces only once. Those double bounces will cause problems unless you are working on a very smooth floor, because any slight deviation on the first bounce tends to get magnified on the second.

Four Four One (441)

The **Four Four One (441)** is a juggling pattern for three balls that looks and feels like a four-ball pattern

•Start with three balls, two in the right and one in the left. Start by making the first two throws of a **Four Ball Fountain** – a right **Self 4**, then a left **Self 4**.

Now **Feed** the third ball from the right to the left hand, which is empty. In terms of numbers, a **Feed** is a **1**.

Then repeat the sequence from the left – left self 4, right self 4, left to right **Feed**.

This six-beat cycle, **441441...** repeats. In effect you are juggling a **Four Ball Fountain** with a **Gap** in it, and every time the **Gap** arrives in one hand the other hand **Feeds** a ball into it.

•There are two shapes you can use for the pattern, depending on whether the **4**'s are thrown *rolling out* or in *columns*. The *rolling out* style makes the pattern look very similar to a **Four Ball Fountain**, whereas the *columns* style makes it into a wild and wacky three-ball something-or-other – to put it another way it's very different.

Feeding a ball under a 4 in the **Four Four One**.

• The basic principle of this pattern can be applied to larger numbers of balls. Start with any **Cascade** or **Fountain** (say a **Five Ball Cascade**) and juggle it with one ball missing. As soon as a **Gap** arrives in a hand you **Feed** a ball into it from the other hand.

Juggling five balls in this way results in a **Five Five Five One** (5551) pattern, six balls gives a 66661 and so on. If you start from a **Fountain** you will get a pattern in which the **Feeds** go in alternate directions. If you start from a **Cascade** the **Feeds** will always go one way, creating an asymmetrical pattern. It's interesting to note that the **Two Ball Shower** (3 1) can be arrived at by applying this idea to a **Three Ball Cascade**.

A **Ladder** chart of the **Four Four One** pattern.

Note that a **Feed** or **1** (the action of one hand placing a ball directly into the other) is shown on the chart by a throw symbol in actual contact with a catch, indicating a sort of "non-throw" with no **Airtime** at all.

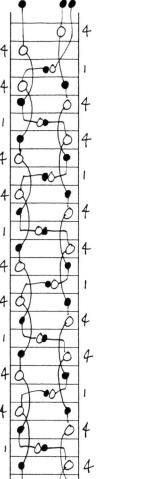

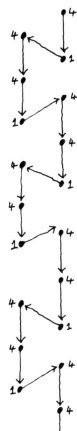

The **Causal Diagram** of the **441** is also interesting, especially since it contains arrows that travel backwards in time.

This is because **Feeds**, or **1**'s, become arrows moving one **Beat** up the chart – indicating that you have to empty your hand <u>before</u> you can **Feed** a ball into it.

To my mind this diagram fits well with the way the pattern feels to juggle – those **Feeds** feel like they are being driven "under" the pattern, which is exactly how the diagram looks.

Four Four One

Four Two Three (423)

This simple **Siteswap** sequence is the basis of so many patterns it deserves its own entry in THE ENCYCLOPÆDIA OF BALL JUGGLING.

• Take three balls, placing two in the right and one in the left. Start by throwing a ball from your right hand, straight up, as if you were starting **Two in One Hand**.

Pause for a moment (that's the **2**) and then make a crossing throw from your right hand to your left, as if you were starting a **Three Ball Cascade**.

Now repeat the same thing on the left-hand side.

Now keep going, that's **423**.

It's the same thing as **Right Middle Left**.

A **4** is a **Two in One Hand** self throw. A **3** is an ordinary **Three Ball Cascade** crossing throw, and a **2** is **Siteswap** language for just holding a ball for a **Beat**.

Your hands juggle in the unusual order *right-right-left-left*.

423 is a simple pattern, but some really spectacular tricks are based on it.

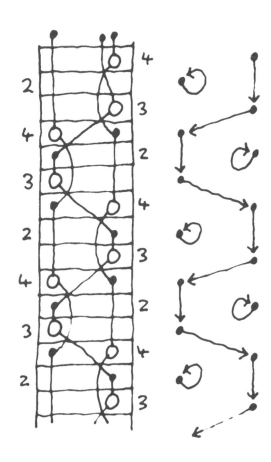

The **Ladder** chart shows how the pattern fits together: note that the two of the balls stay on their own side of the pattern, while the third crosses back and forth. This is spookily similar to the **Box.**

The **Causal Diagram** gives a better picture of the way the pattern *feels*. The **2**'s translate into those weird little arrows pointing to their own tails.

Most of the interesting **423** patterns are *shape distortions* of the "pure" **423**. These include **Right Middle Left, Tennis, Cross Arm Tennis, Burke's Barrage,** the **Fake Mess,** the **Follow** and **Charlie's Cheat.**

• If you throw the **3**'s *straight up in a central column* you end up juggling **Right Middle Left.**

• If you throw the **4**'s right up the middle of your juggling space while throwing the **3**'s **Over the Top** you end up juggling a pattern called **Tennis.**

• If cross your throwing hand *over* your other hand each time you throw a **3**, so that the **3**'s end up going the "wrong" way you are juggling a pattern called **Cross Arm Tennis** which is a just gnat's tickle away from a **Fake Mess.**

• If you juggle the **3**'s **Under the Hand** you are an ant's sneeze away from juggling a **Follow**.

• If you throw the **4**'s **Under the Hand**, so they rise and fall on the "wrong" side of the pattern, you are an amoeba's division away from a **Burke's Barrage** – which in turn is not very far from **Charlie's Cheat**.

• A *shared* **Burke's Barrage** makes a very impressive **Gandini Pattern**. Two jugglers stand close enough to cross their inner arms (their outer arms are not used in the pattern). The **4**'s are thrown *under* your partner's arm. The **3**'s are thrown with arms uncrossed in **Reverse Cascade** throws.

Right after you catch each **4** you should slice your arm right into your partner's juggling space (while they throw their **4**).

See also **Grover**.

Burke's Barrage *(a **423** pattern) juggled as a **Gandini Pattern.***

*Mathematically minded jugglers can use the **Mills' Mess State Transition Diagram** to work out their own **423** patterns. Here's **Burke's Barrage.***

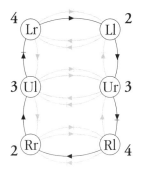

*And here's the **Fake Mess**: note that the throws have just "moved back a space".*

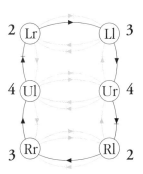

Four Two Three (423)

Gandini Patterns

In the early 1990s Sean Gandini (a highly skilled juggler) and Kati Yla-Hokkala (a rhythmic gymnast) started a collaboration that turned into the GANDINI JUGGLING PROJECT. Together they have developed a very innovative blend of juggling and dance.

Their multi-person ball-juggling patterns are particularly unique and special so I have included a few examples in the ENCYCLOPÆDIA and taken the liberty of calling them **Gandini Patterns**.

A typical **Gandini Pattern** is a relatively simple **Passing Pattern** for two or more jugglers, and will probably involve a frugal quantity of balls. The jugglers work side by side, facing the audience.

*Gandini Patterns are hard to follow with the eye because the performers' arms cross and interweave in elaborate ways as they constantly **Steal** the pattern off each other.*

Before you attempt any **Gandini Patterns** you should find yourself a partner and go and practise some **Steals**.

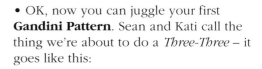

• Call yourselves A and B.

A stands on B's right and juggles a **Three Ball Cascade**.

B then reaches in and **Steals** the entire pattern.

When **Stealing** a **Three Ball Cascade** you reach in *over* your partner's hands. You will be grabbing three consecutive throws and you have the choice of taking the first ball from either the near or far side of their pattern.

•It's a good idea to get proficient at both alternatives.

•Don't forget to swap places so you both get used to **Stealing** every which way around.

Carry on until you are both experts.

• OK, now you can juggle your first **Gandini Pattern**. Sean and Kati call the thing we're about to do a *Three-Three* – it goes like this:

A starts juggling a **Three Ball Cascade** and B immediately **Steals** all three, whereupon A immediately **Steals** all three back. Then you keep going.

To put it another way, A makes *three* catches, then B makes *three* catches. that's why they call it a *Three-Three*.

Note that your arms are starting to do elegant things all by themselves!

•There are two different ways of doing a *Three-Three*. If A starts with a right-hand throw then B will catch that ball in the left hand (the *outside* hand). The Gandinis call this a *Three-Three-Out*.

•On the other hand (literally) if A starts with a left-hand throw, B's first catch will be with the inside hand, hence this variation is called a *Three-Three-In*.

•Don't forget to swap places as well!

When you've mastered all that you are ready to move on to the more exotic stuff.

•The next exercise is a *Two-Two* which is going to turn out a lot more interesting and pretty to watch than you'd expect. This is definitely a pattern to show off to your friends!

The start: A starts with two in the right and one in the left – then tosses the first ball to B's left hand.

Step One: A then throws under B's right arm.

Step Two: A then makes a self throw from right to left.

Step Three: B throws from the left to A's right hand.

Step Four: B makes a self throw from right to left. Now go back to Step One...

By the time you've cracked this pattern you'll really start to get an idea of what **Gandini Patterns** are all about. It's just amazing how such a simple idea can produce such a beautiful pattern.

•The *Two-Two* is not a symmetrical pattern. You'll note that A's first catch is always an *In*, while B's first catch is an *out*.

•If you are doing really well, and would like a serious challenge, you can try a *Three-Two-One*.

A starts juggling, until three catches have been made. Then B makes two catches, then A makes one catch. Now B does three catches, A does two, and finally B does one. Repeat ad infinitum.

Calling the catches out as you go helps.

When you've completed all these exercises you can move on to even higher levels.

See also **Grover, Middlesborough, Cranes, Mills' Mess, Burke's Barrage** and **Eric's Extension.**

And if that isn't enough for you, you can always go and visit the Gandini's web site at **http://www.gandinijuggling.com**.

Gandini Patterns

Gap

A **Gap**, sometimes called a *hole*, is exactly that: a *gap* in a juggling pattern, a missing ball, an invisible ball, a ball that isn't there. Sometimes it's a mistake – the ball *should* be there but it's on the floor. Sometimes it's deliberate – the ball *should* be there, and it is, but only in the juggler's imagination.

• Try juggling a **Three Ball Cascade** using only two real balls and one imaginary one. Mime the throws and catches of the imaginary ball. The missing ball is the **Gap**.

You might find it difficult to make your hands throw at all since, as far as they are concerned, two balls is exactly the right number for doing nothing at all! Persevere. The secret to success in **Gap** patterns is to really *believe* in the gap and treat it just like a real ball.

If you **Drop** while juggling a **Three Ball Cascade** you can continue with a three-ball **Gap** pattern while you bend down and pick up the dropped ball. In this way you can recover the pattern without ever breaking the rhythm of the pattern – see **Picking Up**.

• Any juggling pattern can be juggled with a **Gap**. Try a **Four Ball Fountain** with three balls. You will find yourself juggling **Two in One Hand** on one side with the third ball hopping up and down on the other side.

• **Gap** technology is much used in **Passing Patterns**. You get points for style if you keep going after a **Drop** when passing. Wait until the **Gap** travels around the pattern to the hand that is nearest to the dropped ball, then pick up!

See also **Five Ball Gap** and **Four Four One (441).**

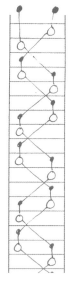

*A three-ball **Gap** pattern, in other words a **Three Ball Cascade** with a ball missing. This is what you should be juggling if you **Drop** a ball out of a cascade.*

*In **Siteswap Notation** this is **330…***

Gorilla

The **Gorilla** is another animal impersonation for the three-ball juggler, along with the **Giraffe**, **Penguin**, **Orangutan** and all the others.

• All you do is juggle a **Three Ball Cascade** and beat your chest at the same time. The chest-beating move is very like a **Chop**.

This trick gets about two out of ten for style, but with animal impersonations it's quantity, not quality, that counts!

Gravity

Gravity is the smoothest force I have ever had the pleasure of working with. It is so utterly constant* and free from variation or turbulence that you can be quite, quite, sure that if your bathroom scales tell a different story from yesterday it's your *weight* that's changed, not the force of gravity.

Gravity causes any object dropped near the surface of our planet to accelerate towards the centre of the earth at a rate of 9.80665 metres per second per second. The *"per second per second"* bit confuses most people; it just means that after one second of free fall the object will be moving downwards at 9.80665 metres per second, and a second after that it will be going 9.80665 metres per second faster and so on until it hits something.

You can work out exactly how far an object will fall in a given time with the formula $d = gt^2/2$, where d is the distance you are trying to work out, g is the acceleration due to gravity (9.80665 m/sec²), and t is the time of the fall in

seconds. Working backwards from this formula you can, if you like this kind of thing, work out the **Airtime** of a throw if you know the height to which it rises. The little t^2 bit in the formula accounts for the fact that the height of a throw increases by the *square* of the **Airtime**.

Contrary to popular belief, the rate at which objects fall is not affected by their horizontal speed. A bullet leaving the muzzle of a gun aimed at the horizon falls just as fast as a bullet dropped out of your hand. It just goes a long, long way before it lands.

It was also thought, in former times, that heavy objects fell faster than light ones. Galileo sorted that one out hundreds of years ago. He dropped two balls of different weights from the Leaning Tower of Pisa in front of assembled VIP's and they both hit the ground together. So if you think that heavy stuff falls faster you are seriously out of date. Of course *very* light objects do fall slower because of air resistance.

Gravity is a strange force that occurs wherever you have *mass*. Every piece of mass in the universe has a slight attraction for every other piece of mass, and this tends to draw them together. Physicists call

the force of gravity a *weak* force because it takes a huge amount of mass (say the whole of planet Earth) to produce a tiny amount of gravity. Science still has *no idea* how gravity actually works. It's a great mystery. **Gravity** tends to cause matter in space to collect into large spherical lumps, like the Earth and the Sun and the Planets.

As you juggle a **Three Ball Cascade**, be aware of the *fourth* ball that makes this wonderful trickery possible – it's the one that you are standing on.

*This is not quite 100% true; gravity *does* vary a tiny bit from place to place on the earth's surface due to the fact that the planet isn't quite perfectly round and parts of it are made of heavier stuff than others. This is of no practical interest to the juggler however, since the variations are ridiculously small. **Gravity** is also about half a percent lower at the equator than at the poles because of the centrifugal force of the Earth's spin.

Gravity

Ground State Pattern

A **Ground State Pattern** is a **Siteswap** pattern that can be started from rest, as opposed to an **Excited State Pattern** which needs to be set up with some prior throws.

The **Three Ball Cascade (33333...)** is a **Ground State Pattern**. You place two balls in the right, one in the left, and just start throwing **3**'s.

The three-ball **Shower (51)** is an **Excited State Pattern** because you can't just grab three balls and start throwing **515151**.

Instead you can go **52 51515151...**

Moreover, even if you are already juggling a **Three Ball Cascade** you *still* can't go right into a **51**: you need to set it up.

33333 52 51515151...

– is one way of doing it.

This terminology is more mathematically interesting than practically useful, but at least you know what it means now.

Grover

I'm not sure why this **Gandini Pattern** is named after a character from Sesame Street*. It is a variation of a *shared* **Burke's Barrage**, which is described under the heading **Four Two Three (423)**.

• Juggle a shared **Burke's Barrage** and pay attention to what you are doing with your *4-ball*.

Normally you would toss this ball up, from under your partner's arm, and then catch it again after throwing your *3-ball*.

• To do a **Grover** you throw the ball as before, but then catch it at the *top of its flight* with your spare (outside) hand. This happens more or less simultaneously with your **3** throw.

You then swing the ball in a large half circle while your empty hand (your inside hand) slices through the pattern. Finally you **Feed** the 4-ball back into your inside hand.

It's big, slow and *very* pretty.

See also **Gandini Patterns, Burke's Barrage** and **Four Two Three (423).**

*Maybe Grover is short for "grab-over"?

A Shared **Burke's Barrage** *juggled normally.*

In the **Grover** *you catch the 4-ball at the top, swing it around with your outside arm, and then* **Feed** *it back into your inside hand.*

Half Shower

This is a rather loose term for any pattern juggled with crossing throws so that one hand throws higher than the other.

I call the term "loose" because, if you are juggling more than three balls, there is more than one distinct pattern that you could call a **Half Shower**.

All showers are *circular* patterns; the balls follow each other around the loop or figure eight as the case may be. **Cascades** and **Showers** are also circular patterns.

•You can juggle three balls as a **Three Ball Cascade** – which is **33*** in **Siteswap Notation** – or a three-ball **Shower** which is **51**. Falling mathematically between these two patterns is a three-ball **Half Shower** which is (**4x,2x**).

Both hands are throwing even numbered throws in this pattern so they both have to throw **Synchronously** (i.e. at the same time). It's a bit of a knack training your hands to do two different things at the same time.

•Start the pattern with two in the right and one in the left. The lead throw is a crossing **4** from the right, thereafter *both* hands throw at the same time, **4**'s from the right and **2**'s from the left.

•Learn the three-ball **Half Shower** both ways, and then try changing direction in mid-juggle. If you change direction on *every* throw you are juggling the **Box**.

•With four balls there are two **Half Showers** that fall neatly and mathematically between the **Four Ball Fountain** (**44**) and the four-ball **Shower** (**71**). One is **Five Three** (**53**) which has alternate throws and the other is **Six Two** (**6x,2x**) which uses simultaneous throws. Both of these patterns have their own entries in the ENCYCLOPÆDIA.

Getting Mathematical!

•Moving up to five balls there are *three* possible **Half Showers** between the **Five Ball Cascade** (**55**) and the five-ball **Shower** (**91**).

They are (**6x,4x**) – quite a common trick with five ball jugglers, **73** – not often seen, and (**8x,2x**) – never seen it.

•For any number of balls you can work out all the possible circular patterns by writing down pairs of numbers that add up to *double the number of balls being juggled.*

Noting that in **Siteswap** we write numbers over **9** as letters (**A** is **10**, **B** is **11** etc.) we can draw up a table of seven-ball patterns like this:

77	Seven-ball **Cascade (Async.)**
(8x,6x)	**Synchronous Half Shower**
95	**Asynchronous Half Shower**
(Ax,4x)	**Synchronous Half Shower**
B3	**Asynchronous Half Shower**
(Cx,2x)	**Synchronous Half Shower**
D1	Seven-ball **Shower (Async.)**

Logic suggests that we can take this a stage further to arrive at (**Ex,0x**) which is mathematically valid, but impossible to juggle since nobody has worked out how to make a crossing throw with an empty hand. **Siteswap**, it seems, has some holes in it!*

However **E0** *is* valid – it's seven balls in one hand!

I've never seen that one either.

---

*Normally we'd just write this a **3**, but we *can* write it as **33** and it makes the mathematics of **Half Showers** a lot easier to follow if we do.

*Or perhaps **Siteswap** doesn't know what you can and can't do with "holes".

Half Shower

Hat Bounce

The **Hat Bounce** is a trick you can do with a **Bouncing Ball** and a hat.

• Put the **Bouncing Ball** into a top hat (or any hat with a flat top) then drop the hat onto the floor. The hat stays down and the ball bounces up out of it! A fabulous way to start a ball juggling routine.

Hat Finish

Catching all the balls you are juggling in your hat is a tidy way to finish a ball juggling routine.

If you are working with three balls there is no problem, but catching four or five is harder because you need to find the time to take the hat off your head! The technique for catching five balls is obviously good enough for four so you might as well learn it!

• Juggle the **Five Ball Cascade**, and then gather one ball into your right hand while you continue to juggle with the other four. This forces the pattern into a **Five Ball Gap**.

As soon as the **Gap** arrives in your left hand it's free to whip the hat off your head and start collecting the balls. No one will spot the cheat – audiences simply cannot follow that many objects at once.

Flashy jugglers like the great and infamous H. H. McLeod throw the last ball **Behind the Back**.

Having Problems?

If you have tied yourself in a knot trying to learn some new trick and you just aren't getting anywhere then you need to learn the art of *sidling up to the problem and catching it unawares*.

• Forget whatever you are trying to learn for a moment and learn this trick instead. Take two beanbags, place one in each hand. Now cross your arms.

Throw both balls *at the same time* so that the right-hand beanbag is caught in the left hand and the left-hand beanbag is caught in the right.

Here's the trick though – catch them *without uncrossing your hands!*

Hardly *anyone* can do this at the first attempt, and that includes seven-ball jugglers. It drives you nuts – but you'll be able to do it after five minutes of practice, I promise!

• Now, flushed with the feeling of success, you can return to your original problem.

High-Low Shower (7131)

The **High-Low Shower** is a three-ball pattern based on the three-ball **Shower**.

You pump out an extra-high throw while showering three balls, then juggle one round of a two-ball **Shower** underneath it.

• Warm up by juggling a two-ball **Shower** as fast and low as you possibly can, preferably *without looking at it!* You'll see why in a moment.

Now pick up a third ball and juggle a three-ball **Shower**; your left hand throws **5**'s while the right throws **1**'s (**Feeds**).

Make one extra-high throw, about double the height of the pattern, and juggle one round of two-ball shower underneath it before catching the high one and resuming your three-ball shower. You'll now see why it was a good idea to practise showering two blind! It's almost impossible to watch the high ball and the low one at the same time.

A two-ball shower uses the throws **31** and that high one was a **7**! So you have just juggled:

5151 7131 5151..

*A **Causal Diagram** of 7131 conveys something of the feel of the pattern.*

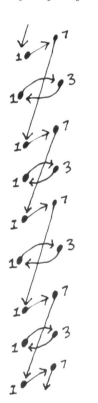

*The shape of a **High-Low Shower**. The problem is where to look!*

• For the full **High-Low Shower** you simply keep going!

713171317131...

• The idea can be taken further if you are feeling keen! If you throw a **9** instead of a **7** you can get *two* rounds of a two-ball shower underneath the high ball:

913131...

The **9** is *very* high!

• You can substitute a quick *double exchange* of crossing **2**'s for the **31** if you're feeling flash – that's **(2x,2x)**.

• If you throw a **9** instead of a **7** you can squeeze in *two* double exchanges before the **7** lands **(2x,2x)(2x,2x)**.

• If you throw a **B** (an eleven) you can get *three* double exchanges in!

I think I'll stop there before it gets silly.

For more of this sort of stuff see **Five Three One (531)** or just try juggling **501**.

High-Low Shower (7131)

Hops

Hops is a very simple three- *or* four-ball trick, best inserted into a routine as a small incidental move.

• Here is a three-ball **Hop**. Start with two balls in your left hand, side by side, and a third in your right hand.

Throw a very low split **Multiplex** throw with your left hand. While the two balls are in the air shoot the ball from your right hand across *under* the **Multiplex** and catch everything!

The right-hand ball ends up in the left hand and the other two balls have **Hopped** one space to the right. Effectively you are back in the starting position, but all the balls have moved round a space. Make that **Multiplex** as low as you possibly can!

It really is that simple!

• You can extend the trick to four balls, by starting with two balls in each hand and doing a **Hop** to the left, followed by a **Hop** to the right. Only three balls are involved in each move. Curiously the four-ball **Hop** is not as visually appealing as the three-ball version.

More is not always better in juggling!

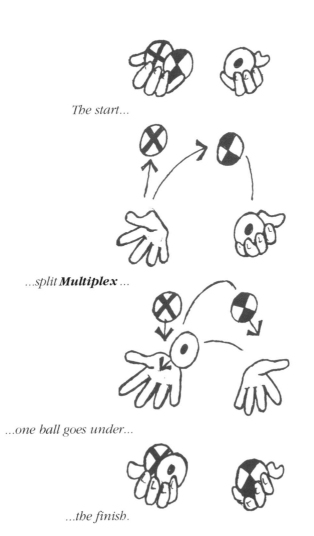

The start...

*...split **Multiplex** ...*

...one ball goes under...

...the finish.

Hopstop

It's good to punctuate the normally smooth and continuous motion of a juggling pattern with *stops*. A flashy finish, like a **Hat Finish,** can be thought of as a juggler's *full stop*. A **Hopstop** then, is a juggler's *comma*.

• Juggle a **Three Ball Cascade** for a few throws, then *stop* in the right hand and *restart*, keeping to the underlying rhythm of the cascade.

That's a simple and not very elegant stop. For the **Hopstop** you add one little "cheating" throw to the plain stop.

As you stop in the right hand, the left hand **Pops** a self **4** and *then* you restart, keeping to the rhythm of the original cascade.

The **Hopstop** is very easy, so make it into a very artistic and expressive move. When juggled well it looks and feels as if the force of the *stop* in the right hand has **Popped** the ball from the left.

• A **Hopstop** starts to look like a very difficult trick if you restart the pattern with an **Under the Hand** throw. To do this, your right hand will be sweeping *under* the left as the *hop* throw is being made.

*A simple **Hopstop** in a **Three Ball Cascade**.*

The important thing is to keep the rhythm of the cascade going right through the move. This is a very easy, but nevertheless very effective, bit of three-ball juggling.

*Make this an **Under the Hand** throw and the **Hopstop** starts to look like a very sophisticated trick.*

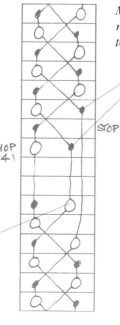

HOP
(4)

STOP

*Make these two catches **Snatches** instead of normal catches and you are really starting to pile on the skill and dexterity!*

You can use the **Hopstop** in the really elegant finish shown below.

•(1) From a **Three Ball Cascade** you gather two balls in your left hand while throwing a **Hopstop** from your right hand.

•(2) Now cross your right hand over your left as you make an **Under the Hand Multiplex** from your left.

•(3) Uncross your hands and throw **Over the Top** from your right.

•(4) Catch some stuff.

•(5) Finish with a final toss right to left. Isn't that nice?

Hot Start

A **Hot Start** is the act of starting a juggling pattern or trick from another already-running juggling pattern. This is the opposite of a **Cold Start**.

See also **Excited State Pattern**.

1

2

3

4

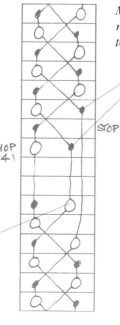

5

Hot Start

How to Juggle Three Balls

Internet Resources

There are now countless web sites devoted to juggling – many of them are really rather good, and it would be quite impossible to list them all. Fortunately there are just three sites you need to know about, since they'll lead you on to all of the rest!

The venerable Juggling Information Service at **http://www.juggling.org** was one of the earliest sites devoted to juggling and has steadfastly retained its original look and feel over the years.

Recently we have seen the debut of the Internet Juggling Database which is at **http://www.jugglingdb.com** and sports a flashy front end which is available in several different languages.

The excellent juggling simulator *Juggling Lab* can be found on the Internet at **http://jugglinglab.sourceforge.net.**

You can find information about this book (and a certain Mr. Charlie Dancey) at **http://www.dancey.net**.

Joggling

Joggling is, on the face of it, a rather silly invention – you can guess what it is from the name.

The idea is that you run and juggle at the same time, perhaps while listening to Vivaldi's *Four Seasons* on your MP3 player.

Of course, jugglers who really get the juggling bug are well known for exploring the potential of juggling and doing X at the same time where X could be anything: catching a bus, driving a car, making a sandwich, holding down a sensible job or even writing an encyclopædia.

This is just one example of such madness, but I suppose it keeps one fit!

Juggle

The word **Juggle**, according to my dictionary, is derived from the Old French verb *jogler* – to perform as a jester. This in turn has its roots in Latin from *joculari* – to jest, and *jocus* – a jest, or joke.

In the past the word "juggler" was applied to conjurers and magicians as well as jugglers in the modern sense.

When one is a specialist in something obscure it is interesting to look it up in the dictionary to see whether the given definition matches your own. Of course it never does exactly, so one is left with a smug feeling of self-satisfaction because it just proves what you suspected all along – you are cleverer than the people that wrote the dictionary.

This isn't quite fair because any definition of exactly what it is to **Juggle** is bound to be flawed because *there are no rules in juggling!* More balls than hands? Always keeping at least one ball in the air? Never holding more than one object in one hand at a time? None of these are absolute rules. If you think you have discovered a rule then I advise you to immediately break it – this is where new ideas come from!

See also **Devil**.

Juggler's Rest Backpackers

Way down south in Picton, New Zealand, there's a small backpackers' hotel called the **Juggler's Rest** where you can stop off on your tour of the South Island of that beautiful country.

There's a nice pool and piles of juggling equipment to play with. They also have a well-stocked library which includes books like this one.

This may be the only hotel in the world operating on a juggling theme. Don't forget to tell them I sent you!

You'll find them at:
8 Canterbury St., Picton, Marlborough, New Zealand
(03) 573-5570
jugglers-rest@xtra.co.nz

Juggling Notation

See **Notation**.

Juggling with Children

Yes – you *can* juggle with children! This is just the sort of thing that street performers like to do.

The problem with using children as juggling props is that they are too heavy to throw easily, they wriggle too much to be easy to catch, and if you drop one its mother will kill you without a moment's hesitation.

• Here is a tried and tested technique that has been performed all over the world. Start with two balls in your right hand and a suitably cooperative child wedged (gently of course) between your left arm and your chest. Juggle a few rounds of **Two in One Hand** in your right hand. Now throw two consecutive high crossing throws – theory says they should be **5**'s but, discretion being the better part of valour, you had better make them **7**'s or better. While they are in the air you **Feed** the child from your left arm to your right. The child doesn't actually change position, you just transfer the grip from one arm to the other.

Catch the high ones and settle back into **Two in One Hand** in the left. Give your assistant a grin and then repeat the sequence the other way around.

That's enough! If your young partner starts to realise that it's *you* that is the centre of attention rather than *them*, they'll squeal!

You should keep the routine short, but as any street performer knows the *buildup* is another matter entirely. You can make that as long as you like.

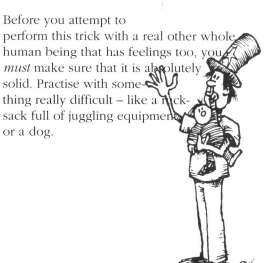

Before you attempt to perform this trick with a real other whole human being that has feelings too, you *must* make sure that it is absolutely solid. Practise with something really difficult – like a rucksack full of juggling equipment or a dog.

Juggling with Children

Kangaroo

The **Kangaroo** is another of those rather silly animal impersonation tricks for the three-ball juggler. Few of these moves have any real *quality* so it's my recommendation that you rattle them all off in a very fast sequence relying on the sheer *quantity* of silliness to do the trick!

• You need to be wearing a big floppy T-shirt for this trick. From a **Three Ball Cascade**, you throw a ball high into the air and then pull your T-shirt out in front of you like a trampoline, bouncing the ball back up again.

Kangaroo? It doesn't make a lot of sense when you actually stop and *think* about it, but then again, somehow it does!

See also **Penguin**, **Orangutan** and any other animals you find lurking in the pages of this book.

Kick Up

• Juggle three balls and let one fall to one side, then kick it back up into the pattern with the outside of your ankle. The expression on your face should be *totally cool*. You'll need to practise the **Kick Up** with one ball until you get your aim right. When you start to feel confident you could try kicking the ball from one foot to the other before kicking it back into the pattern.

• If you want to make a **Kick Up** look really nonchalant, you should *continue juggling* a two-ball **Gap** pattern while the ball falls and gets kicked back up. You can practise getting the timing right by using a **Bouncing Ball** at first – a bounce is much easier to control than a **Kick Up**. See **Six** for more tips on how to do this.

• The previous type of **Kick Up** is fine for balls that are still in the air, but what every juggler needs, sooner rather than later, is a **Kick Up** that works on a ball that has been totally, completely and shamefully **Dropped** onto the ground.

Stand over the dead ball and grip it between your heels. Leap energetically into the air and flick the ball up from behind you. This is *terribly* good for your spine and very hard work, but worth it!

•An easier alternative is to *cheat* the dead ball onto the top of one foot with the other and then simply "lift" it back up into the pattern. It is, admittedly, a rather contrived move, but it's less damaging to the ego than actually bending down and picking the ball up with your fingers (besides, you don't know where it's *been)*. With practice the whole manoeuvre becomes a smooth movement to dazzle and amaze the unbelieving eyes of your spellbound audience.

Cheat the dropped ball onto your foot...

Lift it back into your pattern.

Knee Bounce

This is easy!

•Juggle a **Three Ball Cascade** and let a ball fall past your hands and *knee* it back up into the pattern. If you are feeling flash you can try bouncing off one knee and then the other before resuming the cascade.

This trick combines well with **Off The Elbow**, the **Flick Off** and other body moves.

Ladder Notation

Ladder Notation is the system of juggling **Notation** used to produce the ladder-like charts throughout this book.

Although it is similar in many ways to musical notation, I doubt very much that you will ever see a juggler sight-reading a juggling pattern. Systems of notation for juggling are simply ways of recording patterns on paper that help you to see where all the balls come from, where they go to, and how a pattern actually works.

I devised **Ladder Notation** in 1984, when I was completely stuck trying to work out how to change from a **Five Ball Gap** bounce to a **Five Three (53)** bounce without breaking anything in my kitchen. There is one precise moment in the pattern at which this change can be made, and I had a sneaky suspicion that even when I was getting the *moment* right I was getting the *throws* wrong so I sat down to solve the problem on paper instead – it worked!

Ladder Notation is a fairly simple idea. I know that other people have independently invented almost identical systems since, and I wouldn't be at all surprised if someone had done so before.

Continued overleaf...

Ladder Notation...

Ladder Notation is written from top to bottom on a framework of lines resembling a ladder. The rungs of the ladder divide time into **Beats**. The right- and left-hand sides of the ladder correspond to the right and left sides of the juggling pattern.

Each ball is represented by a line that runs down the chart, moving from left to right as appropriate. Where a ball is caught a solid circle is drawn on the line (solid because the hand is full). Where it is thrown there is an empty circle (because the hand is becoming empty).

Most charts start with all the balls at rest in the hands, and this is shown by placing the appropriate number of catch symbols (solid circles) at the top of the chart.

The chart shown here records a **Three Ball Cascade**, starting with two balls in the right hand and one in the left.

If you examine the chart it should be obvious what is going on, and you can use it to draw some conclusions about the **Three Ball Cascade** that might not be *quite* so obvious from watching the real thing.

*The classic **Three Ball Cascade** in **Ladder Notation**, starting with two balls in the right hand and one in the left.*

These are throws.

These are catches.

*It takes six **Beats** for a ball to cycle once through the pattern.*

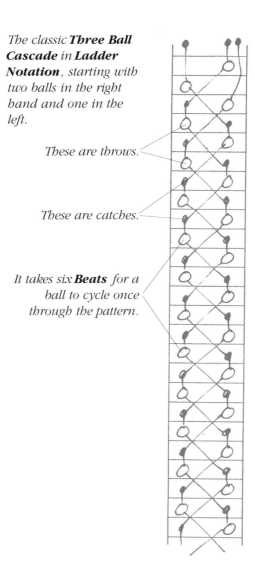

- There is one throw on every **Beat**.
- Throws are made with alternate hands.
- When one hand is throwing the other is catching.
- The airtime of each throw is two **Beats**.
- Each hand (after the start) is alternately holding for a **Beat** and empty for a **Beat**.
- It takes six **Beats** for a ball to cycle through the pattern.
- The pattern resembles a plait.

Sometimes you'll see the side of a chart labelled with the **Numbers** of the throws. The number of a throw is generally one more than the number of **Beats** it spends in the air; it's the number that would describe the throw in the purely numerical **Siteswap Notation**. This information is not absolutely required, but it can make a chart much more readable.

In other cases you may see the side of the chart labelled with **R**'s and **L**'s which help to indicate which hand is responsible for a particular throw. This is helpful in charts that involve crossed-hand throws or catches, like the **Mills' Mess** patterns.

The next chart shows a **Trick** thrown in a **Three Ball Cascade.** The right hand throws a self or **Two in One Hand** throw. You can see that the throw is a **4**, as opposed to the **3**'s used in the cascade. You can also see the extra-long hold that the left hand gets while the trick is being thrown.

You can always tell how many balls are being juggled in a chart by taking a horizontal slice through it anywhere and counting how many ball lines pass through it. One of the nicest features of this system is that so many patterns look so *pretty* when presented in chart form. See especially **Five Three Four (534)** and the **Mills' Mess** patterns.

While the **Ladder Notation** is not as concise as **Siteswap Notation** it *does* understand about hold time, the time that balls spend in the hand. **Siteswap** ignores hold time altogether and cannot distinguish between a three-**Beat** hold and a one-**Beat** throw, calling them *both* a **2**.

You can use **Ladder Notation** to work out new patterns using pen and paper, but be warned! Just because it works in theory doesn't mean you'll be able to juggle it!

*A **Three Ball Cascade**.*

*Every throw in the straight cascade is a 3, spending two **Beats** in the air.*

*Here the right hand throws a **4** to itself.*

This creates a long hold in the left hand...

...then the normal pattern resumes.

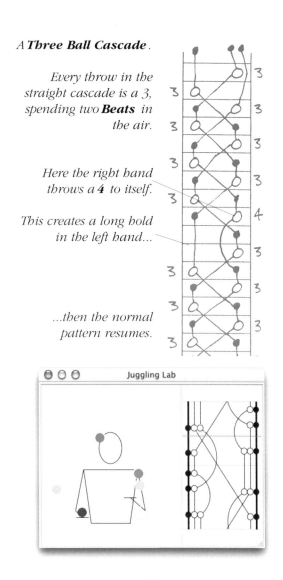

A variant of **Ladder Notation** is used in the juggling simulator *Juggling Lab,* which you'll find on the Internet at **http://jugglinglab.sourceforge.net**.

This is an excellent simulator, developed by Jack Boyce, which allows you to type in **Siteswaps** as well as tweaking the pattern by dragging stuff around on a **Ladder** chart. You can even change the hand movements, so patterns like the **Mills' Mess** are possible.

In the Juggling Lab version of **Ladder Notation** two dark lines are added to represent the hands, while the paths of the balls are represented by lighter lines. The juggling pattern reads from top to bottom, as normal. Throws and catches both appear as white circles, while hand *events* appear as black dots.

Juggling Lab is under development but it's already a very powerful tool, and it is used extensively by juggling net-heads to demonstrate and discuss juggling patterns.

Ladder Notation

Left-handed or Right-handed?

I apologise to any left-handed readers for the fact that this book shows a teensy weensy bias towards the right hand.

Left-handed readers therefore have to suffer their usual fate – translating right-handed instructions to their way of thinking.

But it's not all bad news if you are a left-handed juggler; all those years of swapping everything around in your head have been excellent practice for learning juggling tricks. Juggling is an ambidextrous activity in which the left hand is just as important as the right.

Jugglers should try and avoid favouring their best hand. If you learn an asymmetrical pattern like a **Shower** or a **Five Three (53)**, you should learn it both ways! It's also very important to teach your weaker hand your latest trick *as soon as possible*. Once you get into the habit of juggling a particular move on one side you'll find it increasingly difficult to transfer the skill to the other hand. Your subconscious mind doesn't *want* to do things the hard way, and tries as hard as it can to make the whole thing feel as awkward as possible.

It is also worth bearing in mind that as soon as you can juggle a new trick on one side, the action of juggling it on alternate sides quite often results in a completely new pattern.

The *Guy in the Hat* in the illustrations who demonstrates most of the tricks (the ones he can actually do!) is ambidextrous. Sometimes he demonstrates tricks the same way around as they are described in the text, and sometimes he does them *as if viewed in a mirror*.

So, **Left-handed or Right-Handed**, you are *all* going to have to interpret the instructions in THE ENCYCLOPÆDIA OF BALL JUGGLING both ways around!

Luke's Shuffle

Luke's Shuffle is a three-ball trick – it's a cross between the **Box** and the **Shuffle**.

•**Luke's Shuffle** is a shape distortion of the **Box**.

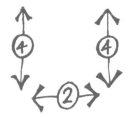

In the standard **Box** three balls move in a U-shape; two balls rise and fall at the side of the pattern, being thrown as **4**'s, while the third ball oscillates from left to right across the bottom of the U on **2**'s. It's the route of the **2**'s that has to change to turn the **Box** into **Luke's Shuffle**.

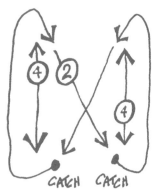

THE ENCYCLOPÆDIA OF BALL JUGGLING

Each **2** is caught in the normal position and then raised outside a rising **4** and *slammed* diagonally downwards to the opposite hand, right through the middle of the pattern. This throw is identical to the slammed throw in a **Shuffle**. If you can't do a **Shuffle** – learn it now!

One way to learn this is to juggle a normal **Box** and then start putting in occasional slammed throws on each side; as your skill builds up you will eventually be able to juggle the full pattern.

*Slamming a ball in **Luke's Shuffle**, the throwing hand has to get back down to catch that **4** double quick!*

Martin

The **Martin**, while it is a complex five-ball pattern, is perhaps a little easier than a **Five Ball Cascade**.

It's *almost* a **Multiplex** pattern because the hands hold more than one ball at a time, though every throw is a single-ball throw.

•Start with three in the right and two in the left. The throwing sequence is *right-right left-left right-right left-left*. The hands take turns to throw a self **6**, followed by a crossing **5**.

Keep those **6**'s on the outside of the pattern and everything should fall into place. The pattern has a fair degree of tolerance – you can throw those 6's as 5's instead if you prefer to make all the throws the same height.

In effect you are juggling a **Slow Cascade** with three balls, while the other two balls rise and fall at the sides.

TECHNICAL NOTE: According to **Siteswap** this pattern is a **690**, we're just throwing the **9**'s as if they were **5**'s, and they conveniently land in the **Gaps** left by the **0**'s. When you say "9" in **Siteswap Notation** you mean that a ball is being thrown in such a way that it will be *ready to be thrown again* in nine beats. Since **Siteswap** knows nothing about hold times we can get away with this trick of throwing the ball lower, and then holding onto it for a few beats to make up the time. Of course you are welcome to try and juggle a *pure* **690** if you wish. Those **9**'s would be *really* high!

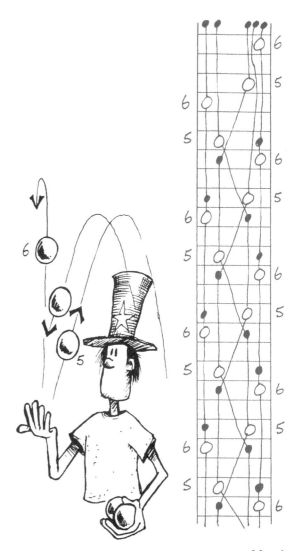

Middlesborough

This is a beautiful **Gandini Pattern** named after the town in England where Sean and Kati had some time to kill, and made this up. It requires two jugglers and just three balls.

It's a *Three-Three-In* which means that each juggler takes it in turn to make three catches, and the first catch (of each three) is made with the *inside* hand.

The tricky bit is that each juggler is using a **Cross Arm Cascade** (**Reverse Cascade** style) as the base pattern – which sounds awesomely impossible, but it isn't.

• Grab one juggling partner and three balls, call yourself A and your partner B. You stand to the right of your partner.

• Place two balls in your left hand and one in your right, then cross your right hand over your left – you are ready to start.

Now, one of the great things about the **Middlesborough** is that you can learn it in slow motion, making one throw at a time. As you become familiar with the sequence you can build up to full speed.

• (Start) A starts the pattern by tossing a ball from their left hand to B's right hand.

• (1) A then throws from their right hand to B's left. Note that A's right hand is crossed *over* A's left but *under* B's right. B should catch A's throw and then *cross* the right hand *under* the right.

• (2) Next A uncrosses hands and makes a left-hand throw to B's right hand.

• (3) B crosses hands, right over left, and makes a throw from the right towards A's left.

• (4) B makes a left-hand throw to A's right hand. Note that B's left hand is crossed *over* B's right, but *under* A's left. A will catch this throw and then cross the left hand *under* the right.

• (5) Next B uncrosses hands and makes a right-hand throw to A's left hand.

• (6) A crosses hands, left over right, and makes a throw from the left towards B's right.

• Now go back to step 1 and repeat.

This can be a pretty confusing exercise, so take it one step at a time, and make sure that you both know what you are supposed to be doing at each step.

As you become familiar with the pattern you'll be able to build up to full speed – concentrating on smooth and steady cooperation.

The result is well worth it – somehow, with **Gandini Patterns**, the whole is greater than the sum of the parts.

This is a pattern well worth showing off.

See also **Cross Arm Cascade, Gandini Patterns, Grover, Turbines, Cranes.**

Start   **1**   **2**   **3**

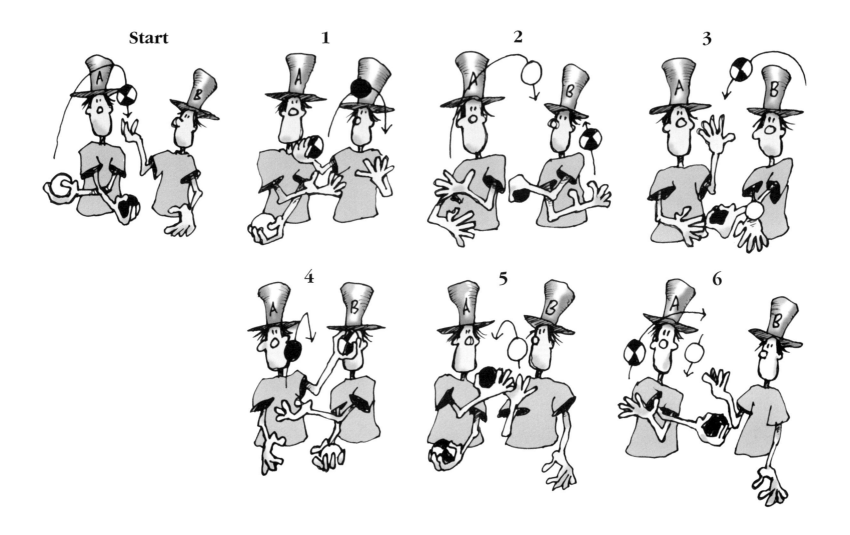

4   **5**   **6**

Mike's Mess

Mike's Mess was invented by Mike Day using his **Mills' Mess State Transition Diagram (MMSTD)**. It's living juggleable proof that a highly mathematical approach to juggling can actually turn out something *useful* that nobody else had thought of before.

The idea is simple: take the pattern **522** (a **Slow Cascade** of three balls) and lay it onto the MMSTD like this so that it follows this loop:

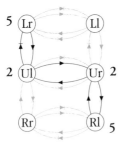

To do **Mike's Mess** you juggle Lr, Ul, Ur, Rl, Ur, Ul and then repeat using the throws **522522**... as you go. The **2**'s are, of course, holds, rather than throws. It's a bewildering pattern to watch, and fairly tricky to learn, but it ranks with the other great and twirly three-ball patterns. I'll explain it in practical terms.

•Start by juggling a **Slow Cascade** with three balls, just to get used to the rhythm.

•Now juggle the same pattern using **Under the Hand** throws instead of normal **Cascade** throws. You'll probably find yourself tending to go into a **Chop** pattern here automatically – very good.

•We're getting there now. Stop juggling for a moment and put one ball down so that you are left holding one ball in each hand. It's time to practise the movement that puts the magic into **Mike's Mess**.

Swing the left-hand ball over the right, then downward as if paddling a canoe on the wrong side. Keep the momentum going so that the ball rises past your right ear, swings back to the left, then continues under the right wrist at which point it is released as an **Under the Hand** throw. *That's* the movement you do before each throw in **Mike's Mess**.

It's very like a move that club-swingers call a *"cross and follow"*. The word *follow* refers to the fact that the *right*-hand ball starts its move as the left hand moves **Under the Hand** for the throw, hence the two balls seem to be *following* each other.

Practise it on both sides until it's completely solid.

•The complete pattern is the **Slow Cascade** juggled **Under the Hand,** with each switch from left-over-right to right-over-left being achieved with a *cross and follow*. Each throw is made at the end of a *follow*.

Got that one? Right, now how about laying **Five Three Four** onto the same **MMSTD** route?

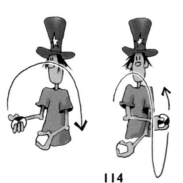

*The "snazzy" bit of **Mike's Mess** being practised with two balls. It's like the club-swingers' move the "cross and follow".*

Mills' Mess

The **Mills' Mess** is the *crème de la crème* of three-ball juggling patterns. A tongue-twister of triple trickery! Anti-gravitational hand jive in the key of three balls!!

Every juggler wants to learn the **Mills' Mess** – two of the questions experienced jugglers most often get asked by beginners are, "How do you do **Four Ball Juggling**?" and, "Do you know that one where the hands cross over and back?"

The **Mills' Mess** is the one where your hands cross over and back. It is a *distortion* of the **Three Ball Cascade**. The balls travel from hand to hand exactly as they would in the cascade, but the hands cross and uncross as they juggle, giving the trick its hypnotic fluidity.

• Start by practising the hand movements with no balls at all – put those beanbags down!

Cross your right hand over the left, look at your right hand and say *"Throw!"* while miming a throw that uncrosses your hands.

Now look at your left hand and say *"Throw!"*, miming a throw that crosses your hands again, this time left over right.

Next, look at your right hand. Say *"Throw!"* and mime an **Under the Hand** throw with your right hand that leaves your hand just where it is.

You have now mimed three throws and your arms are crossed in the *exact mirror image* of your starting position.

If you now repeat the whole sequence of three throws on this side you'll be back at the beginning – it goes like this:

The left hand, *"Throw!"* and uncross.

The right hand, *"Throw!"*, your hands cross again.

Finally, left hand, *"Throw!"* and it stays where it is.

You are back where you started.

This is the sequence of six throws that makes up the **Mills' Mess**. Practise miming that sequence so many times that you have dreams about it. Don't bother to read on until you've got it 100% taped!

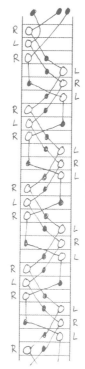

Ladder Notation presents a fairly narrow view of this wonderful piece of juggling since that sinuous curvy style is lost in this network of straight lines.

The characteristic feature of all the **Mills' Mess** patterns is the throwing positions right-left-right on the left, followed by left-right-left on the right.

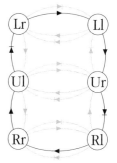

The **MMSTD** shows how the hands cross and uncross as the pattern is juggled. See **Mills' Mess State Transition Diagram** for a full explanation.

Continued overleaf…

Mills' Mess…

...Mills' Mess

• Now you can work with balls, and learn the first three throws of the pattern.

Take two balls in your right hand and one in the left and cross your right hand *over* the left as you would at the start of the mime sequence.

The first throw is a cascade throw, from your right hand, aimed to the right, but you catch it with your *left* hand after you have uncrossed your hands. Try it.

OK. The second throw is an **Over the Top** throw, from your left hand, towards the right. You make this throw before you catch the first one and you catch it in your right hand. Make sure you start with two in the right and one in the left as before.

• Try the first two throws.

The next throw is from the right hand, under the left. It goes straight up like an **Under the Hand** throw. You catch it in your left hand. Try the first three throws until it all fits together. If you get confused then go back to the mime exercise.

Now try the same exercise in reverse. Starting with two balls in your left hand, one in the right, you cross your left hand over the right and you are ready to go.

The first throw is a **Cascade** throw from the left hand towards the left; you catch it in your right hand. The second throw is an **Over the Top**, from your right hand, also

towards the left. The third throw is from the left hand, under the right wrist, and it goes straight up. You catch it in your right hand.

• Now you must take those two sequences and weld them together into the seamless six-throw cycle of the complete pattern (the complete **Mess** perhaps?). It's probably going to take you a while to "click" so be patient, and above all, if you find it tiresome – take a break! You won't learn anything if you get hot and bothered (except perhaps that you can't learn anything when you are bothered and hot, which is quite a valuable lesson in itself).

• Some people find it quite impossible to learn the pattern throw-by-throw. If that sounds like you, then you may need an entirely different approach.

Practise juggling the **Windmill**, first in one direction, and then in the other. If you don't know the trick then look it up.

Once you can **Windmill** both ways, work on those direction changes; when you can change direction every *three throws* you are juggling a **Mills' Mess**!

The **Mills' Mess** is *such* a classic pattern that people have been known to buy THE ENCYCLOPÆDIA OF BALL JUGGLING for the sole purpose of learning this one single trick.

If you are still reading this entry then it's possible that you still haven't cracked it – you're just tying your brain in knots and getting more and more frustrated by the moment. Here's a valuable hint:

If it feels too awesomely difficult you are doing something wrong! Most likely you are trying too hard.

• Take a break, do something else. When a pattern is driving you nuts you *aren't learning anything*. Go and play at juggling **Windmills** for a while and come back to it later.

• You could also check out **Having Problems?**

• The principle of the **Mills' Mess** can be applied to larger numbers of balls. You'll find the four- and five-ball versions listed in THE ENCYCLOPÆDIA.

• The **Mills' Mess** idea was *extended* by Eric Urhane, who adds an extra twist to the pattern by winding the arms up one stage further than would seem to either physically possible. This pattern is called **Eric's Extension**.

• Mike Day invented a special notation for describing hand crossage which goes by the unwieldy name of the **Mills' Mess State Transition Diagram**.

See also **Four Ball Mills' Mess, Five Ball Mills' Mess, Eric's Extension.**

Mills' Mess

Mills' Mess State Transition Diagram (MMSTD)

Mike Day is a juggler (and a computer programmer) well known for his work with the GANDINI JUGGLING PROJECT. He has developed a brilliant system of notation for exploring tricks related to the **Mills' Mess** – a pattern which turns lesser notations to gobbledygook flavoured jelly.

In hand-crossing patterns, according to Mike's theory, there are various distinct *states* that the pattern can be in; each state is determined according to how the hands are crossed and which hand is to throw next.

The fundamental reason for setting out on this very analytical road is that if one can map out all the different states, and then work out the various ways in which a juggling pattern could move from one state to another, then it might be possible not only to chart a pattern like the **Mills' Mess** but also to discover new patterns of similar complexity, patterns that a randomly a practising juggler might never stumble upon by chance.

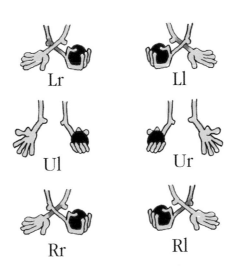

Here are what Mike chose as the six fundamental "states". He argues that there are three ways in which the hands can be crossed: right over left, left over right and not crossed at all. These states are further subdivided according to which hand is just about to make a throw. Next each state is give a two letter code; "Ul", "Rr" and so on. The capital letter tells you how the hands are crossed ("L" = left over right, "U" = uncrossed, "R" = right over left). The small letter ("l" or "r") tells you which hand is about to throw.

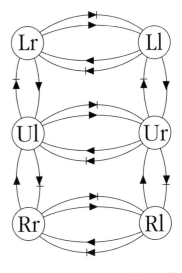

The six states are represented in a diagram as six labelled circles, and these are connected to each other with arrows representing the way in which you can move from one state to the next; either with a normal throw or a **Reverse Cascade** style throw. Mike Day calls this a **Mills' Mess State Transition Diagram** or **MMSTD** for short.

To move from one state to another using normal throws, you follow the ordinary arrows. Moving to another state using **Reverse Cascade** throws is done by following the barred arrows. The two types of throw (normal and reverse) are determined from the *hand's* point of view; a normal throw from the right hand has the hand sweeping to the *left* (whether the hands are crossed or not) and contrariwise for the left hand and contrari-versa for reverse throws.

Here's a route map of a normal **Cascade**. The only states visited are Ul and Ur because the hands never cross.

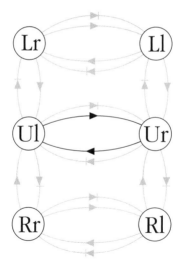

A **Reverse Cascade** would use the two *barred* arrows between Ur and Ul instead of the plain ones.

Now here's the pattern that gave rise to this idea in the first place: it's the **Mills' Mess**.

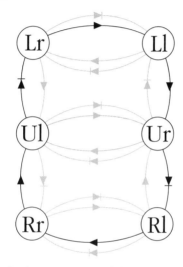

It's a clockwise circuit of the entire diagram. With a little ingenuity you should now be able to map out the paths taken for many simple patterns like the **Windmill** and so on.

So far we have assumed that each throw, whether normal or reverse, is an ordinary **3**, but it doesn't have to be this way. If we made each throw a **4** then our route around the diagram would be describing a **Four Ball Mills' Mess** instead. More exotic patterns (like a **Five Three Four** version

of the **Mills' Mess**, for example) could also be worked out with the **MMSTD**. The more mathematically minded reader should now be experiencing a grand *"Aha!"* as they contemplate the possibilities of the **MMSTD** – yes, it *does* do **Rubenstein's Revenge** and **Burke's Barrage** and more besides!

Here's a significant pattern: **Mike's Mess** that was developed using MMSTD technology. The idea is simple: take the pattern **522** (a **Slow Cascade** of three balls) and lay it onto the MMSTD like this so that it follows this loop:

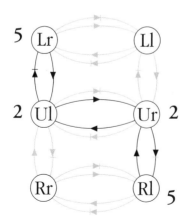

See also **Mike's Mess**.

Mills' Mess State Transition Diagram

Mopping your Brow

After succeeding with a difficult trick you can impress your audience *even more* by **Mopping your Brow** while you are still juggling.

•In a **Three Ball Cascade** it's easy. Throw a self **4** with one hand, as if you are going into **Two in One Hand** for just one throw. This gives you enough time to mop your brow with the other hand. Phew! The hand that mops your brow is holding a ball while you do the trick.

•Four- and five-ball jugglers can also mop their brow, using the time-gaining techniques discussed under **Hat Finish**.

*Phew! I got away with the **Mills' Mess** then!*

Mouth Feed

The **Mouth Feed** is a simple and very silly three-ball trick, closely related to one of the methods for **Eating the Apple**.

•While juggling a **Three Ball Cascade** you catch a beanbag with your right hand and place it in your mouth where you grip it with your teeth. *Keep juggling* the other two balls and as soon as the **Gap** comes to your left hand, take out the beanbag and resume the cascade.

Got it? Now juggle so that *every* right-hand "throw" places a beanbag in your mouth and every left-hand "catch" takes a beanbag out – completely mad!

Multiplex

A **Multiplex** is the act of throwing more than one ball at a time from the same hand.

A two-ball **Multiplex** is sometimes called a *duplex*, it follows that you can throw a *triplex*, a *quadruplex** and so on. These horrendous names are not used in this book but you might read them in other writings on juggling – you have been warned.

•The most common **Multiplex** throw is the two-ball *split* **Multiplex**. Start with two balls in your favourite hand and throw them both to the same height so that one  falls into each hand. Thus you are *splitting* the pair of balls. It sounds a lot harder than it actually is. When you try it you'll discover that your throwing hand can work out what it needs to do all by itself. You should concentrate more on where the balls are going than what your hand has to do to get them there.

* I've never seen a *quinquplex*,
I hope I never see one,
And I can tell you anyhow,
I'd rather see than be one!

When you can juggle the basic throw, you should practise inserting it into three-ball juggling and try all the combinations you can think of, including exotic variations like **Under the Leg** and **Behind the Back** and **Over the Shoulder**.

The two-ball split **Multiplex** is the basis of a very easy five-ball pattern – **Five Ball Splits**.

.•Another common throw is the two-ball *column* **Multiplex**. Start with the same comfortable grip that you instinctively worked out for the split **Multiplex**.

This time throw the ball nearest your index finger two or three times as high as the other one. Again – don't analyse too much, just let your hand try it a few times and it will start to get the idea. You catch the two balls in the same hand – either hand will do! Practise throwing selfs and crosses from both sides.

The column **Multiplex** is used in the five-ball trick **One-up Four-up**.

•If your column **Multiplex** feels solid and reliable then you could start working on the cheat's method of juggling six balls. Simply juggle a **Three Ball Cascade** with six balls, making each throw a column **Multiplex**.

•Another very commonly used throw is a subtle variation of the split **Multiplex**: subtle because the only difference is that the ball that returns to the throwing hand is thrown as a **4**, and the crossing ball is thrown as a **3**. The self throw is therefore about double the height of the cross. Use this throw to change from **Three Ball Cascade** to **Four Ball Fountain**.

You start by juggling a **Three Ball Cascade** with a fourth ball palmed in one hand. Break out of the cascade by throwing the split **Multiplex**. If you do this neatly the **Four Ball Fountain** should continue at exactly the same speed as the **Cascade**.

•Three-ball **Multiplex** throws are commonly used as **Three Ball Starts** – where you begin a three-ball routine by tossing up three balls from one hand.

•A **Reverse Multiplex** or **Squeeze** (as it is more elegantly known) is the action of catching more than one ball in the same hand at once. It might sound impossible, but there is a trick to it! See **Squeeze**.

•**Siteswap Notation** can handle **Multiplexes** fairly elegantly – paired throws are written in square brackets. So a split **Multiplex** made up of a crossing **3** and a self **4** is:

[3x, 4]

Throwing a **3** while holding an extra ball in the hand is also a **Multiplex** as far as **Siteswap** is concerned, so it looks like:

[3x, 2]

That change from **Three Ball Cascade** to **Four Ball Fountain** reads like this:

[3x, 2] 3 [3x, 2] 3 [3x, 4] 4 4 4

See also **Five Ball Splits, Seven Ball Splits, Hops** and **Three Ball Start**.

Multiplex

Neck Catch

Catching a ball on the back of your neck is a great way to finish a juggling routine.

• Throw a ball high, aimed so that it drops straight towards your forehead. At the last moment take a bow, and trap the ball on the back of your neck, just behind your head. It's much easier than it sounds!

• Wait, there's more – now that you have the ball on the back of your neck you can throw it back into the pattern. Straighten up quickly, keeping your head bowed until the last moment, and then flick the ball straight up by raising your head.

With luck and practice it will rise vertically.

Notation

There is no system of juggling notation that can record every aspect of any juggling pattern and still remain readable – though plenty of people have tried to invent one. This is a shame because if there was a perfect juggling notation then it would have been a lot easier to put THE ENCYCLOPÆDIA OF BALL JUGGLING together.

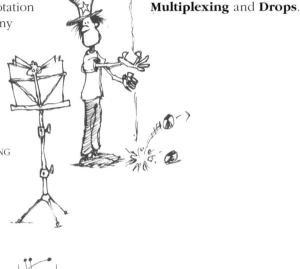

Multiplexing and **Drops**.

Instead I have used thousands of words, hundreds of pictures and diagrams and several different systems of **Notation**.

Ladder Notation

This produces the ladder-like charts sprinkled liberally throughout these pages. **Ladder Notation** is good at expressing the timing structure of a pattern and shows you clearly where every ball goes and where it comes from. It also makes some very pretty plaited and interwoven shapes on the page. While it cannot describe body moves like **Under the Leg**, it *can* handle subtle points like **Gaps**,

Siteswap Notation

This mathematical notation simplifies juggling to the limit. You start with a real juggling pattern and distil this reality down to a string of numbers. This radical transformation throws out even more information than **Ladder Notation** does, but there is considerable power in its simplicity – the strings of numbers it produces can be manipulated mathematically to discover hidden truths about the nature of juggling and sometimes to invent completely new patterns. It's also possible to *speak* a pattern in **Siteswap Notation** and describe throws very concisely, which is why you'll see throws referred to as **1**, **2**, **3**, **4**, **5** and so on throughout THE ENCYCLOPÆDIA.

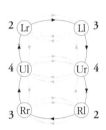

Causal Diagrams

This notation describes the *reason* for each throw in a pattern – which might seem odd and obscure, but it produces diagrams that map neatly onto the way in which a juggler *thinks* about a pattern. The diagram shown here depicts the **Box**.

Mills' Mess State Transition Diagram (MMSTD)

This isn't so much a notation as a road map of possible moves involving the crossing and uncrossing of a juggler's arms as they work a pattern.

You can use the **MMSTD** to work out *shape distortions* of basic juggling patterns such as **Four Two Three (423)**. The example here shows a **Fake Mess** mapped onto an **MMSTD**.

Quite a few of the more complex tricks in this book are cartoon strips, showing either a full or half cycle of a pattern.

Numbers Juggling

Numbers Juggling is the quest to get just *one more* object in the air, a personal crusade between a juggler and the force of **Gravity**.

Three-ball juggling is an easy trick – many people learn it in an afternoon. **Four Ball Juggling** is a little harder, requiring perhaps a couple of weeks of dedicated practice. Five-ball juggling takes months to master, and as you move up through the numbers each extra ball is added with increasing effort.

The benefit of **Numbers Juggling** is that it improves the pure juggling skill of your hands, eyes and mind. Every juggler should own at least one more ball than they can juggle so they can have a go, once in a while, at the impossible. A few attempts at five balls will make your four-ball juggling feel easier and more relaxed. So if you plan to juggle four, buy five; if you are determined to get five solid by Christmas, buy six!

You do not have to be able to juggle large numbers of objects to be a great juggler; there is more to this art form than just keeping objects in the air.

Continued overleaf...

*The reverse is also true, as I know only too well!

Numbers Juggling...

...Numbers Juggling

Think of a juggling pattern as a fragile sculpture, constantly manipulated by the hands of its maker – when the dance of the hands stops, it simply ceases to exist. **Numbers Jugglers** work on increasing the size and breakability of their patterns – others work on the dance. The numbers juggler challenges **Gravity** as an enemy to be conquered, but perhaps it is a friend to be worked with. **Gravity** is, after all, what makes **Toss Juggling** possible.

The gateway to **Numbers Juggling** is surely the **Five Ball Cascade**. Many jugglers feel that they have really achieved something when they get that far, and so they have! The real **Numbers Juggler**, though, is the juggler who reaches this level and then keeps on going.

Curiously, the next target is not six, but seven balls. Seven, like any odd number, can be juggled in a **Cascade** pattern whereas six, like any even number, cannot. By the time a juggler has mastered five they will have spent most of their *learning time* on **Cascades**, from the early experience of learning the **Three Ball Cascade** to the long, long effort required to crack the **Five Ball Cascade**. Four balls seems almost to be an incidental achievement. You won't find a seven-ball

juggler who can't juggle six, but you'll find that they often think of the **Cascades** as the more *natural* patterns.

For each extra ball the number of jugglers in the world to juggle it decreases; there are millions of three-ball jugglers, thousands of four-ball jugglers, hundreds of five-ball jugglers, dozens of seven-ball jugglers, a few nine-ball jugglers and *very few* better than that!

Who knows where it ends? THE GUINNESS BOOK OF RECORDS says eleven. I've heard it said by a great juggler that the physical limit of human ability probably lies at or below fourteen.* However, from time to time throughout recorded history, exceptional people have appeared out of nowhere.

How many balls can *you* juggle?**

See also **Zen and the Perfect Juggler**.

*Fourteen balls in two hands gets a **Difficulty** rating of 6.53 according to Dancey's Juggling Index. This is an astronomical level! Eleven balls in two hands gets 5.04 – keep practising!

**Don't you just *hate* that question? Jugglers get asked it all the time. The snappy comeback is, "One more than you!"

Off the Elbow

Off the Elbow is a very simple move, similar to the **Flick Off**, for three-ball jugglers.

• While juggling a **Three Ball Cascade**, throw a ball from your left hand so that it bounces off your right elbow and back into the left hand. Your right hand misses a throw and holds a ball while the **Off the Elbow** move takes place. It's a lot easier than it sounds!

A neat combination of moves is a **Flick Off** from the fingers, followed by a **Flick Off** from the wrist, followed by **Off the Elbow** – all executed in rapid succession on one side of the pattern.

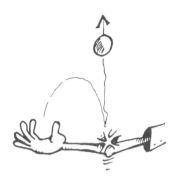

•A variation is the *Greengrocer Trick* – bouncing a ball off the *inside* of your elbow instead. I remember, as a child, watching our local greengrocer do this as he popped an extra potato in the brown paper bag before sealing it with a twirl as he held the corners. (I could manage the **Off the Elbow** move but my paper bag twirl always used to split the bag.)

Throw a ball straight up and bounce it back, off the inside of your elbow, by straightening your arm as the ball hits it. You can get a nice **Popped** throw with a minimum of arm movement.

•It's possible to juggle **Two in One Hand** like this, so that *every* throw bounces off your arm.

Off the Head

Off the Head is a classic ball-juggling move.

•Juggle a **Three Ball Cascade** and put a ball on your head with one hand – then let it roll off to be caught in the other hand. You will find it best to work with balls rather than bean-bags because they have a consistent roll.

The trick is to get the ball to pause on your head for just the right space of time. It takes a little practice to find the perfect spot to place the balls on, but once you have the knack you can keep going all day!

Try all the usual combinations: every right, every left, same ball each way, every ball and so on.

•You can also let the balls roll off the back of your head so they are caught behind your back – just like juggling **Behind the Back**, **Backwards!**

One Count

A **One Count** is a **Passing Pattern** in which *every* throw is a pass to your partner.

•To juggle a six-ball **One Count**, stand face to face with a partner, three balls each, two in the right and one in the left. You both start juggling together. *Every* ball from your right hand goes to your part-ner's left hand and *every* ball from your left hand goes to your partner's right hand.

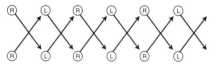

*A **Causal Diagram** of a **One Count**.*

•So simple to say, so much harder to do! Try it as a **Floor Juggling** pattern first.

When you juggle this pattern you and your partner are actually juggling two shared, and totally independent, **Three Ball Cascades**.

•A five-ball **One Count** is much easier. You start with two balls in the right and one in the left. Your partner starts with one ball in each hand.

Continued overleaf...

...One Count

*A five ball **One Count** – a lot simpler!*

Your passes are diagonal 3's (right to right and left to left), and your partner's passes are tramline passes (right to left and left to right), also thrown as 3's.

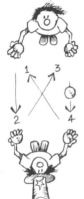

*A five-ball **One Count** with the first four throws numbered in sequence.*

You start first, throwing a right to right pass. On the next beat your partner throws back, right to left. Then you throw a left to left pass and your partner responds with a left to right. Just repeat that sequence of passes and you have the pattern.

There is only one more ball than there are hands, and the passes chase each other around the pattern. It's a **Domino** pattern!

•You can juggle a seven-ball **One Count** using the same layout as the previous pattern. As before, you throw diagonals and your partner throws tramlines.

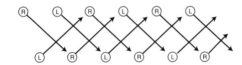

You start with four balls, two in each hand, and your partner starts with two in the *left* and one in the right. Every throw is a very unusual **3.5**! – so make them fairly high. There is one throw on every half beat.

You start first, throwing a right to right **3.5** pass, and then you just keep going at normal juggling speed, throwing alternate right to right and left to left passes.

Your partner starts throwing passes *immediately* after your first pass – for perfect timing their first pass is thrown exactly halfway in time between your first and second passes. They then continue to throw tramline passes from alternate hands at normal juggling speed.

One-up Four-up

One-up Four-up is perhaps the most visually appealing five-ball **Trick** of all. We'll start with the easy version.

•From a **Cold Start** with three in the right and two in the left, you throw one ball, from your right hand straight up through the middle. As it peaks you throw a *column* **Multiplex** from each hand simultaneously. Each multiplex is caught by the throwing hand.

To juggle this from a **Five Ball Cascade** you just gather the balls into your hands, throw the trick and go straight back into the cascade.

•Now for the flashy version! It's the same trick as before, but the two **Multiplexes** cross over. This means that they actually have to pass through each other. Both of them travel over the falling centre ball and a good photographer with split-second timing should be able to catch the instant at which all five balls form a perfect column in the air.

One-up Two-up

One-up Four-up juggled with crossing throws. A major photo-opportunity!

This is a simple three-ball trick; as soon as you can juggle a **Three Ball Cascade** you are ready to try it.

•Start by trying the trick from a **Cold Start**. Put two balls in your right hand and one in your left.

Throw a ball from your right hand, straight up the middle to about head height. When it peaks you simultaneously throw the other two balls straight up the sides.

See if you can keep this going as a continuous pattern.

•Notice that *one* of your hands, most likely your right, is juggling **Two in One Hand** in columns. The other hand just tags along for the ride. It's better practice to share the work evenly between both hands so that they take turns to throw the *one-up* ball.

•Try throwing the *two-up* balls so that they cross over. There is a chance that they will collide, but Murphy's Law says that if you aim for a *hit* they'll miss!

•Now try catching the *two-up* balls with your hands crossed.

If you want to get *really* complicated then throw the two balls so they cross *and* catch them with your hands crossed. Alternatively, catch them with your hands uncrossed and immediately *throw* them with crossed hands.

You could spend days on this.

You *should* spends days on this sort of thing.

One-up Two-up

Orangutan

The **Orangutan** is a gibbous comedy juggling pattern for three balls. It's similar to **Floor Juggling** in that the balls are not really *juggled,* but they change places in the same way that they would in a **Three Ball Cascade**.

•Start with one ball under each armpit and a third ball in your right hand. Let the ball in your left armpit drop into your left hand, and replace it with the ball in your right. Now, let the right armpit's ball fall into the right hand and replace it with the ball in your left hand. Keep going and you are juggling the **Orangutan**.

With a moderate amount of contortion it's possible to juggle the pattern behind your back. You could also add more balls, trapped in other places around your body, one ball in a **Chin Trap** and another balanced on top of your head for example.

Orbit

The **Orbit** is a simple move. A hand that is holding a ball **Orbits** another ball in the air.

•Practise **Orbits** in a **Three Ball Cascade**. As a ball leaves your left hand your *right* hand swoops right around it, counterclockwise. After completing the **Orbit**, the right hand releases its ball in a **Reverse Cascade** throw (**Over the Top**) and catches the ball it has just travelled around. The **Orbit** runs *down through the middle* and it feels very similar to a **Chop**.

•Orbiting the other way, *up through the middle* is another matter entirely. Not impossible, but it just doesn't feel very smooth. **Orbits**, of the first kind, are used in the deadly **Rubenstein's Revenge** and the positively-tame-by-comparison **Orbit Bounce** (see next entry).

Orbit Bounce

The **Orbit Bounce** is a graceful, slow and artistic pattern for three **Bouncing Balls**, more of a dance than a juggling pattern!

•Start by juggling a **Three Ball Bounce**, using the slow and lazy **Reverse Cascade** style. Now start putting in **Orbits**. As a ball approaches your right hand, the hand orbits it once – going *down* through the middle, before throwing its ball **Over the Top** of the approaching ball. Build up the trick until you are making an **Orbit** before every throw. You are halfway there.

•Notice that while one hand **Orbits**, the other is just hanging around feeling bored and left out because the pattern is so slow. In the full **Orbit Bounce** *both* hands **Orbit** continuously. The free hand (the hand that is not about to throw) **Orbits** empty space so that both hands are moving in circles all the time. The hands circle out of phase with each other, so that as one hand is going down through the middle, the other is going up on the outside. Miming a **Reverse Cascade** produces the same hand movements. As a result of this complete overdose of flourishing hand movements, each ball does two **Orbits** before it is thrown; the first turn goes around empty space, the second goes around the ball that is about to be caught.

Over the Head

If you learn to juggle **Over the Head** then you'll be able to juggle in bed!

•Juggle a **Three Ball Cascade** with your hands over your head. You can do this while standing up or lying down. If you can manage three balls try four! Many three-ball tricks, including the infamous **Mills' Mess** can be juggled in this position.

•It is possible, but unlikely, that you might actually be able to juggle a **Three Ball Cascade**, then sit down and do a backwards roll, returning to a standing position – juggling all the way. You'll need the **Over the Head** technique about halfway around. This really *can* been done.

•It is also possible, but increasingly improbable, that you may learn to juggle three balls over your head *without looking* at all!

Over the Head juggled normally and completely blind.

Over the Head

Over the Shoulder

The **Over the Shoulder** throw is a behind the back **Self Throw**.

• Use a scooping action to **Snatch** a ball and throw it straight up, so that it rises behind your shoulder and is caught in the same hand.

Because **Over the Shoulder** throws are **Self** throws, they can be used in **Two in One Hand** and the **Four Ball Fountain**.

• Double **Over the Shoulder** throws look good. *Both hands* throw **Over the Shoulder** at the same time.

Juggle a **Three Ball Cascade**, and then throw one ball up the middle as a **4**, as if you were going into **One-up Two-up**. Now throw both the other balls **Over the Shoulder** simultaneously.

Over the Top

There are a few tricks that **Beginners** should start work on as soon as they have cracked the **Three Ball Cascade** because they form the basis of many other juggling patterns. **Two in One Hand**, **Under the Hand** and **Over the Top** are all in this category.

Throwing a ball **Over the Top** means exactly what it says, throwing a ball *over the top* of the **Cascade**.

• Juggle a **Three Ball Cascade** for a moment and notice how you throw each ball *under* the approaching ball. (That doesn't make sense on paper, you actually have to *do* it!)

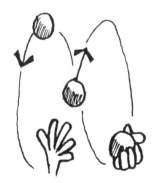

*The normal shape of a **Three Ball Cascade**: each ball goes under the last throw.*

See what I mean? To throw **Over the Top** you just throw a ball *over* the approaching ball instead, it will pass right over the whole pattern. Try it.

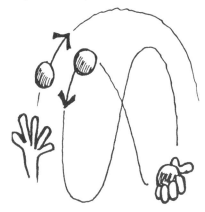

This can be a supremely difficult challenge to the new juggler. Having just got to grips with juggling three balls, you thought you were doing OK. Now you have gone right back to that awful patting-the-head-and-rubbing-the-stomach feeling. You feel dizzy, nauseous, dispirited, cack-handed and hopeless.

Learn to *enjoy* that feeling. It means you are learning something! Juggling has plenty more where *that* feeling came from! Break the trick down, try making the throw and don't worry about the catch. You'll get it.

If you get *really* stuck then work on something else and come back to it later. Often you will find that leaving a trick for a while works wonders. This happens because your mysterious subconscious has been secretly working on the problem for you in your absence. Sometimes you'll find, on returning to a difficult trick after a night's sleep, that you have somehow magically improved.

• Once you can throw **Over the Top** on one side, learn it on the other. Once you can do it on *that side* try all of the combinations of left and right. The possibilities are:

• Every right hand throw **Over the Top.**
• Every left hand throw **Over the Top.**
• The same ball **Over the Top** on every throw.
• Every ball **Over the Top** every time.

Each of these variations produces something that is, effectively, a new pattern. Certainly none of them is a **Three Ball Cascade**.

The first two are sort of **Half Showers**. The third one (same ball every time) has a very hypnotic and clock-like feel to it. You can play with making the **Over the Top** throws wider and wider, while keeping the other two balls as low and tight as you can manage.

The fourth variation (every ball thrown **Over the Top**) creates a pattern called a **Reverse Cascade**. Believe it or not, if you filmed this pattern and played it back **Backwards**, you'd be watching a normal **Three Ball Cascade**!

You should congratulate yourself on getting this far: not only have you learnt to juggle, but you are starting to learn *how to learn* to juggle.

See also (unless you have already) **Under the Hand** and **Two in One Hand** for your next lessons!

Over the Top

Passing Patterns

Many of the tricks and patterns in THE ENCYCLOPÆDIA OF BALL JUGGLING are interesting because they add extra frills, extra balls or just extra complexity to the more basic juggling patterns.

When you juggle **Passing Patterns** you are adding extra *people*. The possibilities are staggering. The **Passing Pattern** is a many-handed, multi-brained juggling monster that can do things with balls that the solo juggler couldn't even attempt.

To juggle a simple two-person **Passing Pattern** you stand face to face with your partner and both juggle **Three Ball Cascades** in time with each other. Every so often you throw a ball to each other instead of to yourself, thus you *lose* a ball from your pattern, but *gain* one from your partner's.

It's important that you both know when the exchange is going to take place, otherwise the whole thing will fall apart (unless you are *very* hot jugglers!). This problem doesn't occur in solo juggling because one brain controls all the hands in the pattern (OK – *sometimes* your left hand doesn't know what the right is doing, but I'm sure that you get the point).

The extra hands are an advantage, the extra *brains* are a problem.

Every **Passing Pattern** is therefore arranged as a *routine*, a set plan of action that both jugglers stick to. This ensures that the brains know what they are doing and that they are both doing the same thing. The simplest routines are of the "every *umpth* throw is a pass" variety. For example, every third throw is a pass (**Three Count**), every second throw is a pass (**Two Count**), or even every single throw is a pass (**One Count**).

With every *umpth* throw routines you just keep going till you drop. They are very popular!

Alternatively you can juggle a prearranged sequence of passes, like the **Three Three Ten** or the **Four Four Eight**. Each of

these two-person routines has a beginning, a middle and an end. Routines like these give you the opportunity to finish on a high note rather than just carrying on until you drop. A great psychological advantage!

Passing routines are part of the popular language of juggling. Most jugglers you meet will know them, so you can get straight down to some friendly social juggling without having to spend time inventing and rehearsing.

You might think that **Passing Patterns**, because they are prearranged routines, remove the potential for improvisation that you have in solo juggling. Not so! When you are juggling a **Four Count,** your partner may be expecting to *catch* a pass from you on every fourth **Beat**, but there are no rules about when you *throw it* – it just has to arrive at the right time. **Passing Patterns** can be *syncopated*; in other words, you can make *out of time* throws without breaking up the pattern, just as a drummer can strike odd beats without losing the rhythm.

When juggling **Passing Patterns** you are not limited to three balls per juggler – see **Seven Ball Passing** to get started on the road of multi-person **Numbers Juggling**. On the other hand, *more* is not always *better*. Instead of increasing the number of balls in your pattern, why not juggle fewer and leave more room for art! See **Steal** and **Beach Ball Juggling** for some good two-person three-ball routines.

Learning all the weird and wonderful syncopated throws that are possible enables complete strangers to juggle **Passing Patterns** that look so complicated to non-jugglers that they surely *must* have been rehearsed. Of course, if you actually *have* rehearsed then even *more* complex patterns are possible.

Apart from juggling different numbers of balls with different numbers of jugglers to different routines, you can also play around with the *arrangement* – the positions of the jugglers themselves. You could stand face to face, back to back, in a circle, on each other's shoulders, at various positions up a ladder – or just about any way that you can think of! In *really* complex arrangements the jugglers *move around* while they juggle.

See **Speed Weave** and **Beach Ball Juggling**.

Passing Patterns

Penguin

The **Penguin** is a comical and rather tricky way of juggling a **Three Ball Cascade**.

•Let your right arm hang down by your side, now turn your hand inward as far as it will go so that the back of your hand rests against your thigh. Now bring your fingers up so that you can (in theory) catch a ball. It's quite a stretch!

Try catching balls from this hand position in a **Three Ball Cascade**, first on one side, and then the other. After each **Penguin** catch your hand turns back to a normal position to make a throw. It's a tremendously good stretching exercise for your lower arm!

When you can catch and throw *every* ball this way you are juggling the **Penguin** and you look very silly!

Picking Up

When you **Drop** a ball you don't have to stop juggling. Just keep on going! Maintain that rhythm while you bend down, reach under the sofa and deftly toss the ball back into the pattern.

The art of **Picking Up** falls into the general area of **Floor Juggling** – there is a lot of fun to be had between the moment at which a ball hits the floor and the recovery.

•If you are juggling a **Three Ball Cascade** when the inevitable happens you can continue juggling the remaining two balls in a **Gap** pattern. *Believe* in that third invisible ball – if you juggle it smoothly enough the eyes of the audience will be bewildered sufficiently. It may not feel like real juggling to you, but make it look like real juggling to *them*.

Depending on how awkwardly placed the dropped ball is, you may be able to pick it up while juggling the **Gap**. If the ball has rolled down a deep dark hole you may need to go into **Two in One Hand** while you grope around for it.

• **Four-ball Jugglers** drop even more frequently.

If (make that *when!*) you **Drop** in a four-ball pattern you can "change gear" instantly to a **Three Ball Cascade** and position yourself within easy reach of the dropped ball.

• Lead into a **Four Ball Fountain** from the left – throw a left self **4**, a right self **4** and *immediately* pick up the dropped ball with the right hand.

• If you find this difficult, practise starting a **Four Ball Fountain** from a **Cold Start** with two balls in the left hand, one in the right and one ball on the floor in front of your right knee.

Lead straight into the **Fountain** from this position. The first throw is from the *left* hand – left **4**, right **4**, *pick up!*

When you are happy with that you should find it quite easy to start by juggling a few rounds of **Three Ball Cascade** before **Picking Up** into four, and that's the trick!

• Instead of immediately executing a deft **Pick Up** when you **Drop** out of a **Four Ball Fountain** you can use the moment to

add a bit of comedy to your routine.

Kneel down in front of the dropped ball and *place* another ball on the floor next to it. This leaves you juggling just two balls in a **Gap** pattern.

As the **Gap** comes to your right hand, pick up one of the dropped balls and "hop" it over the other one, plonking it *back down on the floor*. Repeat the move from alternate sides and mix it up with a few rounds of the **Four Ball Drop** for a guaranteed giggle from the audience.

• A good way of practising **Picking Up** from a **Gap** pattern is to *start* a **Three Ball Cascade** with one ball on the floor.

Kneel down, placing one ball in front of your right knee and hold a ball in each hand. Now start your **Three Ball Cascade**. Make the first throw from your right hand which then *immediately* picks up the ball on the floor – after **Picking Up** you cascade as normal.

Practise *putting down* as well. Juggle a **Three Ball Cascade** and then *place* one ball on the floor instead of throwing it. Combine *pick ups* with *putdowns* until the whole business becomes as natural as juggling the **Cascade** itself. You'll be glad you did because, with these skills, a **Drop** is no longer a disaster.

Continued overleaf...

Picking Up...

• Five-ball jugglers spend more time dropping balls than the whole of the rest of the world put together.

If you drop a ball from a **Five Ball Cascade** you can change the pattern to a **Four Ball Fountain** while you position yourself near the dropped ball. The pick up is tricky because you need to be looking down *and* up at the same time!

Assuming you can deal with that minor problem, the pick up technique is much the same as before. Lead into the **Five Ball Cascade** from the right – right crossing 5, left crossing 5, right crossing 5 and *immediately* pick up the dropped ball with the right hand.

• Recovering a **Five Ball Cascade** from *two* dropped balls is even more impressive. If you've dropped one ball I'd recommend dropping another for the sheer hell of it.

Juggle a **Five Ball Cascade** and let two balls drop "accidentally on purpose". This takes your pattern down to a **Three Ball Cascade**. Jiggle the dropped balls around with your feet, until you can kneel down with one ball in front of each knee.

Look hard at the positions of the balls on the floor and fix them in your mind – when you actually pick up you will be looking *upwards* and reaching for the balls blind.

• Six-, seven- and eight-ball jugglers rarely pick up while still juggling. The pattern they are juggling is hard enough already, and picking up is just that little bit harder still! Nine-ball jugglers? They're so good they never **Drop** at all!

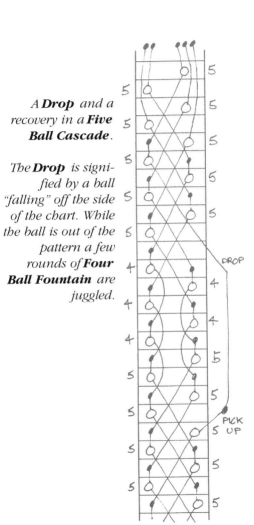

*A **Drop** and a recovery in a **Five Ball Cascade**.*

*The **Drop** is signified by a ball "falling" off the side of the chart. While the ball is out of the pattern a few rounds of **Four Ball Fountain** are juggled.*

Pistons

Pistons is a simple pattern for four balls. It's the equivalent of the three-ball pattern, **Right Middle Left**.

• Each hand juggles **Two in One Hand** in columns with the hands throwing alternately, thus all four balls rise and fall vertically, each in its own column.

While juggling **Pistons** you can give your audience a brief lecture on the technicalities of a four-cylinder petrol engine.

People who *really* understand engines know that it would be more accurate to juggle the pattern on simultaneous throws, with the two inside columns rising together in opposite time to the two outside columns.

To hell with technical accuracy: it looks much nicer if you juggle the pattern with alternate throws. Someday all engines will be built like this.

If you should **Drop** a ball – just keep going. The drop-line is "...and here, ladies and gentlemen, is the more economical *three* cylinder engine!".

Pop

The more ancient books about juggling often mention the skill of **Popping** balls.

A **Pop** is just a throw made with the absolute minimum of hand movement, a throw with no follow-through.

This is a good practice point because it focuses the mind on the finer details of throwing a ball. When you **Pop** a ball it should appear to leap from your hand of its own accord. This is a good throwing style for patterns like the **Box** and tricks like the **Hopstop**.

Some of those ancient dusty volumes* go as far as to say that the **Pop** is the "correct method" of throwing a ball. This is not so – there are *many* ways of throwing a ball. How many do you know?

See also **Slap**.

*I refer in particular to the Vaudeville Artiste's Manual of Prestidigitation, Equilibrism and Antigravitational Befuddlement – now long out of print.

Pop

Powerball

An early hi-tech hi-bounce ball that was produced in the 1960s. They were made of a black rubber-like compound, moulded under very high pressure. The bounce was terrific but they were rather unstable, having a tendency to explode if they hit any rough surfaces, therefore not a single one survives to this day.

Those cheap garishly coloured plastic high-bounce balls you see today don't even come close to the old **Powerball** bounce.

Pyramid

Four balls can be stacked in the shape of a **Pyramid** (or *tetrahedron*).

• If you are working on **Four Ball Juggling** it's a good idea to familiarise your hands with handling four balls in every way possible. The **Pyramid** is the neatest way of holding four balls in one hand.

Form a **Pyramid** in your right hand and practise hopping each ball, in turn, over to the left hand, thus forming a new **Pyramid** there. Then hop them back again. In a little while you'll be able to do it without even thinking about it.

If you want to look really flashy (of course you do!) hop the **Pyramid** from hand to hand using **Cascade** throws and **Under the Hand** throws alternately.

• Use the **Pyramid** as the starting and finishing position for your four-ball routine. It looks especially good if the very last ball is thrown **Behind the Back** to land on the top of the **Pyramid**.

• A **Pyramid** formed from silicone **Bouncing Balls** will roll across a smooth floor *as a unit* without falling to bits – see **Bouncing Beast**.

Quad & Quin

Quad is shorthand for *quadruple*. A **Quad** is a throw that would normally be made with four spins in club juggling. In ball-juggling terms this usually means a **6**, a throw with five **Beats** of **Airtime**. This is the throw used when juggling **Three in One Hand** or a **Six Ball Fountain**.

A **Quin(tuple)** is a throw that might possibly be thrown with five spins in club juggling – but who am I trying to kid? It's a wild and high throw of great theoretical interest. For the ball juggler it's a **7**, having six **Beats** of **Airtime**. It's the throw used in the seven-ball **Cascade**.

While on the general subject of highly numbered throws it's worth noting that THE ENCYCLOPÆDIA OF BALL JUGGLING doesn't have a lot to say on the subject of juggling really big patterns (seven, eight, nine balls and so on). The reason for this is simple – if you are serious about learning to juggle that many, you already know what to do! You certainly aren't going to learn much from a book!

See also **Single, Double, Triple.**

Reachover

A **Reachover** is a quick hiccup that you can throw in a **Three Ball Cascade**.

•Juggle the cascade and then throw a ball from the right hand *straight up* (it's a **3**, not a **4**, because you are *not* going into **Two in One Hand**). Your left hand then reaches *over* the pattern, catches the ball and throws it straight up again.

The *shape* of the cascade is broken for a couple of throws when you do a **Reachover**, but the *logic* of the pattern is unchanged; there are no **Two in One Hand** throws involved. The balls tend to go into a quick columns juggle during the recovery from the **Reachover**.

•If you juggle a **Reachover** on every third **Beat** of the **Cascade** (same ball every time) you are juggling a **Boston Mess** or something *very* similar!

Reachunder

A **Reachunder** is a quick hicdown that you can throw into a **Three Ball Cascade.**

•Juggle the cascade and then throw a ball from the right hand straight up. Your left hand then reaches *under* the pattern to catch it and throw it straight up again. This is almost identical to the **Reachover**.

•Juggle a **Reachunder** on every third beat of the pattern (same ball every time) and you are doing something very like, you guessed it, a **Boston Mess**.

*A **Reachover**.*

Reachunder

Relaxation

If you compare a **Three Ball Cascade** being juggled by a **Beginner** to the same pattern juggled by a more experienced juggler there is one very clear difference – **Relaxation**.

The better the pattern is juggled, the easier it looks, becoming less like a tricky problem being solved by supreme effort, and more like a liquid pouring of balls from hand to hand. It is actually not very difficult to move balls around in the air once your hands have learnt what they need to do. Even complex patterns like the **Mills' Mess** can, and should, be juggled with the minimum possible physical effort.

Of course, while you are *learning* to juggle a new trick it's not easy at all. But you should be very careful not to become resentful and frustrated if the trick just won't work. Let that happen and you'll be fighting against the tension in your body *as well* as trying to keep those balls in the air. Stay relaxed, and if you are having a *really* hard time, take a break and do something that's fun instead!

Jugglers constantly exercise their "learning muscle" and, as time goes on, the juggler cannot fail to realise, consciously or subconsciously, that the best and fastest way to learn is to relax. As more tricks are learnt, the learning muscle becomes fitter, and the art of **Relaxation** becomes second nature.

See also **Having Problems?**

Reverse Cascade

A **Reverse Cascade** is a **Cascade** juggled so that every ball is thrown **Over the Top**.

•Juggle a **Three Ball Cascade** and start putting in **Over the Top** throws, from the right, then from the left, and then *every single throw*.

Notice that your hands are now catching balls on the inside of the pattern and throwing them on the outside, which is the complete opposite of the normal **Cascade**.

It's actually a complete *time-reversal*. If you were to film a **Three Ball Cascade** and then play the film **Backwards** you would see a **Reverse Cascade**.

Five- and seven-ball jugglers can juggle **Reverse Cascades**, and the **Fountains** can be juggled **Backwards** too. A **Four Ball Fountain** juggled *rolling in* (with throws on the outside and catches on the inside) is the reverse of the standard pattern in which the throws *roll out*.

•More complex patterns can be time-reversed with interesting results. **Charlie's Cheat** for example, is a time-reversal of the **Follow**.

• The **Fake Mess** incidentally, is exactly the same either forwards or backwards.

Modern juggling thinking hails the **Three Ball Cascade** as *the* fundamental, basic, normal juggling pattern, while the **Reverse Cascade** is a **Trick**. But rumours filtering down through the many-thousand-year-old past of this art form suggest that this was not always so.

In former times the **Shower** patterns were seen as the basic patterns while the **Cascades** were the tricks.

It's interesting to note that if you juggle a three-ball **Shower** and change the direction of the pattern on *every* throw, you will find yourself juggling a **Slow Cascade**. Whether you get a normal or **Reverse Cascade** depends on the style of the throws you use to change direction, but the **Reverse Cascade** seems to come more naturally!

See also **Backwards**.

Reverse Multiplex

This is exactly what it sounds like – the act of catching two balls (or more) balls in the same hand at the same time. There's a better name for it though!

See **Squeeze**.

Cascade. *Reverse Cascade.*

Rhinoceros

A crude, but sadly effective, animal impersonation that takes advantage of the rather rude and satisfying *"plap!"* that a **Beanbag** makes as it hits the floor.

Grab a big handful of **Beanbags**, bend forwards and mime a **Rhinoceros** horn with the other hand.

I leave the rest to your imagination.

Rhinoceros

Right-handed or Left-handed?

See **Left-handed or Right-handed?**, but while we are on this subject – how is it that a mirror reverses *left and right*, but doesn't reverse *up and down*?

You'll find the answer somewhere in or around **Zen and the Perfect Juggler**.

Right Middle Left.

Right Middle Left

A simple three-ball pattern that is half a bit easier than juggling **Two in One Hand** in columns. **Right Middle Left** is the three cylinder version of **Pistons**.

•Take three balls and imagine three columns in front of you. Start with two in the right and one in the left.

Begin by juggling two throws of **Two in One Hand** (in columns) on the right, throwing *right-middle...*

Now juggle two throws of **Two in One Hand** from the left hand, *left-middle...*

Thus the pattern continues; the hands throw *right-right-left-left*, while the balls bob up and down *right-middle-left-middle* and so on.

Technically, this is a **Four Two Three (423)** pattern, and it's the easiest of the **423**'s to learn.

423, like the humble **Three Ball Cascade**, is an excellent "base pattern" which can be juggled in all sorts of interesting shapes.

See also **Four Two Three (423)**, **Tennis**.

Right-left-self-left-right-self

Right-left-self-left-right-self is a **Passing Pattern** routine that falls exactly halfway between a **Two Count** and a **One Count**. Two throws in every three are passes.

•Stand in front of your partner, three balls each, two in the right and one in the left. All passes are *tramline passes*, that is, right to left and left to right.

Starting together you both throw a pass from the right, immediately followed by a pass from the left, then you each throw a right to left **Self**.

Repeat the sequence the other way around – that's a pass from the left, a pass from the right and a left to right self.

It's not quite as fast as a **One Count**, and not quite as slow as a **Two Count**. I suppose you could call it a *One and a Half Count*.

•If you have trouble getting the pattern going between you, practise it as a **Floor Juggling** pattern.

Robot Bounce

The **Robot Bounce** is a **Square Juggling** pattern for three **Bouncing Balls**.

•The pattern is best learnt by developing it from the **Three Ball Bounce**, juggled in the slow and lazy **Reverse Cascade** style. The **Robot Bounce** is simply a shape (and style) distortion of this pattern. On every throw the throwing hand reaches over the pattern and *drops* its ball *straight down* on the opposite side.

Effectively the pattern has become a **Column Bounce**. The right hand catches in the right column and throws in the left, the left hand catches in the left column and throws in the right.

The robotic effect is achieved by working on a really exaggerated sweep of the hand from the catching position to the dropping position and then *freezing* for an instant before making the drop. The freeze, followed by the perfect vertical fall of the ball looks very mechanical and square.

There is no *lifting* involved in this pattern; the drops are made from points a few inches above the catch points.

Robot Bounce

Robotic Drop

The **Robotic Drop** is a comic **Floor Juggling** pattern with robotic overtones. It is *not difficult,* although you are going to wonder what is going on right up until that magical moment at which everything clicks. It's more like mime than juggling. Read on and discover!

The pattern travels horizontally across the floor, *walking* to the right. It has to be juggled with **Beanbags** because you need balls with an absolutely dead drop.

• Kneel down on the floor. Place three beanbags in a line from left to right, a couple of inches apart. Imagine the point at which a fourth beanbag would sit if it were tagged onto the right-hand end of the line. In your imagination mark that spot with an X. If you have no imagination get a felt tip pen and mark a big X on the carpet.

With your right hand pick up the middle beanbag and lift it about six inches into the air. Your left hand holds the left-hand beanbag as it sits on the floor. This is the starting position.

Simultaneously – your right hand drops its beanbag to *exactly where it came from* and moves to hold the right-hand ball. Your left hand carries the left-hand ball to a point six inches over the spot marked X.

Freeze here for an instant – all robotic moves need freezes!

Simultaneously – your left hand drops the ball so that it lands on the spot marked X and moves to hold the (new) left-hand ball – your right hand lifts the ball it's holding six inches into the air, straight up.

Freeze again. You are back in the starting position after executing two moves and everything has moved one space to the right. Repeat those two moves, with panache and elegance, and you have the pattern.

• The **Robotic Drop** is very closely related to the **Robot Bounce** (see opposite). In fact either pattern can be juggled with **Beanbags** or **Bouncing Balls**. If you juggle the **Robot Bounce** with **Beanbags** you are actually juggling a **Floor Cascade** in which you *drop* balls onto the floor rather than *placing* them there.

See also **Dropswap.**

Romeo's Revenge

This pattern was invented by Michael Karas and it's a big favourite with fans of complex three-ball work. It deserves the "revenge" handle since it has a lot in common with **Rubenstein's Revenge**, in particular it makes great use of **Orbits** as well as adding a couple of **Clawed** catches and throws.

For the numerically minded it is a **52233** – not that this information will help you much. The pattern has an unusual and counter-intuitive start.

• (The start) Place two balls in the right hand and one in the left. Cross your right hand *under* your left. Toss a **Reverse Cascade** throw from your right hand. It's a **5** so make it a lazy one. This is a pretty unusual start – **Mills' Mess** experts would expect to throw from the hand that's crossed *over*.

1. Now *very rapidly* unwind your hands, then *rewind* them so that your right hand is *over* your left – **Chopping** the right hand *under* the ball that's in the air. Now toss a **Reverse Cascade** throw from the left hand.

2. Make a **Clawed** throw from the right hand...

3. ...**Snatch** the other airborne ball with your right hand and **Chop** it to the far left of the pattern, travelling *under* the only ball that's still flying. Simultaneously make a **Reverse Cascade** throw from your left hand.

We're halfway through; now we run those three moves reflected left to right.

4. *Very rapidly* unwind your hands and *rewind* them so that your left hand is *over* your right – **Chopping** the left hand *under* the ball that's in the air. Now toss a **Reverse Cascade** throw from the right hand.

5. Make a **Clawed** throw from the left hand...

6 ...**Snatch** the other airborne ball with your left hand and **Chop** it to the far right of the pattern, travelling *under* the only ball that's still flying. Simultaneously make a **Reverse Cascade** throw from your right hand.

That completes the sequence – loop back to step 1 to continue.

See **Dropswap** for another Michael Karas pattern.

Rubenstein's Revenge

This trick was invented by Rick Rubenstein, but the "revenge" handle was coined by George Gillson who popularised it in his book *Beyond the Cascade*.

Rubenstein's Revenge is to the **Mills' Mess** what the **Mills' Mess** is to the **Three Ball Cascade**. **Rubenstein's Revenge** says to the **Mills' Mess** '..and the same to you with *frilly bits* on!'

Anyone can learn the Revenge! Just don't expect to get it straight away. With all those complex moves it will take you quite a while to even begin to get to grips with it, but remember that the full pattern really does work and does not require brute force! A well juggled **Rubenstein's Revenge** is smooth and liquid, just like a **Mills' Mess** or a **Cascade**.

If you are **Solid** with the **Mills' Mess** you should be having a reasonable amount of success by sometime around the middle of the next week, or two, probably! The secret is to take it in stages.

• Start by practising **Orbits** with two balls. Hold a ball in each hand. Your right hand is going to orbit the left-hand ball anti-clockwise. Swing your right hand *over* the left hand and downwards. Your left hand needs to throw its ball straight up to avoid a wrist collision.

As the left-hand ball rises the right hand continues the orbit *underneath* the rising ball then throws its ball **Over the Top** to the left hand. Both hands catch and the balls have traded places. Practise this on both sides until you can do it without even thinking about it. When your **Orbits** are really smooth you should work them into a running **Three Ball Cascade**.

*The two-ball **Orbit** exercise for would-be revengers. The Guy in the Hat's right hand **Orbits** his left-hand ball and then throws **Over the Top**. At the end of the move the balls have swapped hands.*

• The next stage is to add a *frilly bit* to the beginning of the **Orbit**. The frilly bit is an *outside* **Chop**. If you are not sure what one of those is – look it up!

Start as before, one ball in each hand. Your right hand is going to **Orbit** the left-hand ball as before, but first the *left* hand is going to execute an outside **Chop**, followed by an anti-clockwise circle on your right side.

From a normal starting position (right hand on your right side, left hand on your left) – bring your left hand *over the right*, then swing it in an anti-clockwise circle. Now do an **Orbit** (the previous exercise) with your right hand, around the left-hand ball. This flourishing move needs to be done with smooth speed and grace to either *look* or *feel* right. Practise this *relentlessly* on both sides using two balls and every spare minute of the day until it becomes as natural as swallowing.

• As soon as you can do the **Chop-Orbit** combination solidly you can start to work on the pattern with three balls. You don't have to go for the full Revenge straight away; all you need to do, at first, is to insert one **Chop-Orbit** at a time into a **Three Ball Cascade**.

Juggle a cascade and lead into the move by throwing a ball straight up on the right (as if you were about to go into **Two in One Hand**). This ball gets *outside-chopped* by the left hand, then the right hand **Orbits** it and you recover back to the cascade – phew!

Practise this move on both sides until your hands can do it without any muddling intervention from your poor befuddled brain.

Don't be disheartened when balls fly off at high speed on random angles. This is completely normal – stay relaxed and give your hands time to learn.

When you can do the **Chop-Orbit** move smoothly on both sides of the pattern *without* putting in any little cheats, like the odd tempting **Two in One Hand** throw, you are nearly there!

The full **Rubenstein's Revenge** is just a sequence of **Chop-Orbit** on the left, followed *immediately* by **Chop-Orbit** on the right. This feels downright stressful at first but in time the whole shape and style of your Revenge will settle into a relaxed, smooth and incredible pattern.

Good luck!

*Below, spread across both pages, is the full sequence of **Rubenstein's Revenge**. It's hard to believe that this is simply a shape distortion of the **Three Ball Cascade**!*

*The pattern is entirely symmetrical and the last frame leads back to the first. You can start **Rubenstein's Revenge** from a **Three Ball Cascade** by throwing one ball straight up and outside-chopping it.*

Rubenstein's Revenge

Runaround

The **Runaround** is a pattern for two jugglers, who continuously **Steal** three balls from each other. They end up running round in circles, both juggling the same **Three Ball Cascade**.

•Find three beanbags and a partner and name yourselves A and B, so that you can follow the instructions more easily.

B starts with two balls, one in each hand.

A starts with one ball in the right hand.

Step 1: A throws to A's own left hand, the ball passes *under* B's right arm, in front of B.

Step 2: A moves to B's left side and catches the throw from step one.

Step 3: B throws more or less straight up from the left hand towards A's right hand and starts to move around behind A.

Step 4: A catches B's throw in the right hand.

You are now back in the starting position, except that you have changed places.

Repeat the last four steps contrariwise, swapping A for B, and you have the whole sequence.

That's it! You each have only two different throws to learn! Repeat the sequence, slowly at first and then build up to normal **Three Ball Cascade** speed, unless you collapse in hysterical giggles first.

To do the **Runaround** well you need to move around each other smoothly. When it's done perfectly the three balls cascade fluidly in the middle while two idiots run around each other in circles. Add a bit of chat and it's a performer's dream – audiences love it!

See also **Gandini Patterns.**

Seeing Stars

Seeing Stars is a simple three-ball trick that mimics a cartoon character seeing stars after a bash on the head.

•Juggle **Two in One Hand** while orbiting the third, held, ball around your head.

•A development of the trick, which looks very flashy, is to juggle it on alternate sides. Carry a ball around your head once while juggling **Two in One Hand** in the right hand, then immediately change to **Two in One Hand** in the *left* hand while carrying another ball around your head the other way!

This variation is an extension of the **423** pattern **Charlie's Cheat**.

Seven Ball Passing

Six-ball passing is simple to understand; both you and your partner juggle **Three Ball Cascades** and from time to time (preferably the *same* time) you both throw balls to each other. So maybe to juggle seven you should both juggle three-and-a-*half* ball **Cascades**?

•Not quite! The simplest pattern for seven is a **Two Count** pattern. You and your partner pass to each other on every right-hand throw, catching in the left. Unlike the **Two Count** for six balls, each pass is thrown as a 4 instead of a 3 and you juggle out of time with each other. The 4's need to be about twice as high as your self throws.

The trick to seven-ball passing is to get the start right; it's a **Fast Start**. One juggler starts with four balls, two in each hand, the other starts with three balls, two in the right and one in the left.

The juggler with four balls starts first, throwing a pass on the very first throw. The other juggler *waits until the ball is halfway across* before responding with their first pass. The pattern then continues, both jugglers passing alternately and calling out helpful hints to each other like "Higher!", "Lower!", and "Oops!"

Continued overleaf...

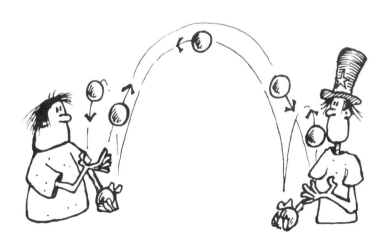

Seven Ball Passing...

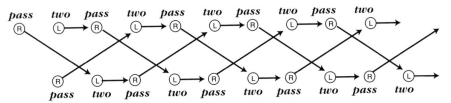

*A **Causal Diagram** of a seven-object **Two Count**, note that your right hand throws in time with your partner's left hand.*

The staggered timing of the seven-ball **Two Count** pattern means that your right hand is throwing in time with your partner's left hand, and vice versa.

You can throw **Tricks** in a seven-ball **Two Count**, just as you can in a six-ball **Two Count**, but they move *up a level*. For example, you can throw a right to right **5** pass on the *pass* beat while juggling seven. (The corresponding throw with six balls is a right to right **4** pass.)

• Seven balls can also be passed between two jugglers as a **Four Count.** You each pass with every other right and all passes are **5**'s. The passes are alternate – first *you* make a pass, then your partner makes a pass.

You start with four balls, your partner with three, and you both start juggling together. You count off:

Pass *and self and pass and self...*

Your partner counts off:

Self *and pass and self and pass...*

• Working with **Bouncing Balls** it's possible to juggle the seven-ball **Four Count** by bouncing all the passes off the floor. Using this technique it's possible to stand side by side with your partner and juggle a *Side-by-Side-Two-Person-Seven-Ball-Bounce.*

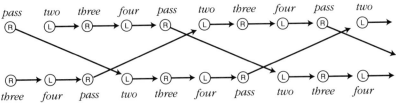

*A **Causal Diagram** of a seven-object **Four Count**.*

• The last in this selection of seven-ball passing patterns is a wonderfully complicated and intricate sequence that has a lot in common with the four-ball solo pattern **Five Three Four (534).**

You and your partner need to be fairly solid with the solo pattern **Five Three (53)** to attempt it.

In this pattern you each juggle a six **Beat** sequence that goes:

Right to left self **5** *-and-*
Right to left pass **4** *-and-*
Right to left self **3** *-and -*

The *and's* are the throws you don't need to think about too much, just normal left to right self **3**'s.

It feels like you are juggling a solo four-ball **Five Three** for two throws (**53**), followed by two throws of normal seven-ball passing (**43**), followed by two throws of **Three Ball Cascade** (**33**).

Your sequence is juggled *out of phase* with your partner's.

So much for the theory, here's what you actually *do!*

You start with four balls, your partner gets three.

You start juggling first. Beginning with the right hand you juggle:

53 43 333...

That **4** is your first pass. Your partner waits until that pass is halfway over and then starts exactly the same sequence. Then you both just keep going, repeating the same sequence of throws.

The key to the pattern is getting the throw heights right. Do that and it runs like clockwork!

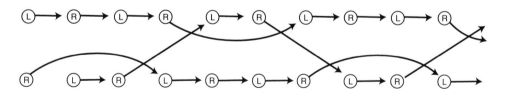

This seven-ball passing pattern is very similar to the solo pattern **Five Three Four (534).**

The key of mastering this pattern lies in getting the throw heights right. Your **4**'s *need to be twice as high as your* **3**'s *and the* **5**'s *twice as high again. It's got a great rhythm once you get it going – definitely worth the effort!*

Seven Ball Passing

Seven Ball Splits

Seven Ball Splits is a **Multiplex** pattern for seven balls that takes the idea of **Five Ball Splits** one level higher.

• You start with four in the right and three in the left and throw split **Multiplexes** from alternate hands just as you would in **Five Ball Splits** – only higher and to a more up-beat tempo (like moving from **Slow Cascade** to a true cascade).

Seven Ball Splits.

*The main problem is starting. Throwing a perfect split **Multiplex** from a grip of four balls in the right hand is not easy!*

*One solution (as shown here) is to start the pattern by throwing just one ball from the right as a crossing 4, then throw the first **Multiplex** from the left hand – throwing a split **Multiplex** from a hand holding three balls is not nearly so tricky.*

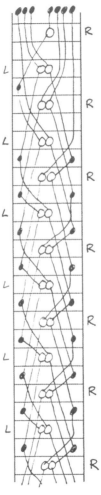

Shower

In solo juggling terms a **Shower** is a pattern (for any number of balls) in which one hand throws to the other and the other hand **Feeds** balls back. In **Passing Patterns** the term **Shower** is used to describe a **Two Count** – a pattern in which every second throw is a pass.

The distinguishing feature of **Shower** patterns, whether of the solo or passing variety, is that the balls all follow each other around *in a single loop*.

• The *two-ball* **Shower** is the simplest **Shower** pattern. The right hand throws **3**'s while the left throws **1**'s (**Feeds**). Many children learn to **Shower** two balls in the school playground. This can cause problems in later life when they try to learn the **Three Ball Cascade** because one hand (usually the left) is so used to **Feeding** that it just cannot get out of the habit!

Make a point of being able to juggle a smooth *two-ball* **Shower** in both directions. Since the pattern is so easy you can work on juggling it as fast and low as you possibly can! You should be able to get it so low that the balls only *just* pass around each other.

•The *three-ball* **Shower** is a harder pattern to juggle than the **Three Ball Cascade.** The right hand throws **5**'s while the left hand **Feeds**. It's not *that* hard though, and you should take the trouble to learn it. Work on getting an even rhythm going by getting the heights of those **5**'s right. Listen to the slap of the balls and remember that a *three-ball* **Shower** should be about *four*

times the height of a **Three Ball Cascade** juggled at the same speed. Practising a three-ball **Shower** in both directions is good practice for the **Five Ball Cascade**.

•Changing the direction of a three-ball shower every *two throws* creates an interesting pattern (**52512** – try making the **5**'s **Under the Hand** throws).

•Changing direction on *every throw* results in a **Slow Cascade** – more evidence of the complex intertwingling of different juggling patterns.

•You can make **Under the Hand** throws in a three-ball **Shower**.

Alternating between **Under the Hand** and normal throws produces a very complex-looking pattern. **Behind the Back** and

Under the Leg are worth experimenting with too!

•In a four-ball **Shower** you throw **7**'s and **1**'s, good practice for seven balls. A five-ball shower uses **9**'s and **1**'s – and so on into the territory of the **Numbers Juggler**.

•The **Shower** is the pattern that is usually drawn by artists who don't know any better. It usually appears as an arch over a clown's head containing an arbitrary and improbable number of balls.

Ah well!

See also **Half Shower.**

Shower

Shuffle

The **Shuffle** is a difficult three-ball pattern with an action that resembles a pack of cards being shuffled. It's difficult because the key throw, the throw that gives the pattern its shape and style, is *hard and downwards*. Miss that catch and the ball will slam into the floor before you even notice that you've dropped it! The **Shuffle** is a shape distortion of the three-ball **Half Shower**. It might be best to learn the much easier **Slow Shuffle** first.

• Warm up by throwing a hundred rounds of a left-handed three-ball **Half Shower**. The left hand throws **4**'s to the right while the right throws **2**'s to the left – both hands throwing simultaneously.

• To juggle the **Shuffle** you change the *shape* of the pattern so that those right hand **2**'s are thrown from top right to bottom left, *over* the approaching ball. The right-hand catch requires very quick and precise movement. The balls move in a figure eight pattern; the right hand does most of the work and the left hand hardly moves at all.

See also **Luke's Shuffle**.

Single

Like **Double, Triple, Quad** and **Quin**, the term **Single** is borrowed from club juggling. It's a loose term describing a throw that a club juggler would usually throw with a single spin.

This is almost always a **3**.

To save you looking it up, **Doubles** are usually **4**'s, **Triples** are **5**'s, **Quads** are **6**'s and so on.

And just to confuse, or perhaps inspire you – a **Single** has two **Beats** of **Airtime** and is called a **3**. A **Double** has three beats of airtime and is called a **4** – and so on. It's mad I know, but it all makes sense really!

See also **Airtime.**

Siteswap Notation

Siteswap Notation was invented independently around 1985 by Bruce "Boppo" Tiemann, Paul Klimek and Mike Day. All three of these people had the same idea at the same time – wow!

Siteswap Notation is a way of describing juggling patterns in which **Numbers** represent throws.

3's are **Three Ball Cascade** throws, **4**'s are **Four Ball Fountain** throws, **5**'s are **Five Ball Cascade** throws and so on. This system of numbering throws is used throughout THE ENCYCLOPÆDIA OF BALL JUGGLING.

To write down a pattern in **Siteswap Notation** you just write down the throws as a list:

333333

– is six throws of a **Three Ball Cascade**.

Reducing a piece of juggling to such a concise form means that a lot of information about the pattern is lost, but there is hidden power in **Siteswap's** stunning simplicity.

Before exploring any further it would be a good idea to understand exactly *why* a

simple list of **3**'s is a fair representation of a **Three Ball Cascade** – and indeed why **Siteswap** is so named.

Lesson One

The core idea is this: *what goes up must come down!*

Let's suppose we are juggling three balls, our hands are taking it in turn to make the throws and the throws are going to the same height. In fact, let's suppose we are juggling a **Three Ball Cascade**.

With a little imagination you can see that, once the pattern is running there is a constant stream of balls falling out of the air, each of which needs to be caught and thrown again to keep the pattern running.

Whenever we catch ball A and throw it again we're actually moving the ball to the *back of the queue* so we won't have to deal with it again until after we've dealt with balls B and C. It only takes a little more imagination to see that the act of throwing ball A could be thought of as moving A *three spaces back in the queue*.

Time rolls on a **Beat** and then B is at the front of the queue, so we throw B, which moves *three spaces back* and so on.

So a **Siteswap** sequence is a list of numbers that tell us how far back in the queue we moved each ball:

333333...

If we call a place in the imaginary queue a *site* and the action of moving to another position a *swap* then we would have a convincing theory for why **Siteswap** is called **Siteswap**.

And we'd be right.

Lesson Two

Here's the queue for our **Three Ball Cascade**.

- - - - - C B A

Ball A is at the front of the queue, followed by balls B and C. If we move A three spaces back and let time move on so that everything moves one space to the right we end up with

- - - - - A C B

..and now it's B's turn to be thrown.

Continued overleaf...

...Siteswap Notation

There is always an infinite number of empty spaces at the *back* of the queue – it's just crowded at the front, so instead of moving ball B back just three spaces, we could move it back four.

3333334!

A **Beat** later, after the whole queue has shuffled along, we get a queue with a hole in it after doing this:

- - - B - A C

Now it's C's turn to be thrown. We have the interesting opportunity of tossing C into the empty slot between A and B. This throw is a **2** – let's try it...

- - - B C A

You'll find, if you play around with pen and paper, that you can juggle:

423423423...

– for as long as you like (see **Four Two Three**).

It's a rule in **Siteswap** that you can only swap balls into empty sites in the queue, otherwise you get collisions.

Here's another pattern, it's called **Four Four One (441)**:

441441441...

The sequence can continue for as long as you care to keep going. Generally a repeating pattern is just written as *one* of its repeats, so we can shorten it to:

441

The **Three Ball Cascade** can be written simply as:

3

Lesson Three

Let's make sure we understand exactly what those numbers mean. A **3** means that a ball will be *thrown again* in three **Beats** time, a **2** means it will be thrown again in two **Beats** time, and so on.

This means we can write out a pattern longhand and then join up the numbers so that we can more easily see where all those balls are going.

Joining up the numbers is a good way of seeing how many balls there are in the pattern – just check to see how many lines there are at any given point! (**441** uses three balls).

Not every sequence of numbers can be juggled, and joining up the numbers is a good way of checking this. It's a rule that *no two lines can end on the same number* (that would be a collision). **432** is an example of a bad pattern.

The first three throws all land in the same place – you'd be catching three balls in the same hand at the same time if you tried this!

*A **3** is the throw you make in a **Three Ball Cascade**; a **4** is a **Four Ball Fountain** throw, and so on...*

It's easy to understand what **3**, **4**, **5** mean, but **0**, **1** and **2** are not so obvious.

A **0** is an *empty hand* or a ***Gap***.

A **1** is a **Feed**, the action of *placing* a ball directly into another hand.

A **2** is a *hold*. Most people find the logic of this elusive, until it's pointed out that a *held* ball in the right hand is ready to throw again *two* beats later.

Which brings me on to the subject of *odd* and *even* numbers.

In **Asynchronous** juggling patterns (that is, patterns in which the hands take it in turns to throw) any *even-numbered* throw goes to the *same hand* while *odd-numbered* throws go to the *opposite hand*.

Even numbers are *selfs*, odd numbers are *crossing throws*.

In **Synchronous** patterns (where both hands throw together) there are only ever even numbered throws.

Cool Siteswap Stuff

Armed with the basic theory, lets see what magic we can do with this new mathematical wand.

• You can check whether a **Siteswap** sequence is juggleable by "joining up the numbers" as described in Lesson Three.

• You can quickly work out how many balls are required for a **Siteswap** sequence by calculating the *average* throw weight.

For example **441** adds up to 9, which you divide by the length of the sequence to end up with 3. **441** is indeed a three-ball pattern.

Similarly **534** adds up to 12, which you divide by three to get 4 – so it's a four-ball pattern.

You can use **Siteswap** to invent new juggling patterns by converting existing patterns according to a few simple rules.

• You can *add the length of a sequence to any of the numbers in it* to create a new juggleable pattern that uses one more object than before.

For example **441** has a length of three. Adding three to the first throw in the sequence we get **741**, which is a valid four-ball pattern.

• It follows from the last rule that you can also *subtract the length of the sequence* from any of the throw weights to generate a new pattern that uses one *less* object. This is only allowable if the subtraction doesn't take any throw weight below zero. Getting an actual zero is OK, it just means a **Gap** or empty hand. Taking **Four Four One** as a starting point again, we can subtract three from the first throw to get **141**.

This is a two-ball pattern (rather a trivial one I'm afraid). If you want to try it, start with the two balls in one hand and throw the 4 first, juggling:

411411...

• Remember that it's up to you whether you write a pattern as a long or a short sequence. By using a different length of sequence you can find your way to more patterns.

Continued overleaf...

Siteswap Notation...

...Siteswap Notation

You could, for example, write the **Three Ball Cascade** as:

3333

This is a sequence of four digits so you can add four to one of the throws and get:

7333

– which is a pretty exotic four-ball pattern.

• The **Three Ball Cascade** could be also written as just:

3

– which you can change to the four-ball pattern:

4

– by adding the length of the sequence (one) to the only number in it. You could equally well have written the **Three Ball Cascade** as **33** which can be changed to **35** or **31** and so on. The possibilities are endless.

And now for the tricky stuff!

When it comes to **Synchronous** patterns (patterns in which both hands throw together), the formerly simple **Siteswap Notation** starts to get more complicated.

Simultaneous throws are represented by pairs of numbers in brackets; **(6, 4)** means the left hand throws a **6** while the right throws a **4**.

All throws in such patterns have to have even weights (**2**'s, **4**'s **6**'s etc.) because the hands only throw every two **Beats**. It's also necessary to distinguish between crossing throws and selfs by tacking an '**x**' onto the crossing throws.

A **Box** becomes:

(4, 2x)(2x, 4)...

A three-ball **Half Shower** (which uses the same throws but in a different arrangement) is:

(4x, 2x)...

The checking process of "joining up the dots" no longer works quite so simply because the throws are now made *every other* **Beat**.

And it's not possible to describe a pattern that changes from **Asynchronous** to **Synchronous** throws in mid-juggle.

Siteswap can also be extended to cover the **Multiplex**. A **Multiplex** is written by putting two numbers together in square brackets:

[3,2] 3 [3,2] 3

– is a **Three Ball Cascade** juggled with one extra ball held in one hand (this counts as a **Multiplex** as far as **Siteswap** is concerned, since a **2** is a valid "throw").

Siteswap threatens to get totally unreadable once you start using throwing weights over **9**'s, because it is at this point that we run out of single digit numbers. You might read **11 11 11 11** (eleven-ball **Cascade**) as **11111111** (shuffling a single ball from hand to hand). For this reason it's usual to start using letters instead of numbers above **9**'s. So **A** becomes **10** and **B** is **11** and so on.

Siteswap begins as a very simple and powerful idea, but as you extend it to cover more of the possibilities of juggling it does start to buckle under the strain a bit.

Siteswap State Tables

Here's a **Three Ball Cascade** juggled with an extra ball in the hand which is then **Multiplexed** out to end up in a **Four Ball Fountain**.

[3,2] 3 [3,2] 3 [3,4] 4 4 4 4 4...

A little hard to read, but it does tell you exactly what throws to make.

The greatest contributions of **Siteswap** to juggling are the simple system of numbers for describing throws and its ability to generate simple juggling patterns that nobody ever thought of before; obscure and clever things like:

501...

– a rather simple pattern for two balls, but not a trivial one! When you juggle it you'll be able to see how it goes against the natural juggler's instinct.

You don't have to use or understand **Siteswap Notation** to be a good juggler. It's just one way of looking at juggling. If you find it useful – great. If not, then leave it to the theoreticians and get on with the stuff you like instead!

What follows is probably only of interest to the more mathematically-minded jugglers.

Here's a diagram of all ten possible *states* a three-ball **Asynchronous** juggling pattern can be in if we limit ourselves to throws of **5** or less.

The vertical bars represent different *states*. Each is labelled with a picture of the queue of balls dropping towards your

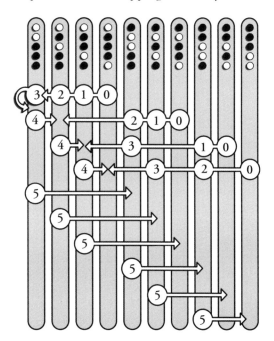

hands: black dots are balls, white circles are gaps. The bar at the far left is the normal state of a **Three Ball Cascade**.

The numbers in circles represent possible throws – if you choose to make a throw you must go to the end of its arrow to find out what state you'll end up in. Note that throwing a **3** in the left-hand bar takes you back to the same state as before.

Let's follow a **Five Three One (531)**. We start in the left-hand bar (in a normal **Cascade**). You'll see a **5** about halfway down that bar, which points to a state four bars to the right. That state contains a **3** which takes us two bars left. That bar contains a **1** which takes us back to the state we started in.

• You can take any route you like through the table. If you write down the numbers as you go you'll always end up with a valid **Siteswap**. Here's an example:

44405253044502

Since I just made that one up I'll name it the **Swiss Bank Account** pattern.

Continued overleaf...

Siteswap State Tables...

...Siteswap State Tables

This is a map of *all* of the possible states for **Asynchronous** juggling patterns using throw weights from **0** to **5**, and *any* number of balls from none to five!

There are 32 possible states, starting from a completely empty queue (the vertical bar at the far left), and finishing with a queue of five balls, which is the normal state of a **Five Ball Cascade** (far right).

Each state is marked with a diagrammatic representation of the queue of balls: black dots are occupied sites, white circles are empty ones. They read, from left to right, like the binary numbers running from 0 to 31.

If a state contains, say, three black dots, then there are three objects in the pattern. You'll discover that normal throws from a three-ball state lead only to other three-ball states, which is what you'd expect.

This diagram also allows you to move between states that contain *different* numbers of balls by means of **Picking Up** (follow the **P** arrows) and **Dropping** (follow the **D** arrows). These moves are not normally considered in **Siteswap Notation** but they are often juggled in the real world (especially the **Drops**).

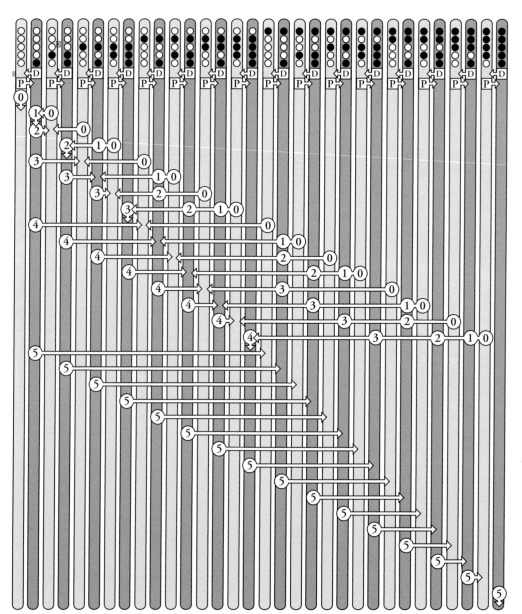

Here's an example of a sequence that represents a juggler going from a **Three Ball Cascade** to a **Four Ball Fountain**.

We start at state ○○●●● (the eighth bar from the left) which is the normal state for a **Three Ball Cascade**. We can keep throwing **3**'s for as long as we like here – the diagram shows that this will keep us in the same state.

Our hypothetical juggler chooses instead to throw a **4**, which takes the pattern into state ○●○●●. From here another **4** is thrown and we end up at ○●●○●. One more **4** takes us to ○●●●○. Note that the last site in the queue is empty, which means that there is no ball to be caught on this **Beat** of the pattern. This is our opportunity to **Pick Up**.

You follow a **Pick Up** by following the arrow labelled **P** – in this case that arrow takes us to state ○●●●●, which is the normal state for a **Four Ball Fountain**.

From here you can carry on throwing **4**'s as long as you like. The whole sequence could be written as:

3 3 3 3 4 4 4 P 4 4 4 4 4

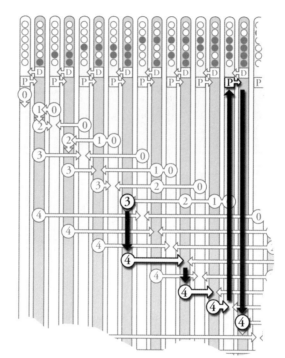

This not exactly conventional **Siteswap**, but it does allow us to navigate the space of all these possible throws in a fairly intuitive way.

The diagram also allows you to play around with **Drops** – see if you can trace out this path: **5 5 5 D 0 5 5 2**

(It's a **Drop** out of a **Five Ball Cascade** leading to a **Gap** pattern – **552**.)

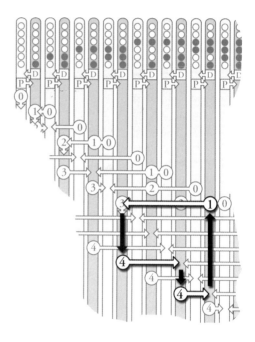

Apart from handling **Pick Ups** and **Drops** the diagram also handles more conventional stuff, like **Four Four One (441)** which is shown here.

I have no doubt that mathematical jugglers will have great fun exploring the diagram.

Siteswap State Tables

Six Ball Column Bounce

All the **Column Bounce** patterns use the same simple rule: add up the number of hands (almost always two) and the number of columns you are juggling in (in this case four) and that's how many balls it takes to fill the pattern!

This **Six Ball Column Bounce** is a logical extension of the **Five Ball Column Bounce**. To the observer the main difference is that in this pattern *four balls* hit the floor in a neat row on every bounce; in the five-ball pattern *three balls* hit the floor at a time. To the juggler it feels very like juggling the four-ball pattern **Spreads**.

• Start with three **Bouncing Balls** in each hand and imagine four columns in front of you. Both hands will throw simultaneously, just as they do in the **Five Ball Column Bounce**.

Lift the first two balls (one from each hand) into the two right-hand columns and let them fall to the floor. As they rise, lift the second two balls into the two left-hand columns so that *all four balls rise together*.

Now that the pattern is started you just continue by making exchanges to the right, then to the left and so on. Every ball bounces twice.

• The **Four Ball Column Bounce**, the **Five Ball Column Bounce** and the **Six Ball Column Bounce** make a neat series. It would be nice to think that you could just keep going! Unfortunately it turns out that the seven-ball pattern is very difficult to keep under any sort of control. Try it if you like! You'll be working in five columns and some balls are going to have to bounce three times! If you want to make bigger patterns then it's best to add more hands as well as more columns. A ten-ball **Column Bounce** between two jugglers works very well! (That's six columns and four hands, juggled just like a **Five Ball Column Bounce**.)

Six Ball Column Bounce.

Six Ball Fountain

The simplest pattern for six balls is the **Six Ball Fountain**, which is just like the **Four Ball Fountain** only much higher and *much* harder.

To juggle four balls you need to be able to juggle **Two in One Hand** in both hands at the same time – make that **Three in One Hand** and you can juggle six. Every throw is, of course, a **6**. The pattern can be juggled *rolling out* (normal), *rolling in* (difficult) or in *columns* (unusual). You also have the option of using simultaneous throws which looks very good!

Numbers Jugglers tend not to do too much work on six balls – by the time they get to this level they have spent so much time working on **Cascades** that the **Fountains** seem awkward. They usually go straight on to the seven-ball cascade.

•There's not much a book can tell you about juggling the **Six Ball Fountain** – you know what it is, so put three in the left, three in the right and go for it!

If you are looking for an easier way of getting six balls in the air (just so that you can say you've done it) then check out the **Multiplex** technique or get some **Bouncing Balls** and learn the **Six Ball Column Bounce**.

Six Three Three (633)

The **Six Three Three (633)** is a pattern for four objects. It's not that widely used because it's rather difficult.

When it's juggled well you see a juggler **Cascading** two balls while two others see-saw very high on each side of the pattern.

•The hands throw alternately. The **6**'s are thrown as **Self Throws**, the **3**'s as normal crossing **Cascade** throws. **6**'s are about five times as high as **3**'s.

Start with two balls in each hand and lead with a right self **6**. Then you juggle two throws of a **Three Ball Cascade** and throw a left self **6** followed by two more **Cascade** throws. This sequence of six throws repeats to give a continuous pattern.

You are going to have trouble with those high throws. Half the trick is keeping the **3**'s very tight and low. The other half of the trick is keeping the 6's accurate. The third half is keeping the whole thing together. It's not easy, but when it's done well it has tremendous visual rhythm.

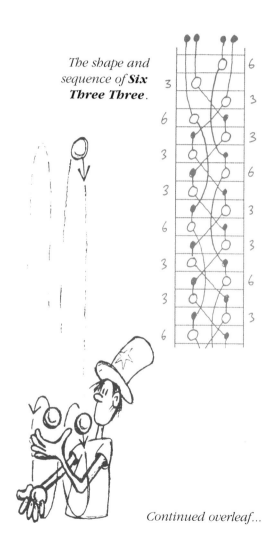

The shape and sequence of Six Three Three.

Continued overleaf...

Six Three Three (633)

...Six Three Three (633)

• Juggling the **Six Three Three** is a bit tricky; practise throwing **6**'s out of a **Three Ball Cascade** first to get the feel of those high throws.

*Juggle the **Cascade** and throw a self **6**, keeping the **Cascade** running underneath it. If you throw the **6** from your right hand then the right hand will make two catches and two throws before the high ball returns.*

Practise this on both sides.

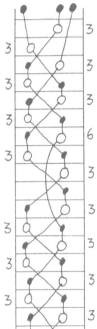

• A much easier way of juggling **Six Three Three** is to use **Bouncing Balls**.

The **6**'s are thrown as self bounces; the **3**'s are air throws as normal. This is much less strenuous, more relaxing and you can see all the balls at once (believe me this *helps*). You can build up to the pattern in the same way as before: start with three balls and work on the self bounce **6**'s. Remember, the pattern *does not stop and wait* for the bounce to come back, it keeps going. Once you are comfortable with the bounced **6**'s in the three-ball pattern start working with four balls.

• You may notice that two of the balls are always thrown as **6**'s and the other two are always **3**'s – so two balls never bounce! Bring on the **Eggs**! It feels very strange juggling the **Six Three Three** with two bouncing balls and two **Eggs**, but it really does work.

A good finish to the *Egg Bounce* is to take the pattern up into a **Four Ball Fountain**, which is quite an easy change. Then change back down to the **Six Three Three** bounce. This is tricky because if you get the sequence wrong an **Egg** (or two) will hit the floor. Of course that might be just what you want!

*A **Six Three Three** juggled with **Bouncing Balls**. The two balls that cascade never hit the floor, so they might as well be eggs!*

Six Two (6x,2x)

The **Six Two** is a four-ball pattern juggled with simultaneous throws. On every other **Beat** of the pattern, one hand throws a 6 while the other hand throws a 2. Both throws cross. But there is more than one way of doing this!

•In the simplest form one hand throws continuous 6's while the other throws continuous 2's, creating a four-ball **Half Shower**.

•It gets much more interesting if you *reverse* the direction of the shower on every throw. First your right hand throws a **6** while the left throws a **2**, then your *left* throws the **6** while your right throws the **2**:

(2x, 6x)(6x, 2x)

In this form you find three balls being juggled in a **Slow Cascade** on **6**'s while the fourth ball hops from hand to hand at the bottom of the pattern on **2**'s.

This particular pattern is actually a four-ball extension of the **Box**, though it is not a **Square Juggling** pattern.

•Another option is for both hands to throw **6**'s, then both throw **2**'s. In this variation you *can* keep the square shape by throwing the **6**'s as **Self Throws**. This variation is none other than the **Four Ball Box**.

(6x, 6x)(2x, 2x)

•It's also possible to juggle *three* balls on **6**'s and **2**'s, but you end up throwing more **2**'s than **6**'s. Here's a 6-2 trick that you can throw while juggling an ordinary three-ball **Box**.

While juggling the **Box**, pump out a self **6** instead of **4** from the right hand. This gives you time to throw two **2**'s as "swapsies" underneath, before recovering back to a standard **Box**.

(4, 2x)(2x, 4)(6, 2x)(2x,2x)(2x,4)

It works!

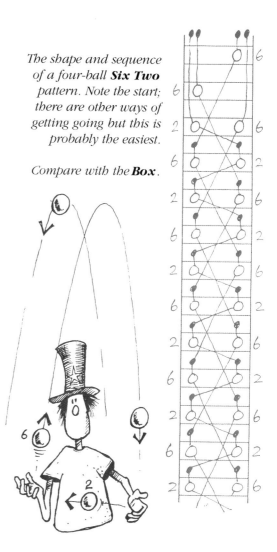

*The shape and sequence of a four-ball **Six Two** pattern. Note the start; there are other ways of getting going but this is probably the easiest.*

*Compare with the **Box**.*

Slap

The **Slap** is a sleight of hand move for the three-ball juggler. The audience hears a "slap" and a ball suddenly leaps out of the pattern as if by magic.

•Practise the **Slap** with one ball first. Place the ball on the *fingers* of your right hand. Now throw the ball from *under* the left hand so that your hands collide as the throw is made. The collision is between the side of your left hand and the palm of your right hand. The impact should stop your right hand dead, but the fingers under the ball *follow through,* giving plenty of height to the throw.

Don't make the painful mistake of thinking that it's the force of the impact that gives height to the throw – it's the spring in your fingers that does the work. The purpose of the **Slap** is to make a noise and to stop your right hand from following through.

Aim to get the highest possible throw with the absolute minimum of right hand movement and a nice clear "slap". As soon as the ball is in the air you should move your hands apart, which improves the illusion of a ball coming from nowhere.

•When you have got the technique you should start working the throw into a **Three Ball Cascade**. Think of the move as a slightly modified **Under The Hand** throw.

Note that when your right hand is throwing a **Slap** your left hand will be *holding* a ball and vice versa. As your **Slap** improves you should concentrate on making it as invisible to your audience as possible. It's also good form not to look up as you make the **Slap** throw – that way it looks like even *you* weren't expecting it!

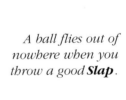

*A ball flies out of nowhere when you throw a good **Slap**.*

Slow Cascade

You can hardly fail to notice that **Beginners** tend to juggle three balls in a pattern that is much higher and slower than the smooth and liquid **Three Ball Cascade** of more experienced jugglers.

The reason for this is that beginners tend to *lock in* to a subtly different pattern for three balls, the **Slow Cascade**.

In the true **Three Ball Cascade** both hands are in constant motion, throwing **3**'s. In the **Slow Cascade** only one hand is working at a time and every throw is a **4**. To put it another way: in a **Three Ball Cascade** one hand is throwing *as* the other is catching, but in a **Slow Cascade** one hand throws *and then* the other hand catches.

Because human beings are naturally rhythmical creatures, it is quite difficult to juggle a pattern that is halfway between these two styles.

If you are a beginner and want to convert your **Slow Cascade** into a true **Three Ball Cascade** then the following exercise will probably help you to "click" into the rhythm.

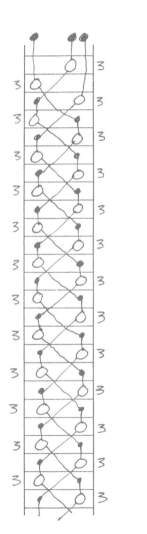
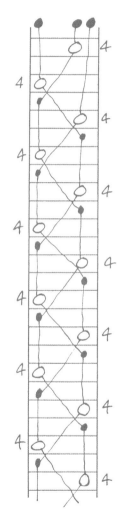

Three Ball Cascade and **Slow Cascade**.

• Put those beanbags down and *mime* the action of juggling three balls. Each hand takes it in turn to move in a circle as if it were catching a ball on the outside and throwing it again on the inside. First the left hand moves, then the right. This is the hand action of the **Slow Cascade**.

Now practise the movement for the true **Three Ball Cascade**. Both hands must circle continuously. As the right comes up through the middle, the left is going down on the outside. Try it, slowly at first, and then settle into normal juggling speed.

Practising hand movements for the true
Three Ball Cascade.

Continued overleaf...

Slow Cascade...

...Slow Cascade

Mime a hundred throws (no **Drops**), and you will feel the **Three Ball Cascade** movement becoming smoother and smoother. You should settle, quite naturally, into the overlapping hand movement of the true cascade.

You are now ready to add the balls. You'll find that the true cascade is easiest to "lock into" if you juggle it at about *half the height* of your most comfortable **Slow Cascade**.

If this doesn't work for you, don't worry: you *will* get it quite naturally anyway! There is nothing *wrong* with the **Slow Cascade**. It's just that it's not the simplest pattern for three balls – despite being the easiest for the **Beginner** to learn.

•If the idea of the **Slow Cascade** is extended then it's obvious that three balls can be juggled with any throw with a weight of **3** upwards. Juggling three balls on **5**'s is quite possible, but the rhythm is not very elegant. Juggling on **6**'s is another matter entirely.

This style is sometimes called *"Hot Potato"* – juggle it and you'll see why!

*A **Slow Cascade** juggled with **6**'s. The empty time of the hands is maximised in this pattern, hence its nickname "Hot Potato".*

*If you compare this chart with **Three in One Hand** you'll see that it's almost exactly the same pattern, except that the hands take it in turn to make the throws.*

*Three balls can be juggled with any weight of throw from 3 upwards but **3**'s, **4**'s and **6**'s create the easiest rhythms to lock into.*

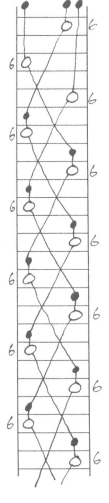

Slow Shuffle

The **Slow Shuffle** is the infinitely easier first cousin to the **Shuffle**. The trick is so named because it resembles the action of shuffling a pack of cards.

•Juggle **Two in One Hand**, in columns, in your left hand. Hold the third ball in your right hand. Position your right hand so that the middle ball peaks *just below it*.

As the middle ball reaches the top of its flight you make a snappy exchange. Your right hand slams its ball diagonally downwards directly into the left hand, then immediately **Snatches** the middle ball out of the air.

This is one of those tricky knacksome moves. On your first attempt you will probably just end up flinging a ball hard at the floor!

With a little perseverance and a few rounds of the **Yo-yo** mixed in for light relief you will get there! Once you can do a single **Slow Shuffle** you should practise making one exchange on *every other* left hand throw. That's the trick!

The difficult version, the **Shuffle** itself, has you making one of these exchanges on *every* left-hand throw.

• The **Slow Shuffle** looks very good if you juggle it on alternate sides. First you make a slam exchange on the right, then on the left.

Curiously, there is quite a close relationship between the alternate-sided **Slow Shuffle** and the very simple three-ball pattern, **Arches**. If you juggle **Arches** by slamming the middle ball downwards you get more or less exactly the same pattern!

See also **Shuffle**, **Luke's Shuffle**.

Slow Start

In **Passing Patterns** a **Slow Start** allows the jugglers to synchronise their patterns by juggling to themselves for four throws before making the first pass.

Starting from the first right-hand throw you both count off *One-and-two-and-PASS!*

The alternative is a **Fast Start** in which the very first throw is a pass.

Snatch

Also known as a **Claw** – a **Snatch** is a catch made with the palm facing downwards, swiping a ball out of the air.

Do a **Snatch** right and it gives great dramatic effect to your juggling; do it wrong and you have never seen anything hit the ground so fast in your life!

Apart from being a good trick in its own right, the **Snatch** is a vital component of many juggling patterns, from the **Slow Shuffle** (opposite) to **Rubenstein's Revenge**.

• Juggle a **Three Ball Cascade** and practise the **Snatch** in all combinations – snatching every right, every left, the same ball every time, and finally every ball.

*A slammed throw in a **Slow Shuffle**. Note that the right hand slams its ball diagonally downwards at exactly the same moment that the left hand throws upwards.*

Continued overleaf...

Snatch...

...Snatch

• As you develop your **Snatch** you can create a picturesque *bubbling up* effect with a **Three Ball Cascade**.

Juggle a low and tight **Cascade** and then let the throws grow higher, acting as if the balls had become lighter than air. Let the pattern rise in front of you until you have to **Snatch** every ball to "pull" the pattern back into line.

• Another much-used effect is that of one ball suddenly leaping far too high out of a **Three Ball Cascade** as if it had a mind of its own, and being **Snatched** back into the pattern.

Juggle the cascade low and fast. **Pop** a ball out as high as you dare and **Snatch** it at the top of its flight.

Timing is the key to getting a good effect – it should look as if you only just managed to catch that ball. Also, be careful that you only throw *one* ball high. The natural tendency is to make the throw after the **Pop** a high one too. Step on that habit!

The effect of this move is vastly improved if you delay looking up at the ball until a millisecond *after* it is **Popped**, rather than anticipating the move.

Solid

When jugglers say that they have got a trick or pattern **Solid** they mean that they aren't **Dropping** any more. The learning process has run its course and they can actually *do* the trick, reliably and every time.

I've noticed that when a juggler really has a trick **Solid**, it actually looks *liquid* – the balls simply seem to flow like water.

You may also hear jugglers referring to a **Two Count** passing pattern as **Solids**.

*Snatching a ball that has tried to escape from a **Three Ball Cascade**.*

Speed Weave

The **Speed Weave** is a complicated **Passing Pattern** in which one juggler **Feeds** three others while they move in a figure of eight pattern like three balls in a **Cascade**. The jugglers juggle themselves while juggling the balls. The **Speed Weave** is tremendous fun – try it at your juggling **Workshop**.

• Warm up by juggling a four-person **Feed**. Three of you stand in a line facing the feeder. Everybody gets three balls each and you begin with a **Slow Start**.

The feeder juggles a right-handed **Two Count**, passing *right-middle-left-middle-right* and so on. This means that the jugglers at the two ends of the line pass *eight counts* while the one in the middle passes a **Four Count**.

• The **Speed Weave** is exactly the same as far as the feeder is concerned – but now the three other jugglers move around each other in a figure of eight as they juggle.

They all juggle *six counts* (every third right is a pass) as they move between the three passing positions. The walk has to be timed so that each pass is made "on the mark" (you can make chalk marks on the floor if it helps!).

It gets very busy in the middle of the pattern – concentrate on walking forwards through the middle quickly or you'll block the next pass.

Note also – from the feeder's point of view – that as one juggler is walking to the *left* the next pass swings to the *right*.

Getting a **Speed Weave** to work tests your organising skills as much as your juggling!

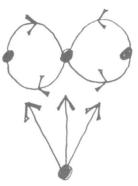

*In the **Speed Weave** the "feeder" passes to three positions in turn while the "fed" move in a figure of eight.*

Spin

By applying **Spin** to a **Bouncing Ball** you can make it change direction when it bounces. A spinning ball is like a wheel – when it contacts the ground the ball tends to be driven in the direction of the **Spin**, just as a car is propelled forwards by its wheels.

Obviously, when a **Bouncing Ball** hits the ground it bounces back up again. What is not so obvious is that the **Spin** bounces too! Depending on exactly how the ball hits the floor it may rise with reversed spin, with more spin, or no spin at all. Also, if an un-spinning ball strikes any surface with a glancing blow, it will rebound with spin.

This may all sound very complicated, but **Spin** is quite controllable, and you can use it to add a new dimension to your **Bouncing Ball** juggling.

When practising tricks that require **Spin** it's best to use multicoloured or marbled finish balls so that you can actually see the spin on them.

Continued overleaf...

...Spin

•Stand over a good floor with one **Bouncing Ball** in your right hand. Drop it vertically, and as you let go give it a good hard clockwise spin by *flicking* it out of your fingers. The perfect action is a hard *snap* – just like snapping your fingers.

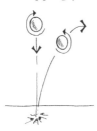

The ball will drop vertically and bounce off to the right (the direction that the spin drove it in) with its spin both reversed and slower.

Now try the same thing, but launch the ball slightly to the left, still with a clockwise spin. This time the ball should rise back to your hand with the spin reversed and about as fast as it was before.

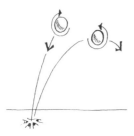

Finally, drop the ball with clockwise spin, thrown slightly to the *right*. The ball will bounce wildly off out of reach with practically no spin at all.

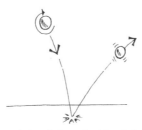

Practise with both hands (the left hand applying anticlockwise spin of course) until you start to get the knack of applying hard spin and some degree of control over where the ball ends up!

•The opposite spin is harder to apply but well worth learning. Throw a ball from the right hand outward to the right with *anti-*

clockwise spin and get it to return to your hand. The better you get, the further you'll be able to throw that ball!

•By throwing a ball forwards from a palm downwards grip you can apply *top spin* so that the ball returns to you. At the exact moment of the release you stroke the ball hard, rolling it off the underside of your hand.

THE ENCYCLOPÆDIA OF BALL JUGGLING

•To apply really massive amounts of spin to a ball, use a Karate chop.

Let a ball bounce once in front of you, and as it rises chop hard on the right-hand side of the ball with your right hand. This applies a huge amount of clockwise spin (if you aim right!) and propels the ball back down to the floor and to the left.

It will then bounce back towards the right with anticlockwise spin – let it go for another bounce. On the second bounce it will go back to the left with clockwise spin and so on until the bounce peters out or you catch it.

•Here's how to apply spin to two balls at once, in opposite directions!

Hold the two balls in your right hand, palm downwards, with your index finger jammed between them. Now squeeze hard so that they pop out and head for the floor. If you get this trick right they both leave your hand with opposite spin, hit the floor and cross on the way up to simultaneous catches in opposite hands.

Continued overleaf...

•The complete opposite of the previous effect is achieved by throwing a ball up, over your head, so that it bounces behind you with *bottom spin*. The ball then bounces up behind you and back into your pattern.

The throwing action is palm upwards this time, rolling the ball off your hand as you throw it. Seriously cool jugglers do this *without looking* to see how the ball is doing!

With a Karate chop you can apply masses of spin to a bouncing ball.

Spin...

...Spin

• Spin is also applied to a ball whenever it strikes a glancing blow on the floor or any other surface (wall, legs, other balls and so on). The most graphic illustration of this is the highly improbable *Table Bounce*.

Find a solid table with a smooth underside. Throw a ball hard, so that it glances off the floor at about forty five degrees and bounces up to hit the underside of the table. The ball comes right back at you! The ball picks up spin by glancing off the floor which causes it to reverse direction when it hits the bottom of the table!

• Another example of glancing blow spin technology is the clever, flashy and comically named *Trouser Bounce*.

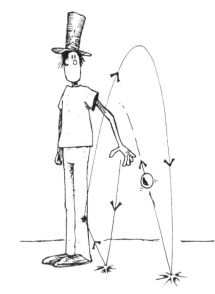

Throw a ball downwards from your right hand so that it bounces off the floor just to the right of your right ankle. If you aim well the ball will rise and strike a very shallow glancing blow on your right leg and fly off to the right, well out of reach. The glancing blow has applied a lot of anticlockwise spin so it will bounce back into an easy catching position.

• A similar trick involves five bounces and a wall. You don't often get an opportunity to do this one because you need to find a good smooth bouncing floor *and* a good wall!

Throw a ball downwards so that it hits the floor (bounce one) just three or four inches from the base of the wall and then glances off the wall, picking up a lot of spin, as it rises (bounce two).

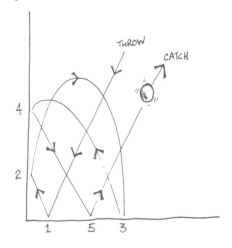

The ball will now rebound off the wall and hit the floor again (bounce three) and bounce *back* and strike the wall again (bounce four).

As the ball comes off the wall it will accelerate,* slamming back onto the floor (bounce five) and bouncing back into your waiting hand.

You'll find that you can get three balls to chase each other around in this pattern. Throw them, in rapid succession, at exactly the same spot on the floor. They all follow the same five-bounce route. With reasonable timing you don't get any collisions. After fifteen bounces and a complex interweaving of balls, they'll pop, one after the other, right into your waiting hand or hat!

*The acceleration is a bit of a surprise. As a young boy I was given a **Powerball**, and I must have driven everyone nuts with it – it practically destroyed my room before exploding into dust and fragments one day.

I discovered the five-bounce trick and noticed the acceleration on the fourth bounce and asked my father (because dads know *everything*) if this was really possible for a ball to rebound from a surface *faster* than it had hit it. I'd been taught about conservation of energy in physics at school and I knew that energy can't just appear from nowhere.

My father is a Professor of Law so he didn't know the answer. He asked two Professors of Thermodynamics at the University for their opinion. Legend has it that they both pondered the question for a moment and answered simultaneously "Not unless the ball *cools* the wall". Which just goes to show how stupid professors can be. It took me years to work out the answer. What happens on the fourth bounce is that the ball hits the wall with terrific spin energy and leaves it with practically none. All the spin energy converts into *speed*, so the ball *does* accelerate, the laws of Thermodynamics remain intact and the wall doesn't get cooled at all.

Spinning Ball

The **Spinning Ball** is the amazing trick of balancing a spinning a ball on the end of your finger, like flashy basketball players do.

You need a ball about the size of a football or basketball with a "grippy" surface and not so light that it skitters around when you try to catch it on the end of your finger. It also helps a bit (while you are learning) if the ball is ever so slightly deflated.

When you balance an object it is always easiest if you have the heaviest end of it at the *top* – hence it is best to balance a broom with the brush head at the top or a pool cue with the fat end upwards. Balls, although round, are almost *always* out of balance, sometimes quite badly. You need to find the heavy end.

• Float the ball in water. The heavy end goes to the bottom and you can mark the light end with a pen. The X now marks the spot you should think of as the *South Pole*. That is where your finger goes when you balance the ball on it. Done that? Right – now dry the ball. You need all the grip you can get. If you bite your fingernails now is the time to stop!

• Grip the ball with outstretched fingers in your right hand, the *South Pole* at the bottom. Give it as much spin as you can while throwing it up a few inches. The spin should be clockwise, looking at the ball from underneath. This is quite a knack in itself. It's very important that the ball spins *flat*. South Pole at the bottom, North Pole at the top and full equatorial spin. If you are more than a couple of degrees out it's going to be very difficult to catch it on your finger!

Continued overleaf...

Spinning Ball...

...Spinning Ball

Assuming that you get the spin right, the next stage is to try and catch the ball on your index or middle fingernail. You have to get your finger to hit the exact South Pole, without any bounce! It's not easy!

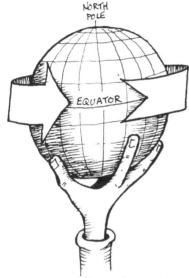

•Once caught you have the problem of keeping it there! The ball has become a gyroscope and gyroscopes are *weird!* They behave quite differently to un-spinning things. As the ball falls to the right your instinct will be to move your hand to the right – *wrong!* Following the tilt on the ball just causes it to tilt in some new and unexpected, direction. Balance it by *feel*

instead. It often helps if you look *away* from the ball. You *will* get the knack, but not straight away. This is not something you can do by *thinking* about it.

•You'll find that the length of time you can keep the ball balanced will always be limited by the length of time it will keep spinning. As soon as the ball loses momentum, it falls off.

Practise *swiping* the ball to build up its speed again. Transfer the ball to your left hand and strike it just below the equator when doing this.

•The classic spinning ball trick is the *Curl*. You spin a ball on one finger, then lower your hand and turn it inward so that the ball passes under your arm, up behind you and back to the starting position. Not only does this trick *look* difficult enough to guarantee you a round of applause, it *feels* even harder! Amazingly brilliantly flash jugglers get two balls going, then they *curl* one after the other!

• You can throw a spinning ball up and catch it again on your finger. A neat variation is to throw it up and bounce it once off your elbow, then catch it on your finger again – still spinning!

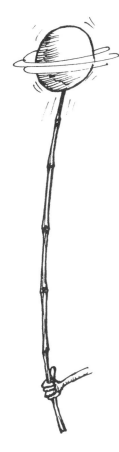

If you transfer a ball onto the sharpened (but not too sharp) end of a bamboo pole about six feet long you'll find that it will balance itself so well that you can hand the pole to a small child and the ball still won't fall off!

Spreads

In **Spreads** you juggle four balls with simultaneous throws, first throwing two balls up on the right, then two on the left. Thus the balls are juggled in four columns. The pattern is surprisingly difficult to juggle but it looks fantastic.

• When you juggle **Spreads** you'll find that you need to look *away* from the side you are throwing on. As you throw to the right you look to the left to spot the balls that are peaking on that side. The technique is similar to throwing **Behind the Back.**

It's quite hard to keep the columns straight and far enough apart to avoid collisions. You should stand with your feet apart and sway from side to side as you throw, keeping your centre of gravity as much as possible below the balls that you are throwing. Think from your stomach!

• Juggling **One-up Two-up** with the *one-up* ball juggled to the side of the pattern instead of the middle is good practice for **Spreads**.

See also **Four Ball Column Bounce** and **Six Ball Column Bounce**.

Your body turns towards the balls you are throwing, while your head turns towards the balls you are catching.

Spreads

Square Juggling

Square Juggling is juggling with *right angles*.

Juggling is normally full of curves and roundness as balls fly through the air in parabolic paths controlled by smooth movements of the hands below them.

So the thing to do, to create a stark contrast, is to throw in a few improbable and sharp *right angles*. The tricks you need for this are the **Box**, the **Factory**, the **Robotic Drop, Robot Bounce** and **Cranes.**

Squeeze

A **Squeeze** is a **Reverse Multiplex**; the act of catching more than one ball at the same time, in the same hand.

This might sound impossible (or at least very difficult) but with a little thought and practice you *can* make it work.

• First we'll try a *pure* **Squeeze**. That is, one with no cheating! Take two balls, hold one in each hand. Now throw them simultaneously (as **4**'s) so that they both go to the same height, but fall to the same place. It's easiest if you send one straight up, while the other arches across. It's also best to start *low!*

Pretty tricky huh?

• Now we'll do an **Asynchronous** *pure* **Squeeze**. This is even trickier. The term "asynchronous" means that your hands are throwing at *different times.*

Hold a ball in each hand, then toss a **4** straight up from your left hand, and *a beat later* throw a crossing **3** from your right hand. Try to get both balls to land in your left hand at the same time.

Amazing!

Now let's suppose that you get really good at this and move on to juggle three- and four-ball patterns containing **Squeezes**. This is all well and good, and you'll feel like a really deft exponent of **Reverse Multiplex** technology – but it doesn't actually look that impressive – in short, it's a lot of trouble for very little effect.

Believe it or not, this is an area of juggling in which *it is better to cheat.*

• Take three balls, two in one hand, and one in the other and throw all three simultaneously so they hang briefly in the air in front of you in a well-separated horizontal line.

Now catch all three at the same time.

It seems like it can't be done, but it can if you *cheat!* All you have to do is catch the two outside balls first, and then *scoop* the middle ball out of the air with one hand (or the other).

OK, so technically you aren't catching two balls in one hand at the same time. Instead you are catching one, then following the falling ball down and scooping it up a moment later.

The point is that it *looks good* – and that's a very good point indeed.

•Concentrate on making those balls move very smoothly and practise the trick every which way around.

Obviously, the closer together you can get that pair of balls, the less *scooping* you are going to have to do and the better the trick will look.

•Now try a four-ball version. Place two balls in each hand, and throw all four so they hang briefly in an evenly separated horizontal row in front of you.

Catch the two outside balls and *scoop* the two inside balls. Good isn't it?

It's quite neat if the two inner balls *cross over* – this adds a little extra impossibility to the whole thing.

•For a really neat effect, hold two balls in each hand and cross your arms. Throw all four balls at once – aim to make the two outer balls stay on their own sides, while the two inner balls cross over. Uncross your hands and catch all four.

There are approximately sixteen variations on that particular theme that I leave as an exercise for the reader.

See also **Multiplex**.

(Thanks to Gary of the **Juggler's Rest Backpackers** in Picton, New Zealand for inspiring this one.)

Squeeze

Steals

Stealing is taking a ball, or even a whole pattern, from another juggler while it is being juggled.

• Begin by learning how to **Steal** a **Three Ball Cascade**.

Stand face to face with a partner while they juggle a **Three Ball Cascade**. You need to *intercept* the balls as they fall into your partner's hands – you *do not* grab the balls out of their hands.

Watch the balls as they fall from the top of the pattern and *count yourself in* mentally – *not that one, not that one, that one!*

Then move positively and decisively. Any indecision or faltering on your part will cause your partner to drop in anticipation. Just insert your hands into the pattern, concentrating mainly on getting the first two balls; the third should follow naturally. Don't **Snatch!**

Take turns practising **Steals** until you are both experts.

• When working in front of an audience it's better to **Steal** from the side. Stand shoulder to shoulder while your partner juggles three balls. Watch the balls falling and tune your brain into their pattern. It is easiest if the first ball you take is on your side of their pattern. Again, avoid indecision and hand collisions and focus on getting the first two balls. As you take ball number two you move into your partner's position and ball number three should just magically appear. You get points for style if the **Three Ball Cascade** stays in the same position throughout.

• While you are in the mood for **Steals** you can practise *sharing* the pattern. Your right hand and your partner's left hand juggle the same **Three Ball Cascade** together.

• With any **Steal**, your partner can steal the pattern back from you as soon as you have taken it from them – or even earlier! Performing *side* **Steals** off each other at the maximum possible rate (every throw is stolen) produces the hilarious **Runaround.**

•You don't have to steal *all* the balls in a pattern. Try taking just one ball and then throwing it back into the pattern.

Stand to one side of your partner and steal a ball from *above* the hand that is supposed to catch it, then throw it back into the pattern below their hand, thus preserving the shape (and timing) of the pattern. You can continuously steal the same ball, first on one side and then on the other, leaving your partner juggling a **Gap** pattern. You stand more or less behind them throwing the same ball from side to side across the front of their body so that it passes *under* one of their arms and then *over* the other.

•If you are taller than your partner you will be able to steal the pattern from behind.

Reach over their shoulders and **Steal** their cascade. They then need to crouch down to escape.

If your partner is taller than you you can crawl between their legs from behind and stand up in the middle of the pattern to steal it.

•For really flashy **Steal**, stand a few paces behind your partner, get them to **Flash** all three balls and bend forwards, you leapfrog over their back, catch the pattern and continue. They will need to throw the **Flash** forwards a little.

•When stealing larger patterns than the **Three Ball Cascade** you'll find that stealing from the front is always easiest.

The **Four Ball Fountain** presents no real problems (as long as you can both juggle four). Once again, the trick is to get those first two balls and take *high*.

Stealing a **Five Ball Cascade** is harder; concentrate on getting the first *three* balls from the top of the pattern – the last two steal themselves!

•Here's a particularly fine stealing routine, made famous by an ancient comic juggling duo who shall remain nameless.* It involves stealing balls one at a time from a **Five Ball Cascade**.

For this trick you need to find a chair and a solid five-ball juggler. Place the chair behind your ace juggler and whisper some suitable words of encouragement – "Keep going whatever I do!" Now stand on the chair and watch those balls as they peak.

It's obvious, from this position, that all you have to do to steal a ball is place your hand in its path, just as it begins to fall. Do this and you will have effortlessly converted their pattern into a **Five Ball Gap**.

Let's assume that you have taken a ball that has just left the star's *right hand* and it's now sitting in your *left*. Immediately move your left hand *directly over* their right-hand catching position, and exactly five **Beats** after the **Steal** you drop the ball. It should drop perfectly into their waiting empty right hand.

Continued overleaf...

*OK, "He's Magic Gold and Cyanide Rachel" – anag.

Steals...

...Steals

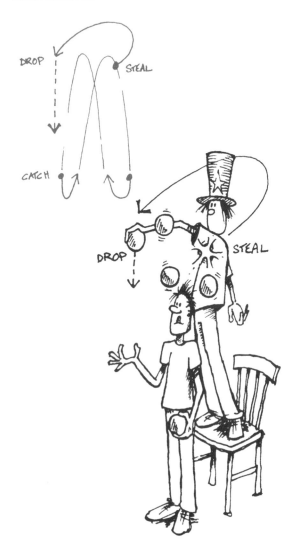

"Exactly five **Beats** later" might sound like a pretty tall order, but you'll find that once you've done it a couple of times you'll get a feel for the rhythm of the trick.

Try this steal both ways and when you have that solid try the incredible *double steal*. Steal two balls from the top of the pattern, one from the right and one from the left, immediately cross your arms over and, at the right moment, drop them back in. Since they were stolen one **Beat** apart, they must be dropped back in one **Beat** apart.

It might take you several attempts to get this working perfectly, but you'll find that the average five-ball juggler is quite happy to participate because it's good practice for them too.

For style it looks best if you make your movements as robotic and square as possible, so that they contrast well with the smooth cascade below. See **Robotic Drop** for a trick with the same flavour of movement.

See also **Runaround, Gandini Patterns**.

Swiss Bank Account

The name of a long **Siteswap** sequence I made up in the section on **Siteswap State Tables**. **"Swiss Bank Account"** can also be used as a general derogatory term for **Siteswaps** with stupidly long "periods".

• Juggle **44405253044502** – three balls, period =14, optional pirouette under the last **5**.

Synchronous

This word is gobbledegook for *at the same time*. In the juggling context it is used by devotees of **Siteswap Notation** to refer to patterns in which both hands throw together, like the **Box**.

Siteswap Notation is most elegant when used on patterns in which the hands throw alternately (**Asynchronous** patterns). It becomes a lot harder to read when the hands throw together – though it does become a useful tool for programming juggling simulators since it is, at least *machine readable*.

This term, and its opposite, are used sparingly in THE ENCYCLOPÆDIA OF BALL JUGGLING.

See also **Siteswap Notation.**

Ten Ball Feed

The **Ten Ball Feed** is a **Passing Pattern** for three jugglers and ten balls. That's three-and-a-third balls each – read on and discover how a third of a ball is juggled.

•The three jugglers stand in a vee formation as they would for a **Feed.** Let's call them **A**, **B** and **C**.

A stands facing **B** on the right and **C** on the left. **A** gets four balls, **B** and **C** get three each.

All passes are 4's, thrown from the right hand; they are all caught in the left hand.

A leads off with a pass to **B**, then continues passing alternately to **C** and **B**. As far as **A** is concerned, it's just like normal **Seven Ball Passing** except that the passes alternate between two people.

B has to *wait* until **A**'s pass is halfway over before responding with a pass to **A**. **B** then continues to juggle a **Four Count**, so every *second* right-hand throw is a pass to **A**.

C has to wait a couple of beats longer before starting. As soon as **A**'s pass to **C** is halfway over, **C** starts doing exactly what **B** is doing, just two beats out of time.

B and **C** are therefore juggling **Four Counts** to **A**'s **Two Count** – which means that nobody is juggling a third of a ball at all. **A** is juggling three-and-a-half balls, and **B** and **C** juggle three-and-a-quarter balls each.

The pattern is pleasant to watch because all the passes are staggered, making a wonderful visual rhythm in the air.

Simple when you know how!

•When you find yourself among four or more jugglers who all know the **Ten Ball Feed** you can team up and juggle the *"Random Feed"*.

One juggler feeds a line of three or more jugglers in random order – it works like this.

The feeder starts with four balls and everybody else gets three. To get the pattern going the feeder and one of the fed start to juggle seven balls between them using a standard seven-ball **Two Count**.

Everybody else waits.

After a few throws the feeder starts to pass up and down the line, in *random* order. The fed jugglers respond to each pass they receive by returning a ball when the feeder's pass is halfway over. They juggle **Three Ball Cascades** in between times.

The whole thing holds together because all the passes are 4's and you have just enough time to react to an approaching pass.

The *Random Feed* is a perfect game for a juggling **Workshop**.

Ten Ball Feed

Tennis

There is a whole family of **Tennis** tricks for the three-ball juggler – all of them share one feature: a *tennis-ball* travels back and forth across an imaginary *net* formed from other balls in the pattern. It's helpful to use a differently coloured ball as the "tennis" ball when learning these tricks.

•The simplest **Tennis** pattern is a **Three Ball Cascade** with the *tennis-ball*, juggled continuously **Over the Top** from side to side over the pattern. Some juggling purists would say that this is not *real* **Tennis** – and of course they would be right, but for the wrong reasons!

•Real (juggling) **Tennis** is based loosely on the **Right Middle Left** pattern. The throwing order is *right-right-left-left-right-right-left-left* and so on.

Start with two balls in the right and one in the left. The first throw is a right self **4** straight up the middle (that's the net). Next throw a right to left **4 Over the Top** (that's the "tennis" ball) and catch the first ball (the "net"). The left hand now does exactly what the right just did: left self **4** up the middle, left to right **4 Over the Top**, then catch the net – easy peasy!

This pattern is called a **Four Two Three (423)** by fans of **Siteswap Notation**.

•A very slightly different form of **Tennis** is based on the **One-up Two-up** pattern. Start with two in the right and one in the left, as before.

Start by throwing *two* balls at the same time straight up the middle of the pattern. Now throw the "tennis" ball **Over the Top**. While it is sailing across catch and re-throw the two *net-balls* and then throw the *tennis-ball* back **Over the Top** from the left. This version is a shape distortion of **One-up Two-up**.

•You can play around with the shape of this **Tennis** pattern by throwing the tennis ball *through* the net, so that it passes under the near ball and over the far ball. If you keep this going on both sides the *tennis-ball* will follow a figure of eight pattern.

•Alternatively, try **Feeding** the tennis ball *under* the net.

•Incidentally, *real* tennis balls make terrible juggling balls; they are far too light and they bounce enough to be annoying, but not enough to be fun. See **Beanbags** for a simple surgical operation on a tennis-ball that will turn it into a reasonable juggler's prop.

*"Real" juggling **Tennis** is a shape distortion of **Right Middle Left**. The "middle" ball flies back and forth **Over the Top** of the pattern.*

The Fastest Trick in the World

•Juggling three balls using tennis rackets instead of your hands is quite a feat. The pattern is much harder than a **Three Ball Cascade** because there is *no hold time*.

•Four-ball jugglers – see **Four Ball Tennis**.

See also **Four Two Three (423)**, **Fake Mess**, **Follow** and **Right Middle Left**.

The Fastest Trick in The World is a seriously difficult juggling trick, based on a very simple idea.

•Juggle **Right Middle Left** with three balls using **Snatches**, that is, with your palms downwards. Speed and control of hand movement is the key, and you'll find that no matter how good you get you can always get better. Aim to make all those throws as low as you possibly can.

When the pattern is juggled really well all three balls seem to hover in a horizontal row as the hands move in a frenzied blur above them. Believe me, it *can* be done.

•I assume that all my readers know the awful old joke about **The Fastest Trick in the World** – you don't?

OK, grit your teeth, here it comes.

Juggle a **Three Ball Cascade** and throw in a few tricks, naming them as you go. You know the thing, do a **Penguin** and a **Yo-yo** or something. Then you ask (*surely you know this one?*) if your audience would like to see **The Fastest Trick in the World**.

They say yes, of course, if only to get your show over a bit more quickly.

"Here goes then... **The Fastest Trick in The World!**"

Do absolutely *nothing*.

"Want to see it again?"

Three Ball Bounce

The **Three Ball Bounce** is the **Bouncing Ball** version of the **Three Ball Cascade**. There are two basic styles which correspond to the normal cascade and the **Reverse Cascade**.

The easier style is the **Reverse Cascade** or *passive bounce* style in which the balls are not so much thrown as *lifted*.

• Starting with just one ball, practise a few crossing bounces. Hold the ball in your right hand and *gently* throw it so that it rises a few inches, bounces once and comes up comfortably into your left hand. You only need to throw the ball high enough to overcome the natural loss on the bounce, hence it is more of a *lift* than a throw. The action is very gentle and relaxed.

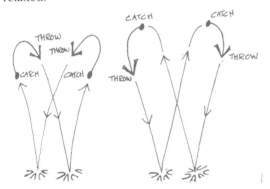

Reverse Cascade and Force Bounce.

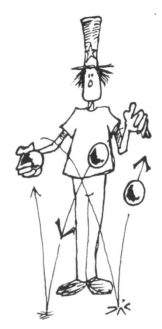

• Now take three balls and try the full **Three Ball Bounce**.

Each hand throws by gently *lifting* its ball *over* an approaching ball. It's very slow and smooth. Balls from the right hand bounce in front of your left foot and vice versa, the balls crossing on the way down. The speed of the pattern is controlled by its height. If you want to go faster you'll have to kneel down!

• To juggle **Under the Leg** while bouncing in the **Reverse Cascade** style you lift your legs *over* the balls as they bounce. Try all the combinations.

• The **Reverse Cascade** style is so slow and relaxed that it is the best method for **Numbers Juggling**. Five and seven balls can be bounced this way.

• The other style is the **Force Bounce**. Instead of lifting the balls gently into the air you throw them at the floor quite hard and the balls cross on the way *up*. The **Force Bounce** is more suited to work on dead or carpeted floors because you can compensate for poor bounce by throwing the balls harder. You can also adjust the speed of the pattern by making harder or softer throws.

Every right-hand throw is aimed to bounce just in front of your right foot and every left goes just in front of your left foot. This is the opposite of the **Reverse Cascade** style. Your throws should be hard enough to make the balls rise comfortably to a point just above your hands, so that they drop in gently.

• To juggle **Under the Leg** in a **Force Bounce** you lift the *right* leg as you throw from the right, so that the ball bounces under it. Learn all the possible combinations!

•Juggle three balls so that every right-hand throw is a **Force Bounce**, while every left is a snappy left to right 2 in the air and you have a *bounced* **Half Shower**. Both hands throw together.

•You can also use the **Column Bounce** to juggle three **Bouncing Balls**.

The three balls are juggled in one column so every ball hits the *same spot* on the floor. All you have to do is juggle **Two in One Hand** as a **Column Bounce** and let your hands *take turns* to make the exchanges.

•Taking this ENCYCLOPÆDIA heading literally, here is the pure **Three Ball Bounce**. It's a single throw trick.

Hold three **Bouncing Balls** in one hand in a triangular grip and throw them at the floor so that they all bounce up together – then catch them, all at once, in the throwing hand. It *is* possible, honestly!

•You can use the move as a **Three Ball Start** with three **Bouncing Balls**. Instead

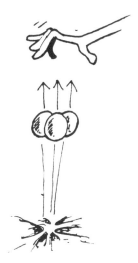

of catching all three as they rebound, just **Snatch** one and go into a normal **Three Ball Cascade**.

•Some jugglers do the **Three Ball Start** by **Snatching** *two* and then letting the third ball bounce off their head before starting to juggle.

•A **Flash Pirouette** is *very easy* with three **Bouncing Balls**. So easy that the trick can be extended so that you make two turns, collecting two balls after the first and turning again to catch the third. Whether you turn a single or double pirouette it's best to throw the three balls in columns or in

One-up Two-up style while you make the turn. If you do go for a double turn it looks great if you collapse dramatically to your knees while catching the last ball.

For more bouncing tricks for three balls, see **Three Ball Doublebounce**, **Orbit Bounce**, **Box**, **Five Three One (531)**, and **Three in One Hand**, to name but a few!

Three Ball Bounce

Three Ball Cascade

There are more cross-references to the **Three Ball Cascade** than to any other entry in THE ENCYCLOPÆDIA OF BALL JUGGLING, and quite right too!

In a **Three Ball Cascade** the hands throw alternately to each other, each new ball passing *under* the one that's in the air.

Beginners usually start their juggling careers with this pattern, unless they have been unfortunate enough to start with the two-ball **Shower**.*

•If you have just arrived on this page after completing the short course in juggling entitled **How to Juggle Three Balls** you'll probably be looking for some tips to help you on your way.

Here are three valuable hints:

1. *Everybody* finds it hard to throw the third ball when they are learning – including you! Either it remains resolutely jammed in your hand or it flies out at orbital velocity, usually more forwards than up.

2. Once you get past the first three throws you may find that the balls keep trying to go forwards. The brutal truth is that *you* are making them do that. Even with that knowledge you may still find it hard to stop, so stand in front of a wall – that should do the trick!

3. You may notice that the more experienced jugglers seem to be able to juggle lower and smoother patterns than yours. This is not just polish – their pattern is subtly different to yours. See **Slow Cascade** for more about this.

•As soon as you can juggle the **Three Ball Cascade** you are ready to start learning **Tricks**. Three good tricks for the **Beginner** are **Over the Top**, **Under the Hand** and **One-up Two-up**. You'll find that the entries for those tricks in THE ENCYCLOPÆDIA lead you on to other tricks, and those tricks in turn lead on to yet more.

Who knows what magic a **Beginner** could be capable of in a couple of weeks' time?

*It's not a bad pattern, but it does tend to pre-programme the left hand to **Feed** instead of throw – which is a hard habit to break.

Three Ball Doublebounce

The **Three Ball Doublebounce** is an easy pattern for three **Bouncing Balls** – but it's not one that you would be likely to discover by accident.

In this pattern *two* balls hit the floor at the same time on every bounce and every ball bounces twice.

The balls are juggled in two columns; the right hand throws in the left column and the left hand throws in the right column so the pattern has a hands-crossed feel to it. It's very slow, very positive and quite hypnotic.

*This piece of **Ladder Notation** shows three balls plaited into a **Three Ball Cascade**. The resemblance to plaited hair is not just superficial! If you tie three ribbons to three balls and juggle them, the ribbons get plaited.*

• Start with two balls in the right and one in the left hand. Imagine two columns in front of you.

The first throw is a gentle **Force Bounce** from the right hand, in the *left* column. As this ball rises, after its first bounce, you throw a gentle **Force Bounce** with the left hand in the *right* column so that both balls fall exactly in time with each other.

Now return to the left column. Your left hand catches the ball that is rising from its second bounce and your right hand throws a **Force Bounce** into the left column exactly in time with the ball in the right column. Just repeat this action on alternate sides and you have the trick!

The pattern is very similar to juggling **Three in One Hand** using the **Column Bounce** technique, except that you are using *both* hands.

Three Ball Doublebounce

Three Ball Flash

Throwing all the balls you are juggling up into the air once and then catching them is called a **Flash**. When jugglers talk about a **Three Ball Flash** they generally mean throwing all three balls up so that *both hands are empty for a brief moment.*

•Juggle a **Three Ball Cascade** and then toss three high **5**'s in succession. You should have time to clap your hands before they land again.

The **Three Ball Flash** is good practice for the **Five Ball Cascade**. Make sure your **Flash** is really smooth, keeping the throws to exactly even heights. Be sure to practise it both ways, leading from the left hand (*left-right-left-CLAP!*) as well as from the right (*right-left-right-CLAP!*). You can throw it from either a **Cold Start** or a running **Three Ball Cascade** and the hand clap is, of course, optional.

When you can throw a really good **Three Ball Flash** you are ready for the **Flash Pirouette**.

Three Ball Start

The **Three Ball Start** is a glitzy way of starting a three-ball routine. What the hell, it's flashy enough to put in the *middle* of your three-ball routine.

•Hold all three balls in the right hand in a triangle and start your routine by throwing a three-ball **Multiplex**. Aim to get two balls to rise a lot higher than the third. The more the air in front of you looks like an extract from **One-up Two-up** the better you are doing!

Snatch the low ball with your left hand *before* it starts to fall. This simple move has converted the situation up there from hopeless (it's hard to catch three balls at once) to manageable. It should now *feel* like **One-up Two-up**.

Throw that first ball up through the middle of its descending companions, catch them and juggle a nonchalant **Three Ball Cascade** while you take your applause. The art of a good **Three Ball Start** is to make it *look* difficult, but *feel* easy.

•**Three Ball Starts** can be thrown **Behind the Back**, **Under the Leg**, or just about any way you can think of. It looks very good if you can manage to bounce one of the balls off your head.

Three Count

•*An alternative is to throw all three balls as a column **Multiplex**.*

It sounds hard but it's very easy if you know the secret. The top and bottom balls are caught by the throwing hand, the middle ball by the opposite hand.

After perfecting your **Three Ball Start** you should work on a good finish – once you have learned a great start *and* a great finish you could miss out the fiddly bits in the middle of your routine altogether!

A **Three Count** is a **Passing Pattern** in which every *third* throw is a pass. The odd numbered count means that you are passing alternately from your left and right hands – so it's a truly ambidextrous and symmetrical pattern (unlike the popular **Four Count** which is usually juggled with right-hand passes only).

•Stand facing your partner, three balls each, two in the right and one in the left. Every throw in the pattern will be a **3**.

Lead straight off with a pass from the right hand and get the count going in your head:

PASS-two-three-PASS-two-three-PASS-two-three-PASS-two-three-

– alternatively:

RIGHT-two-three-LEFT-two-three-RIGHT-two-three-LEFT-two-three-

As soon as you start to pass the **Three Count** you'll notice that it's the *same two balls* that get passed each time. Every time you catch a ball from your partner, *that's the ball you pass straight back.*

•When you **Drop** in a **Three Count** you can keep going. You'll find that the **Gap** naturally stays on one side of the pattern with just one ball being passed back and forth on the other. To pick up you have to manoeuvre yourself and your partner so that the dropped ball is on the *same side* as the **Gap**.

•You can throw **4**'s, **5**'s and so on in the **Three Count** just as you can when passing to other rhythms. All you need to know is where to fit them in. Since the pattern is symmetrical, anything you can throw from one hand can also be thrown from the other, so there's not much point in describing throws as "right to rights" or "right to lefts" because they could equally well be thrown contrariwise (if you see what I mean!).

So we'll describe passes as either "tramline" or "diagonal" and self throws as "crossing selfs" or just plain "selfs". The tricks that follow can be mixed, matched and generally ad-libbed to your heart's content, creating syncopations that may cause the underlying **Three Count** rhythm to become all but lost in a mist of mingling and bobbing balls.

Continued overleaf...

Three Count...

...Three Count

Keep that count, *"PASS-two-three-PASS-two-three.."* going in your head at all times and what follows will seem a lot clearer.

• You can throw a diagonal **4** pass on any *three* beat, giving yourself a brief **Gap**.

• You can throw a self **4** on the *two* beat; again you get the small **Gap**.

• You can throw a tramline **5** pass on the *two* beat; this time you get a decently big **Gap**.

• You can throw a diagonal **4** pass on the *PASS* beat; effectively this means that your pass arrives in your partner's wrong hand one beat late. This is catchable in exactly the same way as a right to right 4 pass on the *PASS* beat is in the **Four Count**. Your partner gets the **Gap**.

• A tramline **5** on the *three* beat arrives in exactly the same way as the previous throw (i.e. the wrong place at the wrong time, but it works!). You both get half a **Gap** each.

• A good sequence of throws (you have to throw *all* of them or it won't work) is a normal pass on the *PASS* beat, followed by a self **4** on the *two* beat, followed by a crossing self **5** on the *three beat*.

When you juggle this sequence you have effectively gone into a complex four-ball manoeuvre for a couple of throws, leaving your partner with the **Gap**.

There are, of course, many other syncopations waiting for you to discover them. Use either your juggler's instinct or pen, paper and **Ladder Notation**.

See also **Four Count**.

Three in One Hand

Juggling three balls in one hand is a difficult trick – about as hard as juggling five balls in two hands.* Every throw is a **6**, which makes sense because you are juggling exactly half of a **Six Ball Fountain**.

• The basic method is broadly similar to juggling **Two in One Hand** – just higher and harder. There are several different shapes you can juggle the pattern in.

Rolling out is generally considered the easiest, though some jugglers prefer to work in *columns*. *Rolling in* is the third obvious variation.

It's also possible to juggle **Three in One Hand** in a one-handed **Three Ball Cascade**, which can either be a normal or a **Reverse Cascade**.

• If you are finding **Three in One Hand** impossibly difficult you might find it helpful to get your hands used to the tempo of throwing **6**'s by juggling an easier pattern that uses these throws, like **Six Three Three (633)** for example.

*Dancey's Juggling Index for **Three in One Hand** is 2.25 which is only a tiny bit more than the **Five Ball Cascade** at 2.08.

Rolling out, and rolling in shapes...

Columns.

Cascade and **Reverse Cascade** *shapes...*

• Five-ball jugglers should have no trouble going from **Five Ball Cascade** into **Three in One Hand** and back again without a stop or a **Drop**.

Start by juggling a **Three Ball Cascade** with two extra balls hidden in your left pocket. Go into **Three in One Hand** with your right hand, casually putting your *left* hand into your pocket and secretly grasping the two extra balls.

Now drop down out of **Three in One Hand** straight into a **Five Ball Cascade**. To the audience it looks like the extra balls have appeared out of nowhere.

Continued overleaf...

Three in One Hand...

...Three in One Hand

•Advanced jugglers can attempt this complex **Three in One Hand** pattern, which is similar to the three-ball **High-Low Shower**.

It uses the **Siteswap** sequence **8040**.

Start with three balls in your best hand and throw alternate **8**'s and **4**'s.

The **8**'s are **Four in One Hand** throws and the **4**'s are **Two in One Hand** throws. The **8**'s need to be about *five times* as high as the **4**'s.

The effect is as if you are juggling **Two in One Hand** very high (on **8**'s) while a third ball bobs around your throwing hand at the bottom of the pattern.

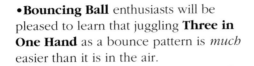

•**Bouncing Ball** enthusiasts will be pleased to learn that juggling **Three in One Hand** as a bounce pattern is *much* easier than it is in the air.

This is a **Column Bounce**. Start with three in the right hand and imagine two columns in front of you – right and left. Every ball is going to bounce twice as you make throws in alternate columns.

Lift ball number one into the right column and let it bounce. As it peaks, release ball number two in the left column so that both balls fall together. B-bump! As the balls peak again you release ball number three, in the right column. Keep making the exchanges in alternate columns and you have it! It's not difficult!

This pattern feels like juggling a **Four Ball Column Bounce** while one hand "takes a breather".

•You can juggle this pattern at double speed, so that every ball bounces *once* only and the two columns rise and fall in opposite time. In this form the pattern resembles a **Four Ball Column Bounce** juggled with alternate rather than simultaneous throws.

You have to move between the columns very quickly with your throwing hand, but it is still a lot easier than **Three in One Hand** juggled in the air.

•Shameless cheats can juggle **Three in One Hand** in the air using the **Two in One Hand** technique.

Juggle **Two in One Hand** while holding a third ball in the throwing hand and toss in a column **Multiplex** on every *third* throw.

Three Three Ten

The **Three Three Ten** is a **Passing Pattern** routine for two jugglers and six balls.

• You and your partner juggle three passes of **Six Count**, three passes of **Four Count**, and ten **Two Counts** – and that's it!

It's a right- or left-handed pattern because all the passes come from one side.

Counting out loud as you go, the sequence is:

*(And) One-and-two-and-pass
and-one-and-two-and-pass
and-one-and-two-and-pass.
And-one-and-pass
and-one-and-pass
and-one-and-pass.**
And-pass-and-pass-and-pass-and-pass-and-pass-and-pass-and-pass-and-pass-and-pass-and-pass!

The *ands* are left to right selfs; the *ones* and *twos* are right to left selfs.

• Written out in longhand the **Three Three Ten** looks *almost* like a limerick. Here's another routine (that I just made up) that's about as close to a limerick as you can get, bearing in mind that the scan of a limerick involves half-beats:

*(And). One-and-two-and-pass,
And-one-and-two-and-pass.
And-pass-and-pass
And-pass-and-pass.
And-one-and-two-and-pass.*

The value of passing routines like these is that there is a good chance that you will get to the end *before* you drop. With practice you can guarantee that you will finish on a high note; this is much better psychology that just juggling a **Four Count** until you drop. It leaves you with that all-important feeling of success.

Can you do the **Three Three Ten**? OK then, juggle it *left handed* and when you can do that you should check out the amazing ambidextrous **Four Four Eight**.

*There is often a bit of confusion here – many jugglers put in an extra self after this pass, converting the routine to a *Three Four Nine*. Don't be fooled – you are right and they are wrong.

Tick-tock

Tick-tock is a simple **Two in One Hand** trick like the **Yo-yo**, **Seeing Stars**, the **Weave** and all the others.

Juggle **Two in One Hand** in columns while holding a third ball in the opposite hand. Mime the ticking of a clock with the third ball, moving it to the top of column A as ball B peaks, and to the top of column B as ball A peaks.

Staccato movement, high ball visibility, and thinking **Square Juggling** all help to turn what is a very trivial move into a great trick.

Tick-tock

Toss Juggling

Toss Juggling is the stuff of which THE ENCYCLOPÆDIA OF BALL JUGGLING is made. The term describes the type of juggling in which you actually *throw* things. You might think that there is no other kind, but you would be forgetting **Contact Juggling** which involves *no throws at all!* Strictly speaking **Floor Juggling** is not really **Toss Juggling** either.

Balls, Clubs and Rings are the three archetypal **Toss Juggling** props. Each of these types of object **Spin** in a different way.

Rings **Spin** like frisbees; clubs **Spin** end over end; and balls – well you don't bother about **Spin** too much.

All three types be juggled in **Showers**, **Cascades** and **Fountains**, though each type of prop requires a slightly different throwing and catching technique.

Causal Diagrams, **Ladder Notation** and **Siteswap Notation** are all designed to record **Toss Juggling**.

Train Rolls

A **Floor Juggling** trick – simple to learn but hard to do well. You can't use **Beanbags** for **Train Rolls** because they don't roll well enough!

• Take three balls and kneel on the floor. Roll the balls from your right hand to your left and **Feed** them back from left to right across the top of the pattern.

This is the **Floor Juggling** equivalent of a three-ball **Shower** – a juggling pattern that doesn't use **Gravity**. The rolling balls need to move *exactly* in time with each other for the trick to look any good, and the wider you can "juggle" the pattern, the better it looks.

• It's quite easy to juggle a rolling version of the **Three Ball Cascade**. Right hand "throws" are made on your right and they roll forwards and to the left – crossing the paths of the throws from the left hand in true **Cascade** style.

Five Ball Cascade? No doubt it's possible.

You can juggle Train Rolls and other rolling patterns either on the floor or on a table.

Triangle

The **Triangle** is an arrangement of three jugglers for a **Passing Pattern**.

Triangles are fun because all three jugglers get to do the same amount of work, unlike **Feeds** in which one lucky or unlucky juggler (depending on your point of view) gets to stand at the "hard end". There are various ways of juggling a **Triangle**.

• *Outs and ins*: all three jugglers juggle right-handed **Four Counts** (**Every Others**) alternating their passes between the person on their right and the person on their left. When you pass to the right it's an *out*, and when you pass to the left it's an *in*. When you can handle this, you can up the speed to a **Two Count** (**Showers**).

• Juggle a **Three Three Ten** so that the passes are thrown alternately *out* and *in*. It's a real brain-bender.

• It's a shame to spoil the symmetry of the **Triangle** by being excessively right handed, so to spread the work evenly between right and left hands you should practise passing **Three Counts** in a **Triangle**.

Start with a **Three Count** juggled on *outs*, then on *ins*. When you can cope with that you should try *out-out-in-in*. Things are starting to hot up!

• The ambidextrous equivalent of the **Three Three Ten** is, of course, the **Four Four Eight** and it's quite a team that can juggle that routine in a **Triangle** with alternate *outs* and *ins*.

• All these sequences can be practised as **Floor Juggling** patterns, which can really help to get the sequence fixed in your head before trying the real thing!

• Finally, try juggling a **Triangle** while standing back to back!

Trick

Anything a juggler does is a **Trick**, as long as they are actually *juggling* at the time; what they do in their spare time is their own business.*

The word **Trick** is also used to describe any deliberate *variation* in a pattern. If a hand throws a ball to itself instead of across the pattern in a **Three Ball Cascade** – that's a **Trick**.

Throwing balls **Over the Top** and **Under the Hand** are **Tricks** that play with the shape of a **Cascade**.

Throwing **4**'s and **5**'s in a **Four Count Passing Pattern** are **Tricks** that play with the timing of the pattern.

You'll find that, very often, a continuously repeated **Trick** leads to an entirely different pattern. For example, juggling constant **Over the Top** throws from one side in a **Three Ball Cascade** is only a hair's breadth from a three-ball **Half Shower**. If you play around with the **Tricks** and patterns that you *know* and keep combining them with each other you are certain to strike gold eventually, and invent a brand new **Trick**.

*When THE ENCYCLOPÆDIA OF BALL JUGGLING was translated into Japanese this paragraph caused more confusion than anything else in the book and was the subject of a lengthy correspondence which contained such gems as "..but *why* is it funny?"

Trick

Turbines

Turbines is a two-person **Gandini Pattern** for five balls and four hands. The name refers to the way in which the two jugglers' inner arms overlap and move out of each other's way – causing a visually dramatic rotation effect in the middle of the pattern.

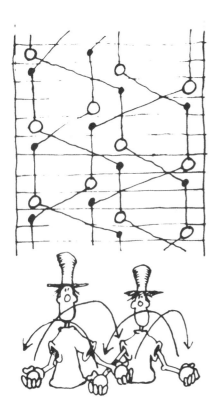

•Grab two balls in your right hand and one in the left. Stand to the right of your partner, so close that you can cross your inside arm over theirs.

•OK, we're ready to go: you'll be juggling *self pass!* and then your partner does a *self pass!* You both throw the *selfs* from your outside hand to your inside hand – and you both throw the *passes* from your inside hand to your partner's outside hand.

•Stand there and *think* about that for a moment; have a *chat* about it. Make sure you know what you're both doing.

•Ah! I forgot one thing – right after you make the *pass* you'll need to swing your inside hand, **Turbine** style, *under* your partner's inside hand.

•Similarly, they'll need to do the same thing right after their *pass*.

•OK, now juggle!

Repeat until you are suitably pleased with yourselves! There's amazing beauty in the simplest things!

•You can add a little extra magic if you like. Note that when you do the **Turbine** bit your hand is *carrying* a ball around your partner's arm. We're going to add a cheeky little throw here.

Just before you make this move you **Drop** the ball in your hand – then swing around underneath your partner's arm and catch it again.

It's a very cool staccato effect!

• The Gandinis also like to play with the held outside ball while juggling **Turbines**. Since it's held for a long time, you have time to do a **Hopstop** throw with it.

The Gandinis make this throw **Penguin** style (but caught normally).

See also **Gandini Patterns**.

Trickledown

Trickledown is a simply adorable name for the trick that Americans usually call the *Statue of Liberty*.

•Juggle three balls with your left hand held up in the air at full stretch. The right hand throws up to the left, which drops the balls it is holding back down into the pattern, allowing them to *trickle down*.

Accurate throws are the key, because it looks best if your left hand stays quite still, releasing each ball just in time to catch the next. One route to mastering the trick is to start by juggling a three-ball **Shower** and then slowly raise your feeding hand higher and higher until it is at full stretch.

If you are putting together an animal impersonations routine, with tricks like the **Orangutan**, **Penguin** and **Gorilla**, you might like to present this one as the *Giraffe*.

•It's worth learning the trick both ways around, that is both right-handed and left-handed, because it looks especially good if two jugglers juggle mirror image **Trickledowns** in time with each other while standing side by side.

See also **Cranes.**

Triple

Club jugglers tend to describe throws as **Singles**, **Doubles**, **Triples** and so on. They are, of course, referring to the number of spins of the club in the air.

Singles usually equate to **3**'s, **Doubles** to **4**'s and **Triples** to **5**'s. In fact the pattern **Five Three (53)** is commonly called *Triple Singles* by skittlespinners because they throw the **5**'s as **Triple** spins and the **3**'s as **Single** spins. So a **Triple** is almost always a **5**, though there are exceptions to this rule. Five-club jugglers, for example, almost always use **Double** spins when cascading five clubs. They are still throwing **5**'s, just with a lazy spin.

Trickledown.

Turnover

A **Turnover** is a simple three-ball move that you can slip into a **Three Ball Cascade** as an incidental move, or juggle as a continuous pattern (in which case it becomes a **Follow**).

•Juggle a **Three Ball Cascade** and **Chop** a ball right across the pattern (an *outside* **Chop**) at the same time as you throw an **Under The Hand** throw from the opposite side.

Thus you carry one ball over the pattern with the **Chop** at the same time as carrying another ball underneath in the opposite direction. Do this with panache and it looks as though you have turned the whole pattern over, hence the name!

•When you can do it one way, do it the other way. And when you can to *that* try turning the pattern continuously one way and then the other. You'll be juggling a **Follow!**

Two Count

A **Two Count** is a **Passing Pattern** in which every *second* throw is a pass. Usually this means every *right* hand because jugglers are mostly both lazy and right-handed. The **Two Count** is sometimes called **Solids** or **Showers**.

• To juggle a six-ball **Two Count** between yourself and a partner simply stand face to face and juggle **Three Ball Cascades** in time, making every right-hand throw a pass to your partner instead of a self throw. As with other passing patterns you can add syncopations, or off-beat throws, without causing the pattern to crash in flames. There are only two **Beats** in the **Two Count** so it's easy to describe (and remember) the possibilities. Here are three commonly used syncopations:

• A right to right (diagonal) **4** can be thrown on any pass instead of the normal right to left **3**.

• A left to left (diagonal) **4** can be thrown in place of the normal left to right self **3** at any time.

• You can immediately follow the previous throw with a right to left (tramline) **5** pass.

See also **Four Count** and **Three Count**.

Two in One Hand

Juggling two balls in one hand is about as difficult as juggling a **Three Ball Cascade** and it is just about the most amazingly useful trick a **Beginner** can learn.

There is an infinity of tricks for three balls that use the **Two in One Hand** technique to leave the other hand free for a moment to do something impressive or improbable – like **Eating the Apple** and **Mopping the Brow** to name but two. When you can juggle two balls in *either* hand you are ready for **Four Ball Juggling**.

• There are three commonly used shapes for the **Two in One Hand** pattern – *rolling out, rolling in* and *columns*.

Rolling out means that your hand throws on the inside and catches on the outside, just like juggling a **Cascade**. *Rolling in* means you throw on the outside and catch on the inside (corresponding to a **Reverse Cascade**). *Columns* simply means juggling two balls so that they rise and fall vertically, side-by-side.

• Practise juggling a **Three Ball Cascade** and going into **Two in One Hand** for a few throws and then dropping back into the **Cascade**.

The **Two in One Hand** throws are **4**'s and should be about twice the height of the **3**'s used in the **Cascade** if your hands are to "keep the beat".

• To practise juggling **Two in One Hand** in *columns* you can use **Right Middle Left** as a base pattern.

Columns are useful for some very visually appealing tricks like the **Factory**, the **Yo-yo** and the **Fake**, so it's worth getting them really **Solid**.

• **Bouncing Ball** jugglers should look up the **Column Bounce** technique for juggling **Two in One Hand**.

• With **Bouncing Balls** you can also juggle **Two in One Hand** so that one ball bounces each time it's thrown and the other always stays in the air.

Start by **Force Bouncing** the first ball straight down. As it rises you throw the second ball *up* and catch the bouncing ball, quickly throwing it back at the floor.

Now catch the air ball and repeat the sequence. One ball always goes *down*, the other always goes *up*, so the *up-ball* never bounces.

• See also **Fork** for a couple of manipulative and interesting **Two in One Hand** patterns.

• See if you can manage all the usual body moves while juggling **Two in One Hand**, like **Under the Leg**, **Over the Shoulder** and so on.

• The **Siteswap** notation for **Two in One Hand** is **40**.

• If you juggle **Two in One Hand** in *both* hands at the same time you are, of course, doing **Four Ball Juggling**.

Two-up

This is roughly half of the pattern **One-up Two-up**.

• Take a ball in each hand, throw them both up and catch them again in the same hands.

Too easy huh?

• Cross your hands for the throw, uncross them for the catch.

Still too easy?

• Throw the balls with hands uncrossed, but cross them for the catch.

Got you that time!

See also **Having Problems?**

Under the Hand

Throwing balls **Under the Hand** in a **Three Ball Cascade** is just as easy as **Over the Top**, so it's a good trick for **Beginners**. It is also a very useful skill to acquire because the technique is used in many other patterns.

•In a normal **Three Ball Cascade** you catch balls on the outside and throw them on the inside. Juggle three balls for a minute and concentrate on the sweep that your hand makes as it brings each ball from the catching to the throwing position.

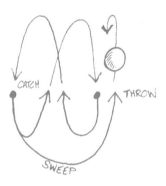

To juggle an **Under The Hand** throw you exaggerate that sweep so that the ball is swept right under the opposite hand and is then thrown straight up. The pattern then continues exactly as before.

The trick looks best if there is absolutely no change in tempo at all – practise it on both sides until it's smooth. When you can do the trick it's time to try all the combinations:

- Every right **Under the Hand**.
- Every left **Under the Hand**.
- Same ball always thrown **Under the Hand**.
- Every throw **Under the Hand**.

Each of these variations produces a pattern that is quite different to the **Three Ball Cascade**.

*After mastering the **Under The Hand** technique you are ready to learn **Chops** and the **Windmill**.*

Under the Leg

Yes – you *can* juggle under your leg.

•Juggle a **Three Ball Cascade** and concentrate on one hand. Notice the sweep that your hand makes between catching and throwing a ball – that's where your leg has to go. Instead of trying to wrap your juggling pattern around your leg, you bring your leg *into the pattern*.

•Once you can do it on one side, try it on the other. Then try all the combinations – every right, every left, and same ball every time.

•Real heroes can juggle *every ball under alternate legs*. To do this you have to combine running on the spot, dancing a cancan and being a very mad juggler indeed!

•Under both legs is much easier if you squat down, poke your hands under your legs and juggle in that rather frog-like position.

•Don't miss out the possibilities of juggling under the *opposite* leg.

Vesuvius

Vesuvius is a five-ball trick, an easy one! It's named after the famous volcano.

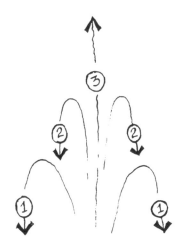

•From a **Cold Start** you hold three in the right and two in the left. Throw a split **Multiplex** from the right – *immediately* followed by a slightly higher split **Multiplex** from the left – passing between the first two balls and *immediately* follow that with the last ball (from the right), thrown through the middle of both **Multiplexes** and higher still. The effect you are trying to get is that of bubbling, erupting lava.

•For a *warm start*, juggle a **Three Ball Cascade** with an extra ball palmed in each hand and throw the trick out of the cascade.

•For a **Hot Start**, juggle a **Five Ball Cascade** and then gather two balls in the right and two in the left – throw a **Vesuvius** and drop back into the cascade.

The trick mixes well with **One-up Four-up** and **Five Ball Splits**.

W-feed

The **W-feed** is a **Passing Pattern** for any number, yes *any* number, of jugglers from four upwards. It's called a **W-feed** because, with five jugglers, you stand in a W formation. If there are more than five of you the W becomes a zigzag.

• Arrange yourselves in formation so that you end up with two lines of jugglers facing each other.

Everybody gets three balls each and battle commences. The two jugglers at the ends of the zigzag juggle **Four Counts** and everyone else juggles **Two Counts**, passing alternately to the jugglers opposite them to their right and their left. In other words, you all **Feed** except the people at the ends who juggle **Every Others**.

It's best to begin with a **Slow Start** to give everyone a moment or two to get in sync. Everyone should throw the first pass to the right, unless they happen to be at the end of the zigzag with nobody on their right.

It's a great thing to do at your juggling **Workshop**, because it's a chance for everyone to work together.

• With careful timing you can walk slowly through the middle of a **W-feed** without getting hit by any of the balls.

A good game is for the person at the end to break off from the **W-feed**, walk through the middle, and join in again. If you keep this going then you all change places and everybody gets to walk through the *Valley of the Shadow of the Deadly Beanbags*.

• You can **Floor Juggle** the **W-feed** if you are all too tired from the day's juggling to stand up!

Weave

The **Weave** is a three-ball trick. To juggle it you need to have mastered juggling **Two in One Hand** in *columns*.

• Juggle **Two in One Hand** in columns in your best hand and then *weave* the third, held, ball through the pattern in a figure of eight.

As each juggled ball rises the weaved ball passes *underneath* it.

The basic idea of the **Weave** is capable of infinite variation as you sweep and slice the held ball through the pattern in improbable directions.

A similar trick, based on **Two in One Hand**, is **Seeing Stars**.

Wheel

A simple distortion of the **Three Ball Cascade**.

•Each throw is made in the centre and is aimed forwards so that the balls travel in circles in a forward plane. The balls are caught at the front and wheeled under the pattern. Some jugglers use **Snatches** for the catches.

Concentrate on keeping all the balls in one plane and when you have mastered it, try rotating the **Wheel** the other way!

Windmill

The **Windmill** is a simple three-ball pattern. The balls wheel continuously in one direction, hence the name.

•Juggle a **Three Ball Cascade** and throw every ball from one hand **Over the Top**, while the other hand throws constantly **Under the Hand**. Try the pattern *before* reading the next paragraph.

OK – you might get a little confused about the routes that the balls are supposed to take and wonder if you have got the pattern right. As long as your **Under the Hand** throws really are **Under the Hand**, and as long as your **Over the Top** throws go over *everything,* your pattern is basically correct. Those **Under the Hand** throws *do* tend to get thrown straight up while everything else wheels around them. This is normal.

•Learn it both ways! Then practise *reversing* the direction of your **Windmill** without putting in any **Cascade** throws during the change.

Continuous changes of direction lead to a new pattern – the awesomely incredible **Mills' Mess**!

Workshop

A juggling **Workshop** is the best possible environment in which to learn, play with and generally have fun with your juggling. Small groups of jugglers all over the world beg, steal, borrow and hire suitable halls and hold regular (usually weekly) sessions. Workshops are usually very informal affairs and there is never any need to feel shy because you are "just a **Beginner**". You'll find that other jugglers are happy to share their skills and their equipment with you – just ask! You'll be glad you went, I promise!

The huge popular interest in juggling in recent years means that there is almost bound to be a juggling workshop held regularly near where you live. You can find out where they are by referring to the web sites listed under **Internet Resources.**

If you cannot locate a workshop, start one up yourself! All you need is a moderately sized hall with good lighting and a high ceiling and a few jugglers to share costs with. If you can't find enough jugglers then teach some of your own! You'll learn much more, and have more fun, working with others than you ever would on your own.

Yo-yo

Kids of all ages love to see this three-ball trick. The **Yo-yo** presents the illusion that two balls are connected by a piece of string.

•Juggle **Two in One Hand** in *columns* with your right hand. Hold the third ball in your left hand and move it up and down directly above and in perfect sync with the middle ball, as if the two balls were tied together: instant hilarity! Now try swapping sides – easier to do than explain. Keep yo-yoing while you do it.

•To build on the gag you can do the *Australian* version (known by Ozzies as the *English* version), moving the held ball *under* the middle ball, as if they were connected by a piece of Australian string. It doesn't make sense I know but – more instant hilarity.

•You can add some amazing sleight of hand to the **Yo-yo** very easily. You won't realise quite how good this next trick is until you have tried it in front of someone.

Juggle the **Yo-yo** as before; your right hand is juggling **Two in One Hand** in columns and the yoing is happening on the left-hand side. Think of the three balls as the *yo-yo ball*, the *string ball* and the *spare ball*. Throughout the next move you keep the *string ball* and the *yo-yo ball* moving in perfect sync. Simply throw the *spare ball* once to the *left* of the *yo-yo ball*, as if you were juggling **Two in One Hand**

rolling out for a throw, and then go straight back to the normal **Yo-yo** pattern. A simple move but the visual effect is surreal. True juggling magic!

•In yet another version of the **Yo-yo** you move the *string ball* alongside the *yo-yo ball*. Now for some curious reason this isn't funny* but it looks good, especially if you swap the trick from one side to the other on every other throw.

Many jugglers do these tricks badly – going through the motions without really *performing* the trick. Concentrate on getting the balls to move in perfect unison. Make sure that you hold the *string ball* so that your audience can see *all* of it, between finger and thumb with your other fingers outstretched. Hold that ball as if you are holding *The Product* in an ad on TV. Your eyes should follow the yo-yo ball up and down as if they were *glued* to it.

The **Yo-yo** is a great trick, easy to learn and easy to impress an audience with. It also illustrates one very important point about juggling: the simple stuff is often the best.

*Humour is a strange thing. It *is* funny if you sync the *string ball* with the *outside* ball. See **Fake**.

Zen and the Perfect Juggler

There once lived a young man who was consumed by a great ambition. He wished, more than anything else, to become the best juggler that there ever had been, or ever would be, in all the world. So instead of seeking sensible employment like his brothers and sisters he decided to devote his whole life to achieving this aim and set out to search for a teacher.

After many years of travelling and adventures he found himself on a rocky ledge, high in the mountains. Before him was a wall of solid rock in which was set a thick wooden door marked with curious symbols. Here dwelt the last living Zen Master of the Art of Juggling.

The young man knocked and the door was opened, just a crack, by a white haired old man.

"What do you want?" he said with a mixture of scorn and contempt as he looked his visitor up and down.

"I wish to become the best juggler that there ever has been, or ever will be, in all the world," said the young man, hoping to be invited in, for the air was blowing with a bitter chill.

The old man sneered. "Tell me, what do you know about juggling?"

"I can juggle two."

The old man laughed even more.

"Well, I know that's not very good," said the young man, "but I can practise, I can get better…"

"It's not so much that you can only juggle two," said the old man. "It's more that you bother to count at all! I don't think I can help you. Goodbye!"

With that he slammed the door shut and would not answer when the young man knocked again. Night fell and it began to snow. Having nowhere else to go, and no reason to go there, the young man lay down on the doorstep and went to sleep resolving to wait for as long as might be necessary for the Master to change his mind.

A week later the door opened and the old man poked his head out into the cold air.

"I'm fed up with tripping over you every morning, and the chattering of your teeth is keeping me awake at night. Take these three balls and go away. You may return when you are an expert in their use. And before you start asking me a lot of stupid questions about which one to throw first and whether the third one goes under or over, I may as well tell you that I don't give lessons, so you'll have to work it out for yourself."

The door slammed shut again.

The joy of being accepted as the Master's new Apprentice filled the young man with a warm excitement that quickly flushed the stiffness and the cold from his limbs. He rose up and went back down the mountain to begin his life's work.

He practised day and night and it was only a week later when he made his way back to the Master's cave and knocked on the door again. Neither weather, nor the welcome had improved.

"Don't come in! You'll let in the cold. Show me what you can do. I can see you well enough from in here."

The young man juggled among whirling snowflakes, wondering how the old man could possibly see through the solid door. He finished his routine and waited for his Master's opinion.

"Is that it?" came the voice from inside. "I suppose it's OK for a week's work."

The door opened slightly. A ball flew out through the gap and landed at the Apprentice's feet. The door slammed shut again.

Thinking it best not to ask any more questions, he went away, resolving not only to master four-ball juggling as quickly as possible, but also to extend his skills with three balls by learning and inventing as many tricks and variations as he could before returning.

A month later he stood confidently outside the cave once more. The worst of the winter was past and the weather was a little better. The Master still refused either to leave his cave or to invite his Apprentice inside.

The young man juggled his best and when he had finished another ball landed at his feet.

"That doesn't mean I think you are any good!" called the Master through the crack in the door, "I just don't want you round here every five minutes pestering me." The door slammed shut.

The Apprentice was thrilled and left with even greater determination. Obviously the Master was impressed with his progress and was encouraging him to move on to the more advanced levels.

"I'll show him how long it takes me to learn to juggle five balls

Zen and the Perfect Juggler

– and I'll amaze him with twelve new three-ball tricks of the most unpronounceable kind."

In the late spring he stood again outside the cave and performed a stunning selection of the very best of three- and four-ball juggling, finishing his routine with a magnificent flourishing cascade of five balls. He felt proud and strong for he knew that his skill was already greater than that of most jugglers. The Master stepped outside to watch him this time, since it was not so cold.

"You don't appear to have learned anything yet."

Two more balls landed at the Apprentice's feet.

"Don't get any big ideas. I'm just worried that you might lose one and come back sooner than I expect."

It is very much harder to juggle seven balls than five and so it was towards the end of summer the following year before the Apprentice was able to return. There are never many seven-ball jugglers alive in the world and his original dream, to be the best juggler that there ever had been, or ever would be, in all the world, seemed far closer to him now.

"Hmph!" said the Master as he threw the eighth and ninth balls at his pupil's feet.

The Apprentice did not return to the cave for another five years.

"You are missing the point! You only get one more ball this time because you seem to be getting tired. In any case, I'm starting to enjoy your company." The door slammed and the nine-ball juggler left, carrying ten balls.

So the Apprentice came and went over the years, and after each visit he remained away for longer than before. Outside in the world his fame grew and his juggling skills became legendary until one day, seventeen years after their first meeting, the Master and the Apprentice stood together again high on the mountain. The Apprentice had just juggled fourteen balls outside the door to the cave.

"Surely I am now the best juggler that there ever has been, or ever will be, in all the world?"

"Here's my answer," the old man replied as he tossed the fifteenth ball to the ground.

The Apprentice slowly bent and picked it up, knowing, as only a fourteen-ball juggler can know, just how serious a problem he was holding in his hand. His shoulders bowed as if under some enormous load and he went back down the mountain with a heavy heart.

It was no longer a young man that stood outside the Master's dwelling carrying eight balls in his right hand and seven in his left. Forty years had passed since his first visit. The great, and formerly young, juggler placed the balls on the ground and did not juggle. He had delayed his visit until the warmer days of summer for he had become familiar with the old man's hospitality.

The Master, who had been old at their first meeting, was now ancient. He came out of the cave and sat down on the stony ground next to his Apprentice. They remained in silence for many hours, which did not concern the Apprentice because he had now learned the Art of Patience.

"So?" asked the Master at last.

"Yes, I have fifteen balls – solid." There was more than a hint of anger in the Apprentice's voice.

"Don't you want to show me?"

"No, I do not. You will just give me another ball and this time I know that I shall fail. You have been leading me on all these years. I can juggle fifteen balls now. Nobody else has ever done that – I know because I looked it up in THE ENCYCLOPÆDIA OF BALL JUGGLING. I can juggle nine balls with my eyes closed. I can juggle an eleven ball *Revenge* backwards! I have dedicated my whole life to the Art of Juggling in a vain attempt to become a Perfect Juggler. And now, after all these years under your tuition, I realise that I have never seen you juggle *even once*. I don't believe that you have taught me anything.'

"Why didn't you say so before?"

"Say what before?" The Apprentice was not sure which of his remarks was being referred to.

"Why didn't you say that you wanted to be a *Perfect Juggler*? I seem to recall, quite clearly, that your spoken wish was to become, 'The best juggler that there ever has been, or ever will be, in all the world'".

"There's a difference?"

"Of course! One is possible – the other is not."

The Master gathered up a handful of stones and threw them up into the air. His hands danced lightly amongst them as he formed a fancifully woven knot of intricately wheeling fragments that hung improbably in the air for a moment. He drew his hands away and let them clatter back into the dust.

"How many, I mean, how do you do that?" The Apprentice stammered in amazement. He had been unable to count the number of objects in the air, somewhere around twenty something he thought, though he had a sneaking suspicion that the old man didn't know either. It wasn't like any juggling pattern he had ever seen before.

The old man's eyes twinkled. He reached into a fold of his cloak and produced a small glass phial that contained a liquid that shone like a pale sunset.

"You use drugs?"

The Master laughed.

"No, I don't use drugs, though I may occasionally indulge in a little, ah, *experimentation* with magic potions. Drink this and we'll see what can be done about your juggling!"

Zen and the Perfect Juggler

The Apprentice took the phial and drank the glowing honeyish liquid. It tasted of fire and spices, sparkling and fizzing in his throat. A warm prickly feeling of excitement surged down to his stomach and rushed out to his fingertips with a shock of fear and adrenalin like a firework exploding inside him. He took a huge slow breath to calm himself as every hair on his body stood on end. The air around him felt suddenly thick and close as if a thunderstorm was about to break.

He looked at his Master who had produced a second phial. With a surreal and incredibly exaggerated slowness, he was putting it to his lips and swallowing. As his long, long gulp continued, the old man stared blankly into the distance, unmoving and unblinking. Everything became still and quite silent. Even the wind stopped.

Suddenly the Master shook himself back to life with a shudder.

"Whoa! Now I've caught up with you. Time to start the lesson. Pick up that stone and throw it into the air. Go on, you're a juggler!"

The Apprentice felt curiously apprehensive as he picked up the stone. Something very strange had happened to him, but he couldn't quite decide what it was. He threw the stone gently upwards and watched it rise into the air. Up it went, and up, and up, and up! It continued its ascent until it became a speck in the sky and then was gone from sight altogether. He looked at his Master for an explanation.

"Quite useless! You threw it too hard! I knew you would. You see, you are almost a Perfect Juggler now, but you still have to learn to control your new abilities. Watch me!"

The Master picked up another stone and held it between finger and thumb. He winked mischievously and spread his hand wide to drop it. The stone didn't fall. Instead it began to creep very slowly toward the ground like a spoon sinking in treacle.

"The potion makes us very quick you see, hundreds of times as quick as we normally are. One day is now a year to us, perhaps more. The world has slowed down, almost stopped. But the potion's effect doesn't last long – let's juggle before it wears off!"

The Apprentice picked up another stone and placed it into the air next to the first. It too started a snail's crawl towards the ground.

"You see! You can put a stone here, put a stone there, move them around like this, swap them over like that, weave your fingers around any way you like. They fall, but we are too quick for them!"

They added more and more stones to the game. Some they set moving sideways so that they slowly curved towards the ground, some they gave a small upwards push so that they rose for a little while before turning. Whenever they spotted a stone getting close to the ground they carefully directed it upwards again. And so they gradually constructed a bewildering juggling pattern of more than one hundred gliding stones that hovered in the air between them.

They crowned their creation with a row of a dozen slowly turning cascades of three stones each, and when they were satisfied they sat together carefully adjusting the fall of each stone in turn so as to maintain the pattern's shape like two mad scientists working dials and levers in some fantastic control room.

The Apprentice's arms began to feel stiff and heavy and he felt a cold shudder.

"Your potion is wearing off," said the Master. "You took yours a little before me. You had better move your hands out of the way if you don't want your fingers broken!"

The Apprentice sat back and everything around him seemed to accelerate. The Master's hands moved faster and faster until they became like a faint blur of mortar amongst the seething wall of untouching stones they had built together. The main pattern was too complicated for the Apprentice's eye to follow but he could still just make out the twelve cascades revolving above the shimmering madness below them.

Suddenly the Master leapt back and giggled as the whole creation dropped to the ground like a descending splash.

The Apprentice thought for a while, feeling that he had learnt something of great importance, if only he could work out exactly what it was. After a while he spoke.

"So that is Perfect Juggling! Just moving things around in the air. Not any particular number, not any particular pattern. Just – just juggling?"

"You're starting to get the idea," said the Master, "but you forgot one thing."

Before the Apprentice could ask what, the Master's hand reached out and a stone fell into it from a great height like a meteorite. It was the one that the Apprentice had lost in the sky. The Master handed it to him. It was hot.

"Ouch!" yelled the Apprentice. But in that moment of pain it seemed to him that he understood everything. A smile spread across his face and his Master grinned knowingly back at him.

"Master, I understand now and I thank you for your teaching which is now complete. But before I leave here I have just one more question."

"And what is that?"

"I don't suppose you can get me any more of that stuff can you?"

The Master got up and walked into the cave where he could be heard rummaging around inside.

After a few moments he emerged and handed his Enlightened Apprentice a parcel.

The Apprentice opened it. Inside there was a set of three juggling clubs.

They never met again.

The End

About the Author

Charlie Dancey was born in 1955 when the cars were all black and The Beatles had yet to be invented. He taught himself to juggle at 3pm in 1977 using a set of perfectly balanced apples.

After eating the apples he moved on to **Eggs** and could soon juggle them well enough to impress people at dinner parties with his **Over the Top** and **Under the Hand** skills. It wasn't until 1982 that somebody passed him a set of **Beanbags**

Charlie describes what came next:

It was just a social thing at first, you know, a few people would meet and start tossing stuff around, just beanbags. It seemed harmless. Nobody was doing more than three but pretty soon I found I had to do more and more just to get the same buzz. Some of the jugglers started were doing four, or even five! Then they started passing them between each other. We didn't worry about dropping them or anything, we'd just pick up and carry on like it was perfectly normal. Slowly it starts to take you over. Somebody turned up with some clubs and a unicycle one day. I honestly never thought I'd go that far but I couldn't help myself. I was getting sucked in. I had to keep learning new tricks and it was taking up every waking hour of the day. I gave up my job and didn't really socialise with anybody but jugglers. I was hooked big time. In the end we had to go out on the streets to busk for money. Sometimes we'd get arrested – but it didn't stop us. We'd even do shows in front of little kids.

I thought that if I wrote this stuff down it might somehow get it out of my system so I started collecting tricks and patterns. I obsessively recorded everything, drawing hundreds of pictures of this funny little guy in a top hat doing tricks. I've no idea where he came from.

Anyway, it turned into this book. Originally it was supposed to be small book, at least that's what they asked me to do, but it just took me over. I guess I'm just naturally obsessive. I can't help it. Then I wrote THE COMPENDIUM OF CLUB JUGGLING which was even bigger. I really promised myself I'd stop after that.

So you can imagine that I was pretty dismayed to wake one morning and discover I'd dashed off a book called HOW TO RIDE YOUR UNICYCLE. I really do mean to stop now.

– which doesn't really explain why Charlie is starting a new project with an almost unimaginably huge and sweeping scope. It is a cartoon strip entitled EVERY TRICK IN THE BOOK.

Charlie would be the first to admit that he is somewhat over-focused in some areas, hence somewhat inept in others.

He is, for example, clinically incapable of living in a house and currently resides in a large caravan towed by "Tugger", the truck, from where he maintains contact with the outside world via a large satellite dish on his roof. This is is mainly used for sending emails to his publishers demanding large advances for books he plans to write some day.

He's also working on a mechanical juggling machine that will read **Siteswap Notation** from paper tape, just like a fairground organ.

If it works then a lot of professional jugglers could find themselves out of a job.

Changes to this edition

This edition of THE ENCYCLOPÆDIA OF BALL JUGGLING has been thoroughly revised and updated. It has a new cover design, and a subtle change of title (formerly it was entitled CHARLIE DANCEY'S ENCYCLOPÆDIA OF BALL JUGGLING).

The following entries have been dropped:

• **1, 2, 3, 4, 5 and so on** – now incorporated in the **Siteswap Notation** entry.

• **English** – this entry used to explain that "english" was the American term for what the English call "spin". It was dropped as part of a general dumbing down process to save confusing Americans.

• **Jurassic Pass** – this was always a frivolous entry. It was originally included to solve a page layout problem by using up a column. Since the dinosaur bandwagon left town many years ago, it's been dropped.

• **Ogie's Nightmare** – this used to describe a **Passing Pattern** that is *really* called **Hovey's Nightmare**[CJ]. This pattern is documented in THE COMPENDIUM OF CLUB JUGGLING.

• **Siteswap Feast** – how long could I keep putting out a book containing three consecutive pages of nothing but numerical digits? **Siteswap State Tables** now do the same job a lot more efficiently.

• **New Mathematical Juggling Ideas** – the contents of this appendix have been relocated.

• **UV (Ultraviolet)** – you can juggle with fluorescent props under UV lighting, which looks great – so now you know!

The following entries are new:

• **Asynchronous**
• **Causal Diagrams**
• **Charlie's Cheat**
• **Cranes**
• **Cross Arm Cascade**
• **Cross Arm Tennis**
• **Dropswap**
• **Eric's Extension**
• **Excited State Pattern**
• **Fake Mess**
• **Follow**
• **Four Two Three (423)**
• **Gandini Patterns**
• **Ground State Pattern**
• **Grover**
• **How to Juggle Three Balls**
• **Internet Resources**
• **Juggler's Rest Backpackers**
• **Juggling Notation**
• **Middlesborough**
• **Mike's Mess**
• **Mills' Mess State Transition Diagram**
• **Romeo's Revenge**
• **Siteswap State Tables**
• **Squeeze**
• **Swiss Bank Account**
• **Synchronous**
• **Turbines**

Other significant (and pedantic) changes:

• **Burke's Barrage** is now correctly described. The old, and incorrect, version turns out to be an original and interesting pattern and it has been named **Charlie's Cheat**. This error has caused a considerable argument over the years. Sorry about that! Hopefully matters are now resolved.

• More use is made of both **Siteswap** notation and **Causal Diagrams**.

• The placement of the apostrophe in **Mills' Mess** was changed – the inventor of the trick is named Mills not Mill.

• **"Siteswap"** no longer has the second S capitalised which is how everyone but me has always written it. I guess I've spent too much time writing software.

• Entries that describe significant **Siteswaps** include the actual numbers in their titles, as in **Five Three Four (534)**.